R

D1356386

DISPOSED OF
BY 3F RY
HOUSE OF LORDS

COMMON WEALTH, COMMON GOOD

OXFORD HISTORICAL MONOGRAPHS

The *Oxford Historical Monographs* series publishes some of the best Oxford University doctoral theses on historical topics, especially those likely to engage the interest of a broad academic readership.

Editors

P. CLAVIN   J. DARWIN   J. INNES

J. McDOUGALL   D. PARROTT   S. SMITH

B. WARD-PERKINS   J. L. WATTS   W. WHYTE

Common Wealth, Common Good

The Politics of Virtue in Early Modern Poland-Lithuania

BENEDICT WAGNER-RUNDELL

OXFORD
UNIVERSITY PRESS

OXFORD
UNIVERSITY PRESS

Great Clarendon Street, Oxford, OX2 6DP,
United Kingdom

Oxford University Press is a department of the University of Oxford.
It furthers the University's objective of excellence in research, scholarship,
and education by publishing worldwide. Oxford is a registered trade mark of
Oxford University Press in the UK and in certain other countries

© Benedict Wagner-Rundell 2015

The moral rights of the author have been asserted

First published 2015

All rights reserved. No part of this publication may be reproduced, stored in
a retrieval system, or transmitted, in any form or by any means, without the
prior permission in writing of Oxford University Press, or as expressly permitted
by law, by licence or under terms agreed with the appropriate reprographics
rights organization. Enquiries concerning reproduction outside the scope of the
above should be sent to the Rights Department, Oxford University Press, at the
address above

You must not circulate this work in any other form
and you must impose this same condition on any acquirer

Published in the United States of America by Oxford University Press
198 Madison Avenue, New York, NY 10016, United States of America

British Library Cataloguing in Publication Data
Data available

Library of Congress Cataloging in Publication Data
Data available

ISBN 978-0-19-873534-2

Links to third party websites are provided by Oxford in good faith and
for information only. Oxford disclaims any responsibility for the materials
contained in any third party website referenced in this work.

In memoriam Florian Lipiński
(4 May 1922/3–29 December 1997)

Acknowledgements

This book is a revised version of a doctoral thesis completed in 2008. My warm thanks must go to all those who offered their help, comments, and support both during my work on the original thesis and during the subsequent revision. Specifically, I would like to thank Richard Butterwick and John Robertson for their advice during my research as well as for their incisive comments when examining my thesis. I have also benefited greatly from the suggestions of the OHM series anonymous reviewer, and from advice from Robert Frost and Jerzy Lukowski while producing this revised version. I would also like to thank Karin Friedrich, Tomasz Gromelski, Andrzej Sulima Kamiński, and Wojciech Kriegseisen for their advice, Christian Preusse for early sight of his own doctoral thesis, and Oliver Thomas for his help on points of Latin translation. I must also offer my warmest thanks to Robert Evans, my doctoral supervisor and editor during the subsequent revision, for his encouragement and invariably perceptive comments over the course of my research and writing.

Last but by no means least, my love and thanks go to my wife Nicola, for all her support and patience through years of research, writing, and re-writing.

Contents

List of Abbreviations

AGAD	Archiwum Główne Akt Dawnych [Central State Archive], Warsaw
APG	Archiwum Państwowe w Gdańsku [State Archive in Gdańsk]
APKr	Archiwum Państwowe w Krakowie [State Archive in Kraków]
Bibl. Czart.	Biblioteka Fundacji im. XX Czartoryskich [Library of the Princes Czartoryski Foundation], Kraków
Bibl. Ossol.	Biblioteka Zakładu Narodowego im. Ossolińskich / Ossolineum [Library of the Ossoliński National Foundation/ Ossolineum], Wrocław
Bibl. PAN Kórnik	Biblioteka Polski Akademii Nauk (PAN) w Kórniku [Library of the Polish Academy of Sciences (PAN) in Kórnik]
Bibl. PAN Krak.	Biblioteka Polski Akademii Nauk (PAN) w Krakowie [Library of the Polish Academy of Sciences (PAN) in Kraków]
BN	Biblioteka Narodowa [National Library], Warsaw
BUW	Biblioteka Uniwersytetu Warszawskiego [Warsaw University Library]
TP	Teki Pawińskiego [Collections of sejmik records assembled by Adolf Pawiński]
VL	Volumina Legum

Introduction

THE POLITICS OF VIRTUE

This study analyses the political culture of the early modern Commonwealth of Poland-Lithuania, with a particular focus on the concept of virtue, and its role within Polish-Lithuanian political culture and discourse. Using the turbulent first two decades of the reign of King Augustus II (r. 1697–1733) as a case-study to explore wider trends, it will argue for two key propositions. First, that virtue was an indispensable part of Polish-Lithuanian political thought, and an indispensable intellectual tool for early modern Polish-Lithuanian political activists and commentators to understand and analyse the polity within which they lived and the challenges that the Commonwealth faced. Second, that adopting a moral rather than structural perspective, analysing the Commonwealth and its evident problems in terms of the moral failings of individuals rather than flaws in laws or institutions, was neither a substitute for nor a barrier to serious discussion of how to tackle the chronic dysfunction of the Commonwealth's government. On the contrary, the belief that public virtue had declined and needed to be revived could inspire substantial proposals for constitutional reform.

The Commonwealth's political culture was, as has been well documented by historians, overwhelmingly a noble culture, as a result of the almost complete domination of public life in Poland-Lithuania by its hereditary nobility, the szlachta. Proportionally and in absolute numbers one of the largest noble estates in early modern Europe, and notable for its religious, linguistic, and economic diversity, the szlachta considered themselves the Commonwealth's political nation: they described themselves as its citizens (*obywatele*), the 'democratic' component of the Commonwealth's government when analysed in Aristotelian terms.[1] The szlachta monopolized both public offices and the ownership of landed property; they even

---

[1] For a discussion of how contemporary political commentators used the Aristotelian *forma mixta* as a model to describe the Commonwealth's political system, see Chapter 1.

propagated a mythical history of their own origins—Sarmatism—that represented them as an entirely separate people from the Commonwealth's other inhabitants (peasants, burghers, and Jews), ruling the land by right of ancient conquest.[2] With the szlachta dominating public life in this way, the political discourse of the early modern Commonwealth was thus one created by nobles and for nobles. The sources that will be used here are therefore almost exclusively of szlachta origin, whether records of public councils such as the Commonwealth's central parliament, the Sejm, or local assemblies, the sejmiki, or political pamphlets or treatises, which were generally produced by szlachta writers and addressed to a szlachta audience. As the noble political arena was also, in theory at least, an exclusively male sphere—members of the szlachta routinely addressed one another as 'brother'—the political discourse that is being examined was also an almost entirely male one.[3]

It is also important to note that szlachta political discourse was primarily a practical one, in the sense that it was a discourse of political practitioners not one produced by writers or commentators observing the Commonwealth's political life from the sidelines. In principle, every adult male *szlachcic* (nobleman, member of the szlachta) was entitled to participate in the Commonwealth's public affairs, either in local fora such as the sejmiki or through central institutions such as the Sejm.[4] Szlachta

---

[2] On the Sarmatian myth and the ideas and culture it supported, see Maria Bogucka, *The Lost World of the "Sarmatians": Custom as the Regulator of Polish Social Life in Early Modern Times* (Warsaw, 1996), Stanisław Cynarski, 'The Shape of Sarmatian Ideology in Poland', *Acta Poloniae Historica*, 19 (1968), pp. 5–17 (p. 5), Cynarski, 'Sarmatyzm: ideologia i styl życia', in Janusz Tazbir (ed.), *Polska XVII wieku: Państwo, społeczeństwo, kultura* (Warsaw, 1969), pp. 220–43, and Tazbir, *Kultura szlachecka w Polsce: rozkwit, upadek, relikty* (Poznań, 1998). Note also that szlachta commentators often glossed over exceptions to their monopoly on political participation, such as the right of the Royal Prussian sejmik (Landtag) to send envoys to the Sejm.

[3] This is not, of course, to deny that individual women could—and did—play influential roles in the Commonwealth's political life: examples of women wielding significant influence would include King Jan III Sobieski's queen Maria Kazimiera (1641–1716), or Elżbieta Sieniawski (née Lubomirska) (1669–1729), the wife of Crown Grand Hetman Adam Sieniawski (1666–1726) and her daughter Maria Zofia (1698–1771), who was the wife first of Lithuanian Field Hetman Stanisław Denhoff (1673–1728) and later of August Czartoryski (1697–1782), head of the Czartoryski 'Family'. Their influence, however, was almost entirely kept behind the scenes as women were strictly excluded from the Commonwealth's public institutions. As will be discussed in Chapter 1, 'private' influence of this sort was the object of profound suspicion among many szlachta commentators, and the late seventeenth and early eighteenth centuries saw several complaints against the alleged 'private' role in public life of women, in particular the queen Maria Sobieska (see Chapter 3).

[4] There were some legal barriers to participation: for example, in theory only szlachta owning property in a given region could attend that region's sejmik, which in principle disenfranchised both those whose property was elsewhere in the Commonwealth and the entirely landless. In practice, however, propertyless szlachta were rarely excluded from the sejmiki. More actively enforced was the gradual exclusion of members of the Commonwealth's

political discourse was thus created inside the Commonwealth's political institutions, and this is reflected in the types of sources that remain, with records of the proceedings of assemblies such as Sejms and sejmiki and polemical tracts on particular debates or controversies by far predominating over abstract treatises on the theory or philosophy of politics and government. To misquote a later eighteenth-century foreign observer of the Commonwealth, the szlachta did not need to spend time discussing in the abstract what should be done: they had the ability to act, or at least to try to.

In some ways, therefore, analysing szlachta political culture is more of an anthropological task than one of political philosophy: the historian must attempt to use the records created by the practice of politics in the early modern Commonwealth to uncover the assumptions and values shared by its practitioners. This includes, perhaps most importantly, those assumptions and values that were so completely and uncontestably shared that they were not, indeed needed not be, openly debated or analysed: the 'universe of the undiscussed'.

This study will argue that one central value in szlachta political culture was that of public virtue. The meaning and historical roots (in particular in classical Greek and Roman political thought) of this concept will be discussed in Chapter 1. But virtue as a political value can be summarized as the belief that each individual citizen is required at all times to subordinate his personal, private interests to the demands of the common good of the political community. It is important to emphasize that this concept of virtue was a political one, relating to the public sphere and the conduct of public affairs, rather than to the personal morality or conduct of citizens in their private lives. Indeed, given the central role of virtue in the Commonwealth's political discourse, it is remarkable how little discussion there was of the relationship between public and private virtue, for example of how a virtuous citizen should dispose of his private property, or behave towards his family. In szlachta public discourse, discussion of virtue concentrated almost exclusively on the political sphere.[5]

---

religious minorities from public life, with for example the last non-Catholic envoy ejected from the Sejm in 1718, and non-Catholics formally barred from the Sejm and from serving as judges on the Tribunal in 1733.

[5] One partial exception to this was religion, where Catholic piety was often acknowledged as necessary for virtue, while the coming of Christianity was often identified as key to the origins of szlachta virtue and liberty in szlachta writers' accounts of the Commonwealth's early history. Anna Grześkowiak-Krawicz, *Regina Libertas: Wolność w polskiej myśli politycznej XVIII wieku* (Gdańsk, 2006), pp. 260–4. Jerzy Lukowski, 'The Szlachta and their Ancestors in the Eighteenth Century', *Kwartalnik Historyczny*, 111, 3 (2004), pp. 161–82, and *Disorderly Liberty: The Political Culture of the Polish-Lithuanian Commonwealth in the Eighteenth Century* (London, 2010).

LIBERTY AND VIRTUE

Virtue was intimately connected to another key value in szlachta political thought, namely liberty. The szlachta concept of liberty, and the institutions it underpinned, in particular the *liberum veto* and the elective monarchy, have generally been the focus of historians' analysis of the Commonwealth's political culture in the early modern period. Arguably the most important figure in modern scholarship on szlachta liberty was Władysław Konopczyński, who was active during the first half of the twentieth century.

Konopczyński presented szlachta liberty as less a single political concept and more an assortment of individual privileges, political, social, and economic, including the freedom from arbitrary arrest, freedom from taxation, and the szlachta's monopoly on public office and the ownership of land. Together, these various privileges sustained the szlachta's position of social and economic predominance in Poland-Lithuania, leaving the szlachta free to lord it over the Commonwealth's peasants, townspeople, and Jews. According to Konopczyński, the capstone of this edifice of individual privileges (described by szlachta writers as their 'golden liberty') was the *liberum veto*, the right of a single *szlachcic* to bar a decision of a local sejmik or of a single envoy to the central Sejm to block legislation and even to disrupt an entire parliamentary session. The *liberum veto* equipped the szlachta to resist any challenge to its privileges, and was passionately defended throughout the early modern period by all but a handful of reformists. However, Konopczyński argued that the *liberum veto* also fatally undermined the effectiveness of the Commonwealth's central government, ultimately leaving it powerless to resist partition at the hands of its neighbours (Russia, Prussia, and the Habsburg monarchy, states more centralized and capable of mobilizing military resources than the Commonwealth) at the end of the eighteenth century.[6]

Konopczyński thus portrayed the szlachta's defence of its 'golden liberty' and the *liberum veto* as a triumph of the szlachta's particular interest over the common interest of Poland-Lithuania in maintaining its independence. In this, Konopczyński echoed the historians of the nineteenth-century 'Kraków School', who argued that the Commonwealth was doomed to partition by its internal weaknesses and the szlachta's selfish preservation of its

---

[6] Władysław Konopczyński, *Liberum veto: studium porównawczo-historyczne* (Kraków, 1918, 2nd edition Kraków, 2002) and *Dzieje Polski Nowożytnej* (2nd edition, Warsaw, 1986). See also Konopczyński, *Polska a Szwecja: od pokoju Oliwskiego do upadku Rzeczypospolitej 1660–1795* (Warsaw, 1924).

privileges.[7] Ironically, both Konopczyński and the 'Kraków School' historians were themselves echoing the moralizing claims of eighteenth-century szlachta politicians and commentators who, as discussed in Chapter 2, frequently attributed the disorder and dysfunction in the Commonwealth's government to the failure of individuals to act virtuously and put aside their 'private' interests in favour of the common good.[8]

Following Konopczyński, historians such as Juliusz Bardach, Władysław Czapliński, Henryk Olszewski, and Jerzy Lukowski have analysed szlachta political thought primarily in terms of the szlachta's ultimately self-destructive attachment to its 'golden liberty' and have focused on attempting to understand why the various attempts to reform the Commonwealth, including attempts to abolish the *liberum veto*, proved unsuccessful until the very end of the eighteenth century, by which point it was too late to preserve the Commonwealth's independence.

Once again echoing the language of early modern szlachta commentators, a running theme in this historiography has been an emphasis on the 'demoralization' of the szlachta during the heyday of the 'golden liberty'. One particular period identified as one of szlachta selfishness and resulting political chaos in the Commonwealth is that of the reigns of Kings Augustus II (r. 1697–1733) and his son Augustus III (r. 1733–63) of the Saxon Wettin dynasty, the so-called 'Saxon period'. The szlachta's defence of their particular privileges at the expense of the Commonwealth's general interest in effective government and independence from foreign domination has thus been identified not just as an isolated failing, but as part of a general moral decline among the szlachta, especially during the Saxon period. In a sense, these historians have remained within the discourse of virtue and its loss as the cause of the Commonwealth's decline, rather than engaging critically with it.[9]

---

[7] See, for example, Michał Bobrzyński, *Dzieje Polski w zarysie* (Kraków, 1879), or Józef Szujski, *Dzieje Polski według ostatnich badań* (Lwów, 1866) and *Historii polskiej treściwie opowiedzanej ksiąg dwanaście* (Kraków, 1880).

[8] The continuity between eighteenth-century polemics and the arguments of the 'Kraków School' may at least in part be explained by the historical context in which historians such as Bobrzyński were writing. Following the Partitions of Poland, and the failed uprisings of 1830–1 and 1863–4 against the partitioning powers, inevitably Polish historians were drawn to the questions of 'what went wrong?' and 'who was to blame?' Lukowski has commented that the 'course of history turned [nineteenth-century historians] . . . into moralists'. Lukowski, *Disorderly Liberty*, vii.

[9] See for example Juliusz Bardach (ed.), *Historia państwa i prawa Polski*; vol. 2, Zdzisław Kaczmarczyk and Bogusław Leśnodorski (eds.), *Od połowy XV wieku do r. 1795* (Warsaw, 1966), Władysław Czapliński, *O Polsce siedemnastowiecznej: Problemy i sprawy* (Warsaw, 1966), Henryk Olszewski, *Sejm Rzeczypospolitej epoki oligarchii 1652–1763: Prawo Praktyka Teoria Programy* (Poznań, 1966), Lukowski, *Liberty's Folly: The Polish-Lithuanian Commonwealth in the Eighteenth Century* (London, 1991). In his more recent work, however, Lukowski has engaged critically with eighteenth-century szlachta rhetoric of virtue and

This negative analysis of szlachta liberty has, however, been challenged by some revisionist historians, most notably Andrzej Sulima Kamiński. Kamiński has argued that the szlachta's elaborate structure of shared political rights, along with the myth of their shared Sarmatian origins, allowed a religiously pluralist, multilingual noble estate whose members were geographically widely dispersed, to forge a common identity. The Commonwealth's decentralized system of government and tradition of decision-making by consensus, enshrined in the *liberum veto*, ensured that the views of all parts of the szlachta state were heard, with no individual region or special interest group being able to impose its will upon the rest. This sense of common identity and equal rights to participate in government were, Kamiński has argued, crucial to ensuring that the vast and diverse Commonwealth held together for as long as it did, despite the various centrifugal pressures that it faced.[10] In a similar vein, Andrzej Walicki and Robert Frost have emphasized that the practice of decision-making by unanimity and the *liberum veto* created powerful incentives for different interest groups to compromise with each other in order to reach consensus.[11]

Another group of revisionists, led by Jacek Staszewski, has challenged Konopczyński's claim that the szlachta's 'golden liberty', including the *liberum veto*, condemned the Commonwealth's central government to dysfunction and ineffectiveness. Staszewski and his followers have emphasized the freedom of action enjoyed by the Commonwealth's kings and their ministers, in particular during the Saxon period when Augustus II

---

corruption, as will be discussed below. Perhaps the most striking example of the tendency to connect szlachta conservatism with stupidity and moral degeneracy is Zamoyski's description of the young Karol Radziwiłł, later head of one of the Commonwealth's most powerful magnate families and a leader of the conservative Confederation of Bar, as a teenage alcoholic who was only taught to read by having metal letters hung in trees as targets for pistol practice. Adam Zamoyski, *The Last King of Poland* (London, 1992), p. 21.

[10] Andrzej Sulima Kamiński, *Historia Rzeczypospolitej wielu Narodów 1505–1795: Obywatele, ich państwa, społeczeństwo, kultura* (Lublin, 2000) and *Republic vs Autocracy: Poland-Lithuania and Russia 1686–1697* (Cambridge, MA, 1993).

[11] Frost has compared the effect of the *liberum veto* in the Commonwealth to that of national vetoes in international institutions such as the European Union, where requirements to reach consensus can help protect smaller member states against bullying by more powerful partners, albeit at some cost to the institution's ability to make rapid decisions. Robert Frost, 'The Nobility of Poland-Lithuania, 1569–1795', in Hamish Scott (ed.), *The European Nobilities in the Seventeenth and Eighteenth Centuries* (2 vols., London, 1995), vol. 2 (*Northern, Central and Eastern Europe*), pp. 183–222. See also Frost, '"Liberty without License?" The Failure of Polish Democratic Thought in the Seventeenth Century', in Mieczysław Biskupski and James Pula (eds.), *Polish Democratic Thought from the Renaissance to the Great Emigration: Essays and Documents* (New York, 1990), pp. 29–54, Andrzej Walicki, *The Three Traditions in Polish Patriotism and their Contemporary Relevance* (Bloomington, IN, 1988) and *The Enlightenment and the Birth of Modern Nationhood: Polish Political Thought from Noble Republicanism to Tadeusz Kościuszko* (Notre Dame, IN, 1989).

and Augustus III were able to draw on the financial, military, and diplomatic resources of their Electorate of Saxony.[12] In his studies of the Swedish Vasa dynasty (Kings Zygmunt III (r. 1587–1632), Władysław IV (r. 1632–48), and Jan Kazimierz (r. 1648–68)), Frost has similarly emphasized the power of the monarchy and its independence from institutions such as the Sejm, while noting how close the Vasa kings came in the middle of the seventeenth century to breaking free of the legal restrictions on the crown and laying the foundations for a strong hereditary monarchy.[13]

Against Konopczyński's view of szlachta liberty as no more than a collection of privileges, Edward Opaliński and especially Anna Grześkowiak-Krwawicz have argued that a single, coherent concept of liberty did exist in szlachta political thought, based on a concept of 'republican liberty'. Drawing on the work of J. G. A. Pocock and Quentin Skinner, Grześkowiak-Krwawicz has argued that in szlachta political culture, liberty was understood above all as independence from the will of a ruler. This concept encapsulated both the szlachta's freedom from interference from government, such as freedom of speech or freedom from arbitrary arrest, and the szlachta's extensive rights to participate in government, for example at sejmiki, Sejms, and royal elections. According to Grześkowiak-Krwawicz's reading of szlachta liberty, it was by their participation in government that the szlachta ensured that their liberty did not depend upon the continued favour of a king with the power to revoke it if he pleased. Liberty was thus a collective pursuit that required that sovereignty in the Commonwealth belong not to the king alone, but be shared with the szlachta citizenry.[14]

Grześkowiak-Krwawicz has also highlighted the close connection in szlachta political thought between this 'republican' concept of liberty and virtue. In particular, she has noted the distinction drawn by szlachta commentators between virtuous 'liberty' (*wolność*) and sinful 'licence'

---

[12] Jacek Staszewski, *August II Mocny* (Wrocław, 1998) and *August III Sas* (Wrocław, 1989). See also Adam Perłakowski, *Jan Jerzy Przebendowski jako podskarbi wielki koronny (1703–1729): Studium funkcjonowania ministerium* (Kraków, 2004).

[13] Robert Frost, *After the Deluge: Poland-Lithuania and the Second Northern War 1655–1660* (Cambridge, 1993).

[14] Edward Opaliński, *Kultura polityczna szlachty polskiej w latach 1587–1652: system parlamentarny a społeczeństwo obywatelskie* (Warsaw, 1995) and 'Civic Humanism and Republican Citizenship in the Polish Renaissance', in Martin van Gelderen and Quentin Skinner (eds.), *Republicanism: A Shared European Heritage* (2 vols., Cambridge, 2002), vol. 1 (*Republicanism and Constitutionalism in Early Modern Europe*), pp. 147–66. Grześkowiak-Krwawicz, *Regina Libertas*, 'Quentin Skinner i teoria wolności republikańskiej', *Archiwum historii filozofii i myśli społecznej*, 45 (2000), pp. 165–74, and 'Deux libertés, l'ancienne et la nouvelle, dans la pensée politique polonaise du XVIIIe siècle', in Grześkowiak-Krwawicz and Izabella Zatorska (eds.), *Liberté: Héritage du Passé ou Idée des Lumières?* (Kraków, 2003), pp. 44–59.

(*swawola*). Liberty was understood as more than just an individual's freedom to act according to his own will, but rather required its practitioners to act in accordance with the common good, that is virtuously.[15] This moral component of liberty was highlighted in the sixteenth century by the cleric, humanist, and political writer Andrzej Frycz Modrzewski, who denied that the freedom to act viciously could be considered true liberty, arguing that 'no one thinks that God is a stranger to liberty, just because He cannot sin'.[16]

In contrast to virtuous liberty, licence (*swawola*) was the freedom to act purely in the pursuit of private interests. Private interests were assumed to be automatically opposed to the common good (see Chapter 1), and hence vicious. Licentious behaviour was to be condemned as harmful to the common interest as well as to the moral nature of the actor. Modrzewski compared licence to the freedom enjoyed by an unbridled horse, which thrashes around wildly in its stable, injuring both itself and others.[17] In the early eighteenth century, the term *swawolnie* (and occasionally the Latin equivalent *licentier*) was frequently used to condemn injuries inflicted on the szlachta, or violations of their legal rights, in particular by troops levying 'contributions' on szlachta property during and after the Commonwealth's involvement in the Great Northern War (see Chapters 5 and 6).

Thus Grześkowiak-Krwawicz has noted that virtue was indispensable to szlachta liberty. At the same time, liberty was in turn necessary to virtue: the preservation of liberty and the free Commonwealth (above all against encroachments by the monarchy) was regarded as the highest common good. Virtue therefore demanded the defence of liberty. Szlachta writers also claimed that only those living in a state of liberty had the capacity to discern and pursue the common good, whereas those who were dependent upon a master could work only for their master's interests.[18] Thus only those who enjoyed liberty could attain virtue. Virtue and liberty were inextricably linked.[19]

---

[15] Grześkowiak-Krwawicz, *Regina Libertas*, pp. 252–3. See also Frost, ' "Liberty without License?" '.

[16] 'Nemo Deum existimet libertatis esse expertem, propterea quod peccare non possit', Andrzej Frycz Modrzewski, *De Republica Emendanda* (1551–9), in *Andreae Fricii Modrevii Opera Omnia* (ed. Kazimierz Kumaniecki, 3 vols., Warsaw, 1953), vol. 2, p. 166.

[17] Modrzewski, *De Republica Emendanda*, vol. 2, p. 167.

[18] Here Grześkowiak-Krwawicz builds in particular on Skinner's argument that seventeenth-century English republicans held that the lack of freedom resulted in individuals becoming 'dis-couraged', 'dis-heartened', and 'dis-spirited', and hence diminished as human beings. Skinner, 'A Third Concept of Liberty', Berlin Lecture to the British Academy 2001, *Proceedings of the British Academy*, 117 (2002), pp. 237–68 (pp. 258–60).

[19] Grześkowiak-Krwawicz, *Regina Libertas*, pp. 249–92. Grześkowiak-Krwawicz has also argued that the importance of virtue to the early modern szlachta concept of liberty

Throughout the early modern period, however, szlachta politicians and commentators bemoaned the loss of virtue among the Commonwealth's citizens, who were becoming corrupted by the pursuit of private interests rather than the common good.[20] Grześkowiak-Krwawicz has noted a near-universal pessimism among szlachta commentators about the decline of virtue in the Commonwealth. She has argued that this moral perspective also coloured szlachta observers' view of the Commonwealth's political situation. Drawing parallels with the fall of the Roman republic after its citizens' supposed moral decline, szlachta commentators saw the Commonwealth's internal turmoil and external weakness in terms of the moral degeneration of its citizens. Indeed, 'for the majority of the szlachta, the loss of virtue was the sole cause of the crisis of the state'. Hence throughout the early modern period szlachta writers argued that it was vital that inculcating virtue be a central part of the education of young noblemen.[21]

This moralizing approach among szlachta commentators has also been highlighted by Lukowski, who has in particular noted the role played in moral accounts of the Commonwealth and its history by the szlachta's (real or invented) ancestors. According to szlachta histories (or pseudo-histories) of the origins of the Commonwealth and of szlachta liberty, these ancestors had, by their selfless service to their fatherland, inspired grateful kings to bestow upon them and their heirs the 'golden liberty' as a reward for their virtuous service. Liberty thus formed a precious inheritance for later generations, who were challenged to live up to the virtuous example of their glorious forebears. Some figures in more recent times had managed to do this, such as Jan Zamoyski (1542–1605), the sixteenth-century champion of the right of every *szlachcic* to vote in royal elections, and Jerzy Sebastian Lubomirski (1616–67), leader of the great seventeenth-century uprising (*rokosz*) against the monarchist designs of King Jan Kazimierz. By the eighteenth century, however, the bulk of the szlachta had lost their virtue, having become devoted to private wealth and luxury rather than to the fatherland. This moral failure, rather than any imperfections in the laws and institutions also passed down by the ancestors, had led to the Commonwealth's decline into internal strife and disorder. That disorder in turn threatened the szlachta's inheritance, by opening

constitutes an important element of continuity between traditional szlachta political thought and the ideas of later eighteenth-century thinkers and reformers such as Stanisław Konarski and Hugo Kołłątaj.

[20] Grześkowiak-Krwawicz, *Regina Libertas*, pp. 273–4. See also Olszewski, *Dokryny prawno-ustrojowe czasów saskich 1697–1740* (Warsaw, 1961), pp. 17–19.

[21] Grześkowiak-Krwawicz, *Regina Libertas*, pp. 262–75.

the way for ambitious monarchs to undermine the Commonwealth's laws and erode szlachta liberty.[22]

Thus Lukowski too has emphasized the extent to which szlachta commentators analysed the Commonwealth and its problems in moral rather than institutional terms. He has, however, taken a sharply negative view of this focus on virtue and on the szlachta's 'ancestral legacies'. According to Lukowski, this moral approach was at best a form of escapism: dwelling on utopian visions of the past and blaming the Commonwealth's present turmoil and paralysis on individuals' lack of virtue allowed szlachta politicians and commentators to avoid addressing the real issue of the Commonwealth's institutional flaws. At worst, the claims that the laws bequeathed to the szlachta by their glorious ancestors were perfect, and that for all their moral decline the szlachta remained ready to emulate those ancestors by laying down their lives for their liberty (a claim given institutional form in the *pospolite ruszenie* or mass levy of the szlachta), legitimated opposition to the reforms (above all the abolition of the *liberum veto*) that Lukowski, following Konopczyński, argues were necessary to revive the Commonwealth's government and preserve its independence. Szlachta commentators' moral perspective thus contributed to the Commonwealth's continuing dysfunction and paralysis and thence its ultimate collapse.[23]

VIRTUE AND REFORM

While building on the work of both Lukowski and Grześkowiak-Krwawicz, this study argues for a different perspective on the role of virtue in szlachta political thought. Contrary to Lukowski, it argues that szlachta political thinkers' portrayal of the Commonwealth's decline in moral terms was more than just naïve utopianism, or an attempt to evade the need for constitutional reform. Rather, during the early decades of the eighteenth century, moral analysis of the Commonwealth's plight informed and inspired a series of attempts to reform the Commonwealth's laws and institutions, aimed at sweeping away a degenerate ruling elite and ensuring government for the common good.

These reform proposals also show that in szlachta political thought virtue was not just a necessary attribute for citizens of the free Commonwealth, as Grześkowiak-Krwawicz had described. In addition, the concept of

---

[22] Lukowski, *Disorderly Liberty*, pp. 13–32. See also Lukowski, 'The Szlachta and their Ancestors'.

[23] Lukowski, *Disorderly Liberty*, pp. 13–32.

virtue was an indispensable analytical tool for szlachta politicians and commentators seeking to understand the Commonwealth's increasing political turmoil and dysfunction. Not only did the loss of virtue explain the decline of the szlachta state: the need to restore virtue pointed towards particular institutional changes that were needed to reverse that decline. So going beyond Grześkowiak-Krwawicz's work, this study argues that the concept of virtue was central to the institutional, as well as the moral or behavioural, analysis of early modern szlachta thinkers.

Chapter 1 sets the scene by following Grześkowiak-Krwawicz in presenting the concept of virtue as an essential part of a coherent ideal of the Commonwealth that brought together szlachta ideas on liberty, respect for the law, and collective sovereignty. The szlachta were not, of course, a monolith, and it would be misleading to speak of a singular 'szlachta opinion', given the repeated controversies and factional quarrels that characterized the Commonwealth's politics throughout the early modern period. The ideal of the Commonwealth was not, therefore, a single political programme, but rather a shared paradigm of ideas and values that set the terms within which political arguments were framed and disputes were pursued. It was the common ground on which the game was played, and battles fought.

Virtue was an indispensable element of this ideal, not just as a necessary condition for liberty, or for citizenship, but also central to the very purpose of government and of the Commonwealth. Given the centrality of virtue to this ideal, it was logical that virtue should be indispensable to szlachta observers' analysis of the Commonwealth's chronic political dysfunction. As Grześkowiak-Krwawicz and Lukowski have recognized, szlachta commentators routinely discussed the Commonwealth's political problems in moral terms, as the result of corruption among the Commonwealth's government and citizens. This was particularly the case during the early years of the reign of Augustus II, when the Commonwealth's political system came under unprecedented strain.

If a loss of virtue was the cause of the Commonwealth's problems, it followed that the key challenge was how virtue could be restored. Chapter 2 examines a purely moralizing response to that challenge during the late seventeenth and early eighteenth centuries. Starting from the assumption that the Commonwealth's problems lay not with its laws or institutions but with the character of its citizens, some szlachta writers sought different means of engineering a moral reformation among their fellow citizens. The argument that institutional tinkering could not be the right response to a problem that was ultimately a moral one was perhaps best represented by Stanisław Herakliusz Lubomirski, Grand Marshal of the Crown (i.e. Poland), in his 1700 dialogue *De Vanitate Consiliorum*, which looked for a solution to the Commonwealth's problems in trust and harmony between its estates, rather than changes to the law. Chapter 2 discusses the calls by Lubomirski and others for a moral reformation of the szlachta, to be achieved either through straightforward exhortation, by rallying the szlachta in a new holy war, or through the appointment of a government of worthy men by the king.

These proposals did not involve any reform to the Commonwealth's laws or institutions of government. Against Lukowski's claim that the focus on virtue was a substitute for, or a barrier to, consideration of institutional change, Chapters 3 to 6 argue that during the late seventeenth and early eighteenth centuries, and in particular in the first two decades of the reign of Augustus II, the aim of restoring virtue lay behind a number of attempts to reform the Commonwealth's government.

The first of these, discussed in Chapter 3, came from below, from the regional szlachta assembled in the sejmiki. Sejmik records, this chapter argues, show a conviction among the regional szlachta that the Commonwealth's government had been usurped by a corrupt clique of self-interested senators, ministers, and courtiers clustered around the throne, and that this usurpation was primarily responsible for the Commonwealth's descent into turmoil. The restoration of the Commonwealth therefore required the removal of this corrupt clique. To this end, working within the existing constitution, the sejmiki lobbied for only virtuous men, drawn from the wider szlachta, to be appointed to office. At the same time, however, the regional szlachta also increasingly took matters into their own hands, by expanding the role and powers of local government in the Commonwealth. Chapter 3 argues that the development of local government, a long-running trend which accelerated markedly in the early eighteenth century (especially following the outbreak of the Great Northern War), represented an attempt by the szlachta of the Commonwealth's various regions, working through the sejmiki, to build from the bottom up the government of worthy men that they were simultaneously urging the king to appoint at the centre.

During the years of the Great Northern War, a small group of szlachta politicians and writers sought to go further than either the moral exhortations of Lubomirski or the evolutionary changes being implemented by the sejmiki. Chapter 4 discusses a set of proposals for radical reform of the Commonwealth's government: Stanisław Dunin Karwicki's *De Ordinanda Republica* of around 1705, Jerzy Dzieduszycki's *Traktat o elekcyi królów polskich* of 1707, and the anonymous *Eclipsis Poloniae Orbi Publico Demonstrata* of 1709. It argues that restoring virtuous government was the central objective of these radical reformers (whom some historians have labelled 'republicans').[24] This goal was to be achieved by reforming the Commonwealth's government in such a way as to allow only virtuous men to rise to positions of power, while at the same time encouraging the development of virtue among the Commonwealth's szlachta citizens. A key theme of these proposals was giving the entire szlachta an effective voice in electing men to the Commonwealth's highest offices, including the crown. Making office-holders subject to the judgement of their fellow citizens would ensure that they only served the common interest of the whole Commonwealth, rather than working for private gain.

Chapters 5 and 6 then discuss attempts to reform the Commonwealth's government at the end of the Great Northern War, first at the Sejm of 1712–13 and then during the General Confederation of Tarnogród (1715–17). These chapters argue that central to the programmes of the Sejm envoys and the Tarnogród confederates were proposals to make the Commonwealth's ministers accountable to the szlachta for their actions, with a particular focus on holding the hetmans to answer for the forced 'contributions' levied on szlachta property by their armies. The Sejm envoys and confederates argued that accountability to the szlachta was necessary to ensure that ministers acted in accordance with the law and the common good, and ministers could be punished for any 'licentious' (*swawolny*) conduct. To this end, they pressed for the establishment of new judicial institutions to investigate ministers' conduct, with the power either to force those found guilty of 'licence' to pay compensation or to remove them from office. The goal of restoring virtuous government was thus central to the programmes of the Sejm envoys and the Tarnogród confederates, and both groups attempted (though ultimately unsuccessfully) to implement significant reforms to the Commonwealth's government in order to achieve this objective.

The majority of this study thus focuses on the turbulent early years of the reign of Augustus II, and Chapters 5 and 6 offer new interpretations of two significant episodes towards the end of this period. The primary intention is not, however, to present a comprehensive narrative of these years,[25] but rather to use the period as a case-study to illustrate broader themes in szlachta political thought, in particular the centrality of the concept of virtue and its potential to inspire significant attempts to reform the Commonwealth's government.

The two decades from the election of Augustus II in 1697 to the 'Silent Sejm' of 1717 serve well as a case-study owing to the exceptional turmoil that

---

[24] Chapter 1, however, argues that identifying a distinct 'republican' tradition within szlachta political thought is problematic, given the near universal adherence to the ideal of the Commonwealth.

[25] A chronology of key dates is, however, included as Appendix A.

they witnessed. During this period the Commonwealth's political system came under immense, perhaps unprecedented, strain. This was the result of a combination of internal political conflicts (over the 1697 election between supporters of Augustus II and his rivals Jakub Sobieski and François de Conti, only settled in 1699, and then in the Grand Duchy of Lithuania between supporters and opponents of the magnate Sapieha family); the arrival on the throne of a king possessed of external diplomatic and military resources far beyond those of any of his predecessors; the decade of devastating warfare started by Augustus II's attack on Swedish Livonia in 1700; and repeated intervention by foreign powers, most notably Sweden and Russia.

This combination of internal and external challenges tested the szlachta state as never before, and threw into sharp relief some of the biggest challenges facing the Commonwealth as a political system: how to ensure that government could function (not least in protecting the Commonwealth from external attack) without being autocratic; whose interests government should serve; and how questions of policy (in particular of war and peace) should be decided. In other words, faced with the turmoil that the early years of Augustus II brought, the question of how the Commonwealth should be constituted and should function politically was unavoidable. At the same time, the patent failure of the Commonwealth to deal with these challenges and to determine its own destiny made clear that the szlachta state was in some fundamental way broken and in need of repair.

At the beginning of the eighteenth century, szlachta politicians and commentators were thus forced to confront the Commonwealth's profound political and constitutional failings. The scale of those failings required a return to first principles both to analyse the problems facing the Commonwealth and to produce and propose solutions. That virtue was central to szlachta observers' analyses of and responses to the crisis of the early eighteenth century demonstrates how the concept of virtue was an indispensable element of szlachta political thought, and of contemporaries' understanding of the szlachta state.

Given the widespread acknowledgement among the szlachta at the start of the eighteenth century that the Commonwealth was in need of reform, and the number of different reform efforts that this period saw, the early years of Augustus II's reign should arguably be considered a 'reforming moment' in the history of the szlachta state. Chapter 7 examines why the fruits of this reforming moment proved to be so meagre, arguing that the political stalemate of this period was not only the result of innate conservatism and disunity among the szlachta or foreign intervention, but also of the collision of competing reform efforts, including the authoritarian, monarchist programme adopted by Augustus II. With this clash of reform proposals preventing any one from achieving a decisive victory, arguably the Commonwealth suffered in this period not from too little drive for reform, but too much. Chapter 7 then considers whether an alternative outcome was possible, based on co-operation rather than competition between king and szlachta aimed at restoring effective but still collective government, expressed through the language of virtue and the common good.

Chapter 8 then examines the szlachta political tradition in international context, comparing szlachta ideas with those of other early modern republican traditions, in particular in England, Scotland, and Great Britain. This chapter argues that a continuing preoccupation with virtue was not only a central but also a distinctive feature of szlachta political thought. Despite some similarities between both the language used and some of the policies advocated by British and szlachta republicans in the late seventeenth and eighteenth centuries, during this period a gulf gradually opened up between the conceptual foundations of the szlachta republican tradition relative to its British counterparts. For whereas szlachta political thinkers continued to consider that the maintenance of a commonwealth required that citizens be virtuous, and subordinate their private interests to the common good, British contemporaries increasingly rejected the necessity of virtue, and instead accepted self-interest as an inevitable and even positive force in society. Rather than suppressing self-interest in the name of the common good, British political (and later economic) thinkers explored how self-interest might instead be harnessed for the common interest, through the skilful construction of laws and institutions, a technique termed 'political architecture'.

The suggestion that the distinguishing feature of the szlachta republican tradition was its retention of classical assumptions that republicans elsewhere were increasingly abandoning, prompts the question of whether szlachta political thought was distinctive in its backwardness relative to more 'progressive' developments elsewhere in early modern Europe. This question is discussed in the Conclusion, which argues that despite the apparent triumph of 'political architecture' and the general acceptance of individual selfishness, all political (and indeed economic) systems nevertheless depend to some extent on individuals sharing certain values, adhering to norms of behaviour and trusting others to do the same—even when they might profit from contravening those norms. To some degree, therefore, all polities, if they are to survive, require that citizens accept a common interest in the maintenance of the system itself, and subordinate their private interests to that common good. The szlachta Commonwealth was therefore distinctive not in requiring deference to the common good, which szlachta thinkers termed virtue, but in the extent to which it did so.

1

The Ideal of the Commonwealth

COLLECTIVE SOVEREIGNTY AND THE *FORMA MIXTA*

Throughout the early modern period, a key characteristic of the Polish (later Polish-Lithuanian) polity was its mixed form of government. As a result of a series of concessions made to the Polish nobility dating from the late middle ages, Polish kings did not rule their realm alone, but were obliged to govern in partnership with the szlachta, Poland's wider political nation. Usually in return for support in war or to secure the succession to the throne, from the late fourteenth century onwards Polish kings granted the nobility a series of rights and privileges that gradually expanded their role in the kingdom's government. Thus under the privilege of Košice, in 1374, the szlachta were exempt from taxation except by their own consent, and in 1454 it was conceded at Nieszawa that the szlachta's agreement, expressed through their local assemblies, the sejmiki, was required before they could be summoned for military service. The principle of government by agreement with the szlachta was then extended to all areas of government by the 1505 statute *Nihil Novi*, which provided that no new legislation at all could be passed without the consent of both the Senate and the szlachta's envoys at the Sejm.

The increasing role of the szlachta in government was reflected in changes in the language of politics during the sixteenth century. By the middle of that century, statutes identified the legislating authority not as the king but as the *Res publica*, or in its Polish form the *Rzeczpospolita* (Commonwealth). The *Rzeczpospolita* was identified variously as the Sejm, consisting of three deliberating estates, the king, the Senate, and the Chamber of envoys chosen by the szlachta, or as the entire szlachta estate. Sovereignty was thus asserted to be not the exclusive possession of the king, but rather shared with the szlachta: a principle articulated in the much-repeated szlachta slogan, '*nic u nas bez nas*': 'nothing [should be decided] concerning us, without us'. The szlachta described themselves not as subjects of their king, but as citizens (*obywatele*), 'as the creators, owners and heirs of the state'.[1] This edifice of collective government was arguably completed in 1573. Following the death of King Zygmunt August, the last of the Jagiellonian dynasty, who had been more or less hereditary rulers of Poland and Lithuania since the fourteenth century, the General Confederation of Warsaw instituted a fully elective monarchy for the combined Polish-Lithuanian state, complete with both contractual limitations on the prerogatives of the crown and repeated interregna, that served to prevent Polish-Lithuanian kings from ruling independently of their szlachta citizens.

Analysing their constitution, from the mid-sixteenth century onwards, szlachta political thinkers described the Commonwealth's government as a *forma mixta* as described by classical authors, in particular Aristotle and Cicero. This mixed constitution combined monarchic, aristocratic, and democratic elements, which szlachta commentators identified in their own state as respectively the king, the Senate, and either the Chamber of Envoys or the szlachta citizenry as a whole. In particular, the sixteenth-century churchman and writer Andrzej Frycz Modrzewski analysed the Polish government of his day as a mixed constitution, which following Cicero he termed a *res publica*.[2] The description of the Commonwealth's constitution as a combination of three elements became standard in szlachta political discourse: by the eighteenth century, one preacher to the Sejm even compared the threefold state to the Holy Trinity itself.[3]

Both Aristotle and Cicero had identified the mixed constitution as the best of all forms of government, holding up as classic examples the governments of ancient Sparta and republican Rome. Modrzewski even claimed divine sanction for this model too, citing the constitution given by Moses to the Israelites as another example of the *forma mixta*. Szlachta writers congratulated themselves on having adopted the mixed constitution, but then adapted and improved on previous examples, for instance by having membership of the aristocratic element (the Senate) depend on virtue not birth, and giving the power of veto not just to a small number of Ephors or Tribunes, but to the entire szlachta.[4]

[1] Opaliński, 'Civic Humanism and Republican Citizenship', p. 156. See also Opaliński, *Kultura polityczna szlachty polskiej*. Note, however, that many szlachta accounts of the early history of their state dated the development of szlachta liberty and collective government even earlier, to the semi-mythical beginnings of the Polish monarchy. Lukowski, 'The Szlachta and their Ancestors'.

[2] Modrzewski, *De Republica Emendanda*, vol. 1, p. 32. *Res publica* was the Latin equivalent of the Greek term *politeia*, used by Aristotle to signify political society in general, the mixed constitution, and the pure form of the rule of the many.

[3] Lukowski, 'Political Ideas among the Polish Nobility in the Eighteenth Century (to 1788)', *Slavonic and East European Review*, 82, 1 (2004), pp. 1–26 (p. 1).

[4] Modrzewski, *De Republica Emendanda*, vol. 1, pp. 32 and 70.

The forum in which the three elements of the szlachta state's compound government came together was the Sejm. Since the *Nihil Novi* statute of 1505, the Sejm enjoyed the exclusive right to make legislation, but in the absence of the doctrine of the separation of powers, the Sejm was also held to be the supreme decision-making body in the Commonwealth on matters that would today be considered executive (such as decisions over diplomacy, peace, and war), as well as, at least in theory, sitting at the top of the Commonwealth's judicial system. Throughout the early modern period, the authority of the Sejm was a key principle of szlachta political thought, and szlachta politicians and writers were quick to denounce any 'usurpation' of the Sejm's decision-making authority, either by kings or bodies such as the Senate Council.[5]

Legality and the law were of very great importance in szlachta political thought. Grześkowiak-Krwawicz and Lukowski, among others, have noted the szlachta's great reverence for the law, with little distinction drawn between what today would be considered 'constitutional' law, pertaining to the institutions of government and the processes for making policy decisions, and other law (the term *constitutio/konstytucja* was used for any statute). Law was both the product, or expression, of the sovereign authority of the Sejm and the *Rzeczpospolita*, and the guarantor of that authority, since it was through law (not least *Nihil Novi*) that the prerogatives of institutions such as the Sejm, as well as restrictions on the powers of the monarchy, were laid down. Hence failures to respect the established roles of different institutions, in particular violations by the king of the restrictions placed upon him, which today might be termed 'unconstitutional', were frequently criticized by szlachta writers

---

[5] The Senate Council was a council of senators resident with the king in the intervals between Sejms. In theory, the Council's function was to advise the king and ensure his compliance with the law. Any decisions it took on urgent business were subject to ratification by the Sejm. During the seventeenth and early eighteenth centuries, however, several kings, in particular Augustus II, attempted to build up the Senate Council into a more substantial institution of government: this was strongly opposed by the Sejm and the sejmiki. See Chapter 3 for calls from the sejmiki for the Senate Council to be either abolished or made more subject to, and accountable to, the Sejm. Jarosław Poraziński, 'Funkcje polityczne i ustrojowe rad senatu w latach 1697-1717', *Kwartalnik Historyczny*, 91, 1 (1984), pp. 25–44. Note that there were some instances during the early modern period when the authority of the Sejm was challenged by an appeal instead to the sovereignty of the entire szlachta, for example during the Zebrzydowski uprising (*rokosz*) of the early seventeenth century. Echoes of the idea that even the Sejm must bow to the authority of the entire citizen body can also be seen in the occasional calls for a Mounted Sejm (*sejm konny*, a mass gathering of the entire szlachta, which was periodically suggested but never in fact summoned during the Commonwealth's history). Opaliński, 'Civic Humanism and Republican Citizenship'. Usually, though, the Sejm was acknowledged as the Commonwealth's supreme authority. Olszewski, *Sejm Rzeczypospolitej epoki oligarchii*.

as illegal (*przeciw prawom, contra leges*). For example, one 1702 pamphlet attacking Augustus II for having waged war without the consent of the Sejm accused him specifically of acting 'not in accordance with the laws'.[6]

The law also guaranteed the szlachta's precious liberty. This included not only protecting the szlachta from interference by government (for example, the szlachta's freedom from arbitrary arrest, enshrined in the *Neminem captivabimus nisi jure victum* statutes of 1430 and 1433). Also, by providing for the authority of the Sejm, the functions of other institutions and the restrictions on the monarchy, the law established the szlachta's 'republican liberty', which Grześkowiak-Krwawicz has argued was founded on their right to participate in government and thus avoid dependence upon the will of the king.[7]

Collective sovereignty, law, and liberty were thus inextricably linked in the ideal of the Commonwealth, and were so interdependent that the loss of any one component of that ideal threatened the entire structure. If the law were subverted, the szlachta might be left vulnerable to coercion by their ruler, and the basis of their participation in government would be undermined. If the supreme authority of the Sejm were undermined, the szlachta could be shut out of government. Excluding the szlachta, and leaving the government of the Commonwealth solely to the will of the king would make the force of the law dependent on the king's good will, effectively negating the law and with it the szlachta's legal protections against arbitrary taxation, arrest, or coercion.

The ideal of the Commonwealth thus rested on three pillars, collective sovereignty, law, and liberty, each of which supported the others. The loss of any one pillar would risk the whole edifice collapsing into *absolutum dominium*, the state in which matters were decided solely according to the king's arbitrary will. Even individual challenges to any of the three pillars could be described, and condemned, by szlachta politicians and commentators as acts of *absolutum dominium*, the term not requiring the complete establishment of what modern observers would recognize as 'absolutism'. Thus in the 1710s sejmiki protested that the levying on szlachta property of forced 'contributions' by soldiers amounted to an exercise of *absolutum dominium* over the szlachta. Similarly, the 1702 pamphlet quoted above could argue that by the single act of waging war unilaterally, 'the King [had acted] without the consent of the Commonwealth, and without having

---

[6] 'nie podlegaiąc o prawom', *Smętna Mowa Strapioney Oyczyzny* ('The Sorrowful Speech of a Tortured Fatherland'), 1702, Bibl. Czart. MS 1682, p. 127.

[7] Grześkowiak-Krwawicz, *Regina Libertas*.

called a Council, usurping for himself the position of an absolute Monarch, which the laws of Your Fatherland forbid'.[8]

THE PURPOSE OF THE POLITY

Absolutum dominium was not, however, to be avoided for its own sake. Rather, the purpose of resisting *absolutum dominium*, and preserving the collective sovereignty of the Commonwealth, was to ensure government according to the common good.

The principle that government should serve the common good was fundamental to classical political philosophy. Whether government served the common good of the whole community or just the narrow private interest of the ruler had been key to the distinction drawn by Aristotle between 'pure' and 'corrupt' forms of government. Key principles of classical political thought, including Aristotle's taxonomy of constitutions (mediated through the work of Cicero) were introduced into szlachta political thought in the sixteenth century by the churchman, politician, and writer Andrzej Frycz Modrzewski.

In his 1551–9 work *De Emendanda Republica*, Modrzewski began by defining a commonwealth (*res publica*)[9] as 'an assembly and a league of men formed according to law and made up of many neighbours, established for the purpose of living well and propitiously' (*ad bene beateque vivendum*).[10] This definition was almost a direct quotation of that in Cicero's *De Republica*,[11] and followed Aristotle's argument that humanity could only realize its nature (*telos*) as a 'political animal' (*politikon zōion*) by living in a political society formed 'for the sake of noble actions'. The collective pursuit of the common good was thus necessary for the realization of human nature, and a solitary individual could not be fully human.[12] Modrzewski accepted Aristotle's argument that living in a commonwealth was the natural state of humanity, quoting Aristotle's claim that an individual living outside political society 'must be considered to be either a wild beast or a God'.[13]

---

[8] 'Krol sine Scitu Reipub: et non convocatu Consilio, usurpando titulum absoluti Monarchae conferuie, czego prawa Oyczyzny Waszey zakazuią', *Smętna Mowa Strapioney Oyczyzny*, p. 123.

[9] Using the term in the general sense of a political society, rather than referring to a specific form of government.

[10] 'concilia coetusque hominum iure societos, ex multis viciniis perfectos et ad bene beateque vivendum constitutos'. Modrzewski, *De Emendanda Republica*, vol. 1, p. 29.

[11] Cicero, *De Republica*, I, 39 (trans. Niall Rudd, Oxford, 1998, p. 19).

[12] Aristotle, *Politics*, I, 2 and III, 9 (ed. Stephen Everson, Cambridge, 1996, pp. 14 and 73–5).

[13] 'vel bellua, vel Deus putandus est'. Modrzewski, *De Emendanda Republica*, vol. 1, p. 31. Quoting Aristotle, *Politics*, I, 2.

Using the metaphor of the body politic (*corpus reipublicae*), Modrzewski argued that citizens of a commonwealth had a duty to pursue the common good, just as individual limbs were obliged to act not in their own particular interests, but in that of the body as a whole. Modrzewski followed Aristotle and Cicero in identifying six simple forms of government, the 'pure' and 'corrupt' forms of the rule of the one (monarchy and tyranny), the rule of the few (aristocracy and oligarchy), and the rule of the many (*res publica* and democracy). In each pairing, what distinguished pure from corrupt government was whether it served the common good of the whole commonwealth or just the private interests of the ruler(s).[14]

Aristotle had argued that each of the pure forms of government had a natural tendency to degenerate into its corresponding corrupt form, as whichever individual or group held power came to put their own interest above that of the whole. Modrzewski similarly observed the tendency of both individuals and governments to degenerate, as a result of human fallibility and predisposition towards selfishness and vice. Once, Modrzewski suggested, good customs alone might have been sufficient to ensure that all men behaved well and in the common interest (in which case, the form of government presumably mattered little). But human nature had long since degenerated: this meant not only that individual conduct had to be regulated by laws, but also that rulers would tend toward pursuing their own interests, with government thus tending toward corruption.[15]

Modrzewski argued, however, that the tendency to corruption could be overcome through adopting a seventh form of government, the mixed constitution that combined elements of monarchy, aristocracy, and democracy. Following Aristotle and Cicero, Modrzewski deemed this to be the best of all forms of government. The mixed constitution avoided corruption by balancing the powers of the different elements against each other, countering the natural tendency of each to degenerate. Thus the involvement of the citizens in public business (which Modrzewski described as

---

[14] Modrzewski, *De Emendanda Republica*, vol. 1, pp. 31–2. Modrzewski followed Aristotle in using the same term (*res publica*, the Latin equivalent of the Greek *politeia*) to describe political society in general, the mixed constitution, and the pure form of the rule of the many. In contrast *democratia* described the corrupt form of the rule of the many, serving the private interests of the poor *populus*. A generation after Modrzewski, the burgher scholar Sebastian Petrycy (1554–1626), who published a translation and commentary on Aristotle's *Politics* in Kraków in 1605, modified Aristotle's terminology, using *Demokracja* to describe the pure form of the rule of the many, and *Timokracja* or *Anarchia* its corrupt counterpart. Petrycy continued to denote both the mixed constitution and political society in general as *Rzeczpospolita*. Sebastian Petrycy, *Przydatki do Polityki Aristotelesowej* (Kraków, 1605) in *Pisma Wybrane* (ed. Wiktor Wąsik, 2 vols., Kraków, 1956), vol. 2, pp. 141 and 223–6.

[15] Modrzewski, *De Emendanda Republica*, vol. 1, pp. 162–5. Note that Modrzewski's imagined virtuous past in which laws were not necessary to ensure all men behaved well was somewhat at odds with the doctrine of original sin.

part of their 'liberty') restrained the power of the monarch, preventing a king from acting only in his own interests, that is tyrannically. The power of the king to enforce the law in turn regulated the citizens' conduct, stopping their liberty from degenerating into selfish licence. The aristocratic element, the Senate, advised the king and shared in the administration of the laws, while also mediating between monarch and citizens.

The unique advantage of the mixed constitution (which Modrzewski argued was the form of government that Poland enjoyed) was thus that by balancing the three elements against each other, it ensured that government always served the common interest. A well-constructed mixed constitution could thus endure over time, without degenerating into corruption.[16]

Very similar arguments in favour of the mixed constitution were also advanced by Modrzewski's contemporary, Stanisław Orzechowski (1513–66). In his 1564 pamphlet *Dyjalog albo rozmowa około egzekucyej Polskiej Korony*, Orzechowski gave a virtually identical definition of a commonwealth as 'an assemblage of citizens united in a community of the law for the good of society'. Orzechowski similarly identified Poland as a mixed constitution, and claimed that the szlachta's ancestors had consciously chosen this form of government in order to avoid the flaws in each of the simple rule of the one, the few, or the many, and their tendency to corruption. The Aristotelian/Ciceronian ideas of Modrzewski and Orzechowski, and in particular the claims that the Commonwealth possessed a mixed constitution and that this was the best of all forms of government, were subsequently universally accepted in early modern szlachta political discourse.[17]

The szlachta's defence of the Commonwealth and its mixed government against the threat of *absolutum dominium* was thus based on the premise that it was only through the collective sovereignty of the three estates (established by law, and encompassing the szlachta's liberty) that government in the common interest, that is virtuous government, could be maintained. As the sejmik of Liw put it at the beginning of the eighteenth century, it was only 'by common consultation' that 'common good of the

---

[16] Modrzewski, *De Emendanda Republica*, vol. 1, p. 32. This repeated a claim made by Cicero that a mixed *res publica* was the most enduring form of government. Cicero, *De Republica*, I, 69. Note that although Modrzewski identified the Poland of his day as a mixed constitution, he did not claim that it was a perfect example of the form, but instead called for a number of reforms, including a loosening of the szlachta's monopoly on political participation and a greater role for Poland-Lithuania's peasants and burghers. See Waldemar Voisé, *Andrzej Frycz Modrzewski 1503–1572* (Wrocław, 1975).

[17] Opaliński, 'Civic Humanism and Republican Citizenship'. Orzechowski's definition of a *res publica* was a direct quotation from Cicero, *De Republica*, I, 39.

fatherland' could be advanced.[18] By contrast, the state of *absolutum dominium*, in which government depended solely on the will of an individual ruler, was described as 'licentious' (*swawolny*) and 'private' (*prywatny*), as it pursued only the ruler's particular interest, rather than the common good. *Absolutum dominium* was thus by definition contrary to virtue.

PATRONAGE AND CORRUPTION

As well as the threat from overt acts of *absolutum dominium* such as the unilateral decision-making condemned by the author of the 1702 *Smętna Mowa* pamphlet quoted above, szlachta politicians and commentators were keenly aware of another, more insidious threat to the collective sovereignty of the *Rzeczpospolita*: that of corruption by royal patronage. Polish-Lithuanian kings enjoyed the sole power of appointment to a huge range of public offices in the Commonwealth, some of which conferred on their holders vast political influence or personal wealth. From at least the mid-seventeenth century, szlachta politicians and writers had expressed the fear that kings seeking to expand their own powers could use patronage to suborn a portion of the szlachta to their cause and thus take over the Commonwealth's government by bribery.

The dangers of corruption by royal patronage were discussed at some length by the prominent senator Łukasz Opaliński in his *Rozmowa plebana z ziemianinem* ('Dialogue of a Priest and a Squire') published in 1641. This work took the form of a debate conducted over two days between a priest and a nobleman returning home from an inconclusive Sejm. Both characters are frustrated at the dysfunction of the Commonwealth's chief public council, and lament the descent into corruption of both the Sejm and the szlachta more generally. They agree that strict enforcement of the Commonwealth's laws, and greater virtue and public spirit on the part of the szlachta are needed, but disagree over how this should be achieved. The priest argues the case for a stronger monarchy, claiming that only the king has the power to compel citizens to behave virtuously (and following the logic of Modrzewski's argument that the power of the monarchy should serve as a check on the tendency of popular liberty to degenerate into licence).

---

[18] 'in communi consultatione provideant communi bono ojczyzny', Resolution of the sejmik of Liw, 5 June 1708, TP vol. 5, p. 312. This conviction can be compared to that described by J. G. A. Pocock in Florentine government, that overcoming the vicissitudes of fortune through the exercise of virtue could only be achieved through collective participation in government. J. G. A. Pocock, *The Machiavellian Moment: Florentine Political Thought and the Atlantic Republican Tradition* (Princeton, 1975), pp. 88–91.

The squire, however, disagrees on two grounds. First, he rejects stronger monarchy as offensive to liberty. But second, he argues that a stronger monarchy would be unnecessary, as the king already possessed sufficient power to promote virtue, if only he chose to do so. This power, the nobleman explains, is that of patronage, for 'above all the distribution of all offices and honours in our fatherland is given over to [the kings'] will'. At present, the squire claims, the king is misusing this power, rewarding 'ambition', 'private support', and even bribery instead of 'disinterested virtue' and 'public service'. But '[l]et the king distribute [these rewards] with attention to virtues', and this would be 'the way not just to maintain but even to expand his majesty's power, win over the hearts of his subjects and [to bring about] a reform of the Commonwealth and a fatherland fundamentally flourishing under good government'.[19] Opaliński's squire thus attributed the Commonwealth's political dysfunction to corruption brought on by the kings' abuse of their powers of patronage.[20]

The claim that the Commonwealth's government, and with it szlachta liberty, were under threat from corruption was repeated by sejmiki and szlachta pamphleteers throughout the early modern period.[21] One particularly blistering attack on the corruption of the Commonwealth's great magnates was contained in the anonymous 1709 pamphlet *Eclipsis Poloniae Orbi Publico Demonstrata*. This pamphlet lambasted the Commonwealth's

---

[19] 'naprzód wszystkich w ojczyźnie naszej urzędów i nadgród wolny szafunek wolej ich [królów] jest podany'; 'Niech pan rozdawa z uwagą cnót . . . sposobem nie tylko zatrzymawszy, ale i utwierdziwszy powagę swego majestatu, serca poddanych sobie powabiwszy, kwitnącą ojczyznę w rządzie dobrym i gruntowną Rzeczypospolitej naprawę', Łukasz Opaliński, *Rozmowa plebana z ziemianinem* (1641) in *Łukasz Opaliński: Wybór pism* (ed. Stanisław Grzeszczuk, Wrocław, 1959), pp. 72–3.

[20] Which, if either, of the arguments put forward by the priest and the squire represented Opaliński's own views has been the subject of some debate among historians. Ignacy Chrzanowski and Stanisław Grzeszczuk have seen Opaliński as a supporter of a stronger monarchy, and hence have identified the priest as his true mouthpiece. By contrast, Kamila Schuster and Władysław Czapliński have instead presented Opaliński as a conservative 'oligarch' opposing any reform, thus closer to the squire. A third interpretation has been offered by Maria Pryszlak, who has instead emphasized Opaliński's support for the mixed constitution and argued that contemporaries would have read between the lines of the dialogue a call for the Senate (the only institution criticized by neither the priest or the squire) to step forward to enforce the law and restore good government. Whichever was in fact Opaliński's own view, for the dialogue to read convincingly to his szlachta audience the arguments put forward by both priest and squire would have to have been familiar ones to Opaliński's contemporaries. For a summary of the debate over Opaliński's own views, see Maria Pryszlak, '"Forma Mixta" as a Political Ideal of a Polish Magnate: Łukasz Opaliński's "Rozmowa plebana z ziemianinem"', *Polish Review*, 3 (1981), pp. 26–42.

[21] Grześkowiak-Krwawicz, *Regina Libertas*, pp. 273–4. Olszewski, *Dokryny prawno-ustrojowe*, pp. 17–19. Lukowski, *Disorderly Liberty*, pp. 33–5. Szlachta politicians were not alone in this period in fearing the subversion of parliamentary government by royal patronage: see Chapter 8 for a discussion of similar fears in contemporary England and Great Britain.

mightiest nobles for putting the pursuit of personal enrichment and luxury ahead of the common good. It alleged that the magnates had been seduced by (and become addicted to) the wealth they had gained from royal patronage. Instead of working for the public interest, the *Eclipsis Poloniae* claimed, they devoted their energies simply to obtaining lucrative offices or royal estates for themselves. Competition between magnates over these prizes had led to the formation of factions, which had brought the Commonwealth's government into disorder. Meanwhile the great lords' pursuit of royal favour and patronage both undermined szlachta liberty, by opening the way to greater royal influence, and threatened the moral character of the wider szlachta, who no longer had an example of public virtue set before them.[22]

The argument that the Commonwealth needed to be defended against the threat of corruption was also developed in the seventeenth century to justify the *liberum veto*, most notably by Andrzej Maksymilian Fredro in his 1652 *Responsum*. Fredro's defence of the veto was far from disinterested: as Marshal of the 1652 Sejm, when the envoy Władysław Siciński had attempted to use his veto to break up an entire Sejm, Fredro had played a key role in admitting that this use of the veto was legitimate, and allowing the breaking of the Sejm. It is therefore hardly surprising that Fredro subsequently presented the *liberum veto* as essential to preserve the Sejm and uphold the common good.

In the *Responsum*, Fredro argued that the *liberum veto* was necessary to guard against corruption, and in particular the risk that individual envoys to the Sejm might be suborned away from promoting the common good and instead captured by some private interest, such as that of the king. Given the extent of the king's powers of patronage, and the imperfection and corruptibility of human nature, Fredro argued that it was all too likely that virtuous individuals would be rare, and that a majority of Sejm envoys might be corrupted into the service of a private interest. It was therefore vital that a virtuous minority, even a minority of one, should have the ability to veto the decisions of a corrupt majority.[23]

Fredro thus presented the *liberum veto* as essential to the preservation of government in the common interest, and the maintenance of the edifice of collective sovereignty, law, and liberty that was the Commonwealth.

---

[22] Candidus Veronensis [pseud.], *Eclipsis Poloniae Orbi Publico Demonstrata* (1709). Polish translations of excerpts from this text are included in Józef Gierowski (ed.), *Rzeczpospolita w dobie upadku 1700–1740: Wybór źródeł* (Wrocław, 1955), pp. 242–6. The proposals in the *Eclipsis Poloniae* for reform of the royal power of appointment to tackle the problem of corruption will be discussed in Chapter 4.

[23] Andrzej Maksymilian Fredro, *Responsum* (1652), reproduced in Biskupski and Pula (eds.), *Polish Democratic Thought*, pp. 163–7.

Neither the apparent paradox in protecting collective government through a single individual's veto, nor Fredro's failure to recognize the risk that the veto would also allow a single corrupt envoy to block the decisions of a virtuous majority stopped his arguments being widely accepted by the szlachta and the *liberum veto* being regarded as the capstone of szlachta liberty.[24] This illustrates the extent to which fears about the threat to the Commonwealth from corruption were prevalent in szlachta political culture.

ALL REPUBLICANS?

Throughout the early modern period, the ideal of the Commonwealth, bringing together liberty, law, and collective government in the common interest, was virtually unchallenged in szlachta political discourse.[25] Virtue and the need to subordinate private interests to the common good were thus parts of the prevailing orthodoxy of szlachta political thought. In practice, this required szlachta politicians repeatedly to proclaim their allegiance to the Commonwealth and its laws, and their support for the common good over any 'private' interests or policies.

Given the breadth of this orthodoxy, it was not unusual for the ideal of the Commonwealth and the common good to be invoked by multiple opposing groups, and by all sides in any particular political dispute. For example, in the Lithuanian civil war, both the Sapieha family and their self-proclaimed 'republican' opponents claimed to be upholding the law, denouncing the other side for undermining the sovereignty of the Commonwealth.[26]

---

[24] Konopczyński, *Liberum veto*.

[25] Those few who may have privately supported an alternative form of government (such as Konstanty Szaniawski (1688–1732), Bishop of Kujawy and Kraków and a close ally of Augustus II who in 1717 privately claimed to support an absolute monarchy in preference to the *Rzeczpospolita* to a Prussian diplomat) dared not state such a view publicly. Lukowski, *Disorderly Liberty*, p. 23 and passim. Comparing the Commonwealth to early modern Great Britain, Butterwick has also remarked on the absence in szlachta political discourse of any significant tradition of monarchist thought. Richard Butterwick, *Poland's Last King and English Culture: Stanisław August Poniatowski, 1721–1798* (Oxford, 1998), p. 17. See Chapter 8 for further discussion of the comparison between Poland-Lithuania and England/Great Britain.

[26] The charge that the Sapieha family had, by amassing multiple offices contrary to law and intimidating the Lithuanian szlachta, violated the sovereignty of the Commonwealth was set out in *Acta Stanow Wielkiego Xięstwa Litewskiego na Pospolite Ruszenie vigore Laudum Wileńskiego 14 Augusti 1698* (printed Wilno, 1699). For the opposing argument, that the Sapiehas' opponents were a private faction rebelling against the legal authority of the Commonwealth and its magistrates (the Sapiehas), see *Reflexya Iednego Senatora Koronnego Na zgromadzenie y Postanowienie Niektorych W.X.L. Woiewodztw y Powiatow Pod*

Similarly, although during the Great Northern War opponents of Augustus II denounced him for violating the sovereignty of the Commonwealth by waging war illegally, Jarosław Poraziński has argued appealing to the sovereignty of the Commonwealth was crucial to the king's ability to build support among the szlachta in the face of the Swedish invasion and demands for his dethronement. In particular, supporters of the king argued that the king was simply fulfilling the commitment in his *pacta conventa* to reconquer lost territories (*avulsa*), and thus serving the will and interest of the Commonwealth. They claimed it was the king's Swedish-backed opponents who had violated the Commonwealth's sovereignty and laws, in particular with the forced election of Stanisław Leszczyński as a pro-Swedish puppet king. Supporters of Augustus II presented themselves as defenders of the szlachta's right to elect their kings freely, and thus of liberty and law more generally. Poraziński has thus emphasized the elasticity of the Commonwealth's political system, noting in particular the range of different institutional channels through which the king was able to reach out to the szlachta, including ad hoc 'general councils' and confederations.[27]

This flexibility nevertheless had its limits, as Poraziński has recognized. Most importantly, although the szlachta were often willing to accept the legitimacy of ad hoc institutions in times of emergency, sovereign authority was reserved for the Sejm alone. For example, in 1710 the szlachta would not accept the right of the General Council of Warsaw to enact permanent fiscal and military reforms, but instead insisted that any changes be ratified by a Sejm. For it was the sovereignty of the Sejm, where all three estates of the Commonwealth were gathered, and where the *liberum veto* ensured collective decision-making, that was supposed to ensure virtuous government seeking the common good.

The range of groups and interests that appealed to the ideal of the Commonwealth in political disputes illustrates how widely, and unquestioningly, that ideal and its core principles of liberty, law, and collective sovereignty were accepted among the szlachta. So although the label was at various times adopted by particular groups, all of mainstream szlachta political thought can be fairly described as 'republican'.

Grodnem miane, y Odprawione (1699). For a further discussion of Lithuanian 'republicanism', see below.

[27] Jarosław Poraziński, *Epiphania Poloniae: orientacje i postawy polityczne szlachty polskiej w dobie wielkiej wojny północnej, 1702–1710* (Toruń, 1999). Examples of pamphlets defending Augustus II include *Respons Szlachcica Pewnego Na Manifest Pseudo-Principis J. W. I. M. P. Woiewody Poznanskiego* (1704), and an untitled pamphlet of the same year that mocked Leszczyński as king 'by the Grace of Sweden' (*z Szwedzkiey Laski*) not 'by the Grace the God'. Bibl. Czart. MS 2447, pp. 141–50.

Some historians have instead sought to apply the term 'republican' to only a sub-set of szlachta political writers and activists. For example, Gierowski and Staszewski have distinguished 'republican' reformers in the early eighteenth century from 'magnate' or 'oligarchic' conservatives. Kamiński has suggested that the term 'republican' should denote those among the szlachta suspicious of the royal court and keen to defend the rights of the Commonwealth's localities, as opposed to 'constitutionalist' supporters of stronger central government. Michalski and Lukowski have characterized as 'republican' szlachta politicians and commentators who sought to restrict or abolish the king's power of appointment to public office in favour of having officials elected by the szlachta.[28]

All of these attempts to isolate a distinct 'republican' tradition within szlachta political thought suffer, however, from the problem that it is extremely difficult to identify any 'anti-republicans' among the szlachta, apart from a tiny fringe of monarchists attached to the royal court. No szlachta politician, for example, ever advocated a 'magnate oligarchy', or admitted to pursuing the interests of any individual group or faction instead of the common interest of the Commonwealth. Similarly, those who defended the powers of central bodies such as the Sejm, or established customs for the distribution of offices claimed to be upholding the traditional laws and institutions of the Commonwealth, and thus its principles of liberty, law, and collective government.

There is also little evidence to support a connection between a distinct 'republican' ideology and a particular socio-economic group within the szlachta. In the context of enforced Marxism under the Polish People's Republic, historians such as Gierowski identified the so-called 'middle szlachta' as the key constituency for 'republican' reforming ideas.[29] The 'middle szlachta' were necessary to Marxist analysis as an 'anti-feudal' force opposing the power of magnate 'oligarchs', a substitute for the politically active bourgeoisie that the Commonwealth almost entirely lacked. Historians have had difficulty in defining the 'middle szlachta', not least because the term had no legal meaning in the Commonwealth (legal distinctions within the szlachta being considered contrary to the principle of szlachta equality), and neither it nor any similar term was used until the

---

[28] Józef Gierowski, *Między saskim absolutyzmem a złotą wolnością: z dziejów wewnętrznych Rzeczypospolitej w latach 1712–1715* (Wrocław, 1953), pp. 100–1. Jacek Staszewski, 'Pomysły reformatorskie czasów Augusta II', *Kwartalnik Historyczny*, 82 (1975), pp. 736–65. Kamiński, *Republic vs Autocracy*, p. 26. Jerzy Michalski, 'Z problematyki republikańskiego nurtu w polskiej reformatorskiej myśli politycznej w XVIII wieku', *Kwartalnik Historyczny*, 90 (1983), pp. 327–38. Lukowski, 'Political Ideas among the Polish Nobility'.

[29] Gierowski, *Między saskim absolutyzmem a złotą wolnością*, p. 100. Note that this book, published in 1953, was written at the height of Polish Stalinism.

end of the eighteenth century.[30] The 'middle szlachta' have been described as the driving force behind the mid-sixteenth-century 'Movement for the Execution of the Laws', which asserted the rights of the mass of the szlachta against the power of the great magnates. Gierowski saw the programme of those he termed 'republicans' in the early eighteenth century, such as Stanisław Dunin Karwicki, as the natural continuation of that movement. Karwicki and his fellow 'republicans' did not, however, appeal to the Executionist movement as a precedent in their own works: nor did contemporary resolutions of the sejmiki that attacked magnate corruption and called for a greater role for the mass of the szlachta.[31] There is thus very little evidence for any continuous 'middle szlachta' group consciousness, or attachment to a distinct 'republican' ideology.

It is not clear, therefore, that 'republicanism' can be identified as a distinct tradition within szlachta political thought, or as the exclusive programme of a discrete component of the szlachta. Rather, with the principles of collective sovereignty, law, and liberty that together made up the ideal of the Commonwealth more or less universally accepted among the szlachta, it is more helpful to describe szlachta political thought in general as republican.

The significant exception to the Commonwealth's broad republican orthodoxy was the political discourse of the Grand Duchy of Lithuania. Historians have traditionally accepted that the culture of citizenship and participation was less developed in the Grand Duchy than in the Crown (i.e. Poland), and that the Lithuanian magnates had a decisive influence on the politics of the Grand Duchy until at least the 'republican' uprising against the hegemony of the Sapieha family at the end of the seventeenth century. Revisionists have argued that this understates the political

---

[30] Kamiński and Kriegseisen have each proposed different definitions of the 'middle szlachta', as part of complex taxonomies of the szlachta defined on the basis of the size of individuals' land-holdings, adjusted for differences in land yields in different regions of the Commonwealth. Kamiński, *Republic vs Autocracy*, p. 30. Wojciech Kriegseisen, *Samorząd szlachecki w Małopolsce w latach 1669–1717* (Warsaw, 1989), p. 52. In 1699 the use of the term 'lesser szlachta', which had been employed in a statute of 1690 to denote those paying taxes at a lower rate, was specifically banned by law as offensive to szlachta equality. Olszewski and Grześkowiak-Krwawicz have noted the strongly egalitarian tone to szlachta political discourse at the turn of the eighteenth century. Olszewski, *Dokryny prawno-ustrojowe*, pp. 17–19. Anna Grześkowiak-Krwawicz, 'Anti-Monarchism in Polish Republicanism in the Seventeenth and Eighteenth Centuries', in van Gelderen and Skinner (eds.), *Republicanism*, vol. 1, pp. 43–59 (p. 50). The earliest known use of a term similar to 'middle szlachta' was a reference by King Stanisław August Poniatowski in 1787 to the 'middling to wealthy szlachta' (*średnia Szlachta maiętna*) whom the king hoped to enlist as political allies. Richard Butterwick, 'Political Discourses of the Polish Revolution, 1788–92', *English Historical Review*, 120, 487 (2005), pp. 695–731 (pp. 707–8).

[31] For a discussion of early eighteenth-century sejmik political activism, see Chapter 3. The reform proposals of Karwicki and other radical thinkers are discussed in Chapter 4.

consciousness and activism of the mass of the Lithuanian szlachta, which began to develop during the first half of the seventeenth century, but concede that magnates, and conflict between magnates, continued to dominate Lithuanian politics. It was only with the emergence at the end of the seventeenth century of the anti-Sapieha movement, who significantly called themselves 'republicans', that mass political activism and a widespread desire to participate in politics as citizens manifested itself in the Grand Duchy.[32] The anti-Sapieha 'republicans' campaigned for a *koekwacja* intended to secure for the mass of the Lithuanian szlachta similar political rights to their Polish brethren, and succeeded in having a *koekwacja* legislated at the Sejm of 1699. The Sapiehas, however, retained sufficient support to fight back against the 'republicans', leading by 1700 to civil war in the Grand Duchy, before the conflict became subsumed into the broader fighting of the Great Northern War.

Thus in the Grand Duchy it could be argued that republicanism was more the ideology of one part of the Lithuanian szlachta, rather than the prevailing orthodoxy as in Poland. On the other hand, it is notable that even the 'republicans'' pro-Sapieha opponents appealed to the authority of the Commonwealth and its laws in their denunciations of the 'republicans' as rebels acting according to a private interest. The Sapiehas may even have arranged for the slander of their opponents through the publication of the so-called 'Wilno Resolution' as supporters of absolute, hereditary monarchy, the worst possible crime against the sovereignty of the Commonwealth.[33] Thus even in Lithuania the ideal of the Commonwealth arguably had some rhetorical power as a source of legitimacy.

So with the partial exception of Lithuania, szlachta political thought can be described as broadly republican, and differences of political programmes as variations within that broad republican consensus. The various proposals for reform made in the late seventeenth and early eighteenth centuries can thus be seen as suggesting different means by which the commonly adhered to principles of the Commonwealth could be put into practice, and the challenges facing the Commonwealth overcome.

For common adherence to the ideal of the Commonwealth was matched in this period by a general recognition among the szlachta that

---

[32] Gintautas Sliesoriūnas, 'Problem separatyzmu Wielkiego Księstwa Litewskiego w końcu XVII wieku', in Andrzej Link-Lenczowski and Mariusz Markiewicz (eds.), *Rzeczpospolita wielu Narodów i jej tradycje* (Kraków, 1999), pp. 85–94. Artūras Vasiliauskas, 'The Practice of Citizenship among the Lithuanian Nobility c.1580–1630', in Karin Friedrich and Barbara Pendzich (eds.), *Citizenship and Identity in a Multinational Commonwealth: Poland-Lithuania in Context, 1550–1772* (Leiden, 2009), pp. 71–102.

[33] For a summary of the continuing debate over the origins of the 'Wilno Resolution' see Lukowski, *Disorderly Liberty*, pp. 28–9.

the Commonwealth was under threat. This threat was analysed by szlachta politicians and commentators primarily as a moral one, rooted in the loss of virtue among the Commonwealth's rulers and citizens, leading to the abandonment of the common good in favour of the pursuit of private interests. The key challenge facing the szlachta state was therefore how virtue could be revived, and the Commonwealth's government thus restored. Some contemporaries proposed a range of institutional measures in order to achieve this objective, which are discussed in Chapters 3 to 6. Others, however, argued that a moral problem could only be solved through a moral reformation among the Commonwealth's rulers and citizens. Chapter 2 discusses some of the different ideas put forward for how this moral revival could be brought about.

2

Calls for a Moral Revival

PESSIMISTIC MORALIZING?

Not all szlachta observers who saw the Commonwealth's problems as stemming from the corruption of its rulers and citizens looked for an institutional solution to that corruption. Indeed, some made the case that a moral problem could only be tackled through moral solutions: and so looked for a revival of the Commonwealth from within the hearts of its szlachta citizens.

To the modern observer, this may seem a rather naïve approach, and some historians have presented it either as romantic nonsense or as a means of the szlachta (perhaps deliberately) avoiding hard truths about the flaws of their political institutions. However, it should be recognized that the view that 'if the men who control the institutions of government are corrupt, the best possible constitutions cannot be expected to restrain them, whereas if men are virtuous, the health of the institutions will be a matter of secondary importance' had a long historical pedigree both in Poland-Lithuania and elsewhere in early modern Europe, and continues to have some resonance even in modern political discourse.[1] So if the szlachta were naïve in taking this view, they were not alone in their naïvety. There may also be a case that in practice it is difficult to observe whether institutions function well because of their inherent design or because of the commitment by the individuals acting within them to make them work: it is conceivable that imperfect systems of government that nonetheless function well because of the 'virtue' (in classical and szlachta terminology) of their participants have their success subsequently ascribed to the quality of their institutional design.

It is also worth noting that whereas naïvety is commonly associated with an over-optimistic, rose-tinted assessment of the state of the world, the

---

[1] Quentin Skinner, *The Foundations of Modern Political Thought* (2 vols., Cambridge, 1978), vol. 1, 44–5. For a discussion of some of the modern resonances of this idea, see the Conclusion to this book.

pessimistic tone of late seventeenth- and early eighteenth-century szlachta 'moralizing' analysis is difficult to mistake. As Olszewski has shown, szlachta pamphleteers bemoaning the corruption of the Commonwealth frequently questioned whether it could continue to exist, or rather was likely to collapse, a risk that even radical reformers acknowledged.[2] Arguably, placing moral considerations at the heart of their analysis of the Commonwealth's problems represented less the hope of a quick fix, but more szlachta commentators' fear that the Commonwealth's troubles were so deep-seated that only a collective change of heart could address them. The moral roots of the Commonwealth's dysfunction were thus a measure of the difficulty, not the ease, of solving the problems facing the szlachta state. That the ideas of virtue and corruption continued to form the principal paradigm for szlachta analysis of their political system even when those ideas appeared to offer so few solutions to the Commonwealth's difficulties may illustrate the enduring power of those ideas in szlachta political discourse.

Some 'moralizing' szlachta commentators did, however, continue to hold out some hope that a revival of the Commonwealth from within could be brought about, either as a result of appealing to the ideal of szlachta brotherhood, or through a revival of the szlachta's supposed ancient military virtues, or simply through a purge of corrupt individuals from the Commonwealth's ruling elite. This chapter will examine proposals for restoring the szlachta state through these means, before more 'institutional' solutions are discussed in Chapters 3 to 6.

VIRTUE IN FELLOWSHIP

The most notable and widely circulated appeal in this period for a revival of the Commonwealth from within was a work of 1699–1700 by Stanisław Herakliusz Lubomirski (1642–1702), Grand Marshal of the Crown, entitled *De Vanitate Consiliorum* ('On the Vanity of Counsels'). Lubomirski was a scion of one of the Commonwealth's mightiest and most renowned magnate dynasties, and the son of Jerzy Sebastian Lubomirski (1616–67), the leader of the mid-seventeenth-century uprising against King Jan Kazimierz who was later lionized by szlachta pamphleteers as the greatest recent paragon of szlachta virtue. By the end of the seventeenth century, Stanisław Herakliusz Lubomirski had risen to the most senior public office in the Commonwealth, the Grand Marshalcy, and following the death of King Jan III Sobieski in 1696

---

[2] Olszewski, *Dokryny prawno-ustrojowe*, pp. 18–19. On the doubts harboured by radicals such as Stanisław Dunin Karwicki over whether the Commonwealth could survive, see Chapter 4.

may well have hoped to become one of the new king's closest and most trusted advisers. In this, however, Lubomirski was to be disappointed, as the newly elected King Augustus II turned instead to other councillors, and Lubomirski gradually withdrew from public life, finally resigning his various offices a few weeks before his death in 1702.

De Vanitate Consiliorum was thus composed at a time of great disappointment for its author, and this may well have informed the generally pessimistic tone of the work, not least its title. Staszewski has interpreted *De Vanitate Consiliorum* as just the angry polemic of a disappointed man, containing no positive proposals for improving the Commonwealth's government, a view largely endorsed by Lukowski.[3] Kriegseisen, however, has argued that *De Vanitate Consiliorum* does represent sincere reflection upon the state of the Commonwealth, and a programme for restoring peace and order based on mutual trust and public spirit among the szlachta.[4]

De Vanitate Consiliorum is structured as a dialogue between two participants: *Vanitas*, an energetic and well-intentioned figure keen to reform the Commonwealth and who suggests a variety of apparently reasonable proposals to this end; and *Veritas*, a wiser (and perhaps older) character who critiques the ideas of his interlocutor, whom he portrays as misguided and having failed to grasp the true nature of the problems facing the Commonwealth, or of the harm that *Vanitas*' proposed solutions would in fact unwittingly cause.

A sceptical, rather negative tone is thus established throughout *De Vanitate Consiliorum*, and is visible from the very beginning of the dialogue, which *Vanitas* begins by arguing that government ('*consilium*') is an inherently good and beautiful thing, and that a wise government of worthy councillors can be formed to make good laws for the Commonwealth. *Veritas* sternly rejects all of these propositions, and instead warns that those in love with government have often found it to be their ruin. *Veritas* similarly denies the proposition that a government of worthy men could be established, arguing that given the corruptibility of human nature, even the best of men would soon degenerate, and apparently wise men would turn out to be fools once in office.[5]

Having dismissed *Vanitas*'s proposals for forming a good government, *Veritas* is similarly pessimistic about his interlocutor's enthusiasm for

---

[3] Staszewski, 'Pomysły reformatorskie', pp. 738–9. Lukowski, *Disorderly Liberty*, pp. 33–5. Lukowski does concede that 'less jaundiced interpretations of *De Vanitate Consiliorum* are possible'.

[4] Wojciech Kriegseisen, 'Zmierzch staropolskiej polityki, czyli o niektórych cechach szczególnych polskiej kultury politycznej przełomu XVII i XVIII wieku', in Urszula Augustyniak and Adam Karpiński (eds.), *Zmierzch Kultury Staropolskiej: Ciągłość i kryzysy* (Warsaw, 1997), pp. 15–39 (pp. 20–1).

[5] Stanisław Herakliusz Lubomirski, *De Vanitate Consiliorum Liber Unus* (Warsaw, 1700), pp. 1–3.

writing good laws, again basing his argument on the weaknesses of human nature. *Veritas* notes gloomily that whatever the laws require the people will fail to do, and whatever they forbid the people will do anyway. So not even the best of laws could be counted upon to bring harmony to the Commonwealth, as vices such as ambition, which would always tend to disrupt the state, could never be eliminated. Not even the laws given to the Israelites in the Old Testament were obeyed for long, *Veritas* notes, so for a legislator to be successful in his task, he would need to be wiser than Moses and luckier than God Himself.[6]

Despite his negative tone, however, and despite his rhetorical claims that governments are just 'the most elaborate hindrances to [public] business', that 'where laws flourish, men wither', and that the Commonwealth 'will survive less well, if smothered by laws', *Veritas* does not give up completely on the need for laws and government, or on making them work in practice.[7] On the contrary, at the end of the dialogue *Veritas* argues that laws are essential to prevent the people from degenerating into licence, and large sections of the work are devoted to a discussion of how Sejms should be held and individuals appointed to office. Rather than attacking the very ideas of law and government, *Veritas* therefore appears to be challenging more the presumption that the Commonwealth's problems lie with its laws and institutions, and are therefore susceptible to a legislative or institutional solution. This *Veritas* regards as a misguided, perhaps lazy, notion that distracts from the Commonwealth's real problem, which is one of behaviour and culture. So although 'it is easier to establish laws than customs',[8] *Veritas* argues that the true task of reviving the Commonwealth is one of restoring good behaviour, not of institutional tinkering.

Veritas similarly takes issue with the objective of would-be reformers such as *Vanitas*, who seek to end all discord and bring peace and calm to the Commonwealth. *Veritas* denies that tranquillity is necessarily positive, arguing that the Commonwealth could be ruined by simple inactivity, just as a sailor could be harmed by a dead calm just as much as by a storm. On the contrary, *Veritas* distinguishes between idleness or inactivity and true, harmonious peace. The key characteristic of true peace is that it is based on the citizens' virtue, that is their collective concern for the common good, rather than the selfish abandonment of public business that characterizes

---

[6] Lubomirski, *De Vanitate Consiliorum*, pp. 8–9.

[7] 'elaboratissima negotiorum impedimenta', 'Florescunt Jura, marcescunt homines', 'Minus stabit; si illis [legibus] obruetur'. Lubomirski, *De Vanitate Consiliorum*, pp. 3, 7–8.

[8] 'Facilius enim est praecepta dare, quam mores', Lubomirski, *De Vanitate Consiliorum*, p. 7.

idle inactivity, which *Veritas* denounces as 'the most pernicious poison of virtue and security'.[9] This distinction between self-interested passivity and virtuous peace mirrors that drawn by Modrzewski and others between the two types of freedom: selfish licence and virtuous liberty.

According to *Veritas*, therefore, the Commonwealth could only be restored to peace, order, and good government if individuals would set aside their private interests and collaborate sincerely for the common good. If this could be achieved, the result would inevitably be an atmosphere of trust and fellowship (*'amicitia'*) among the virtuous citizens, for 'Good men cannot long maintain discord, just as Bad men cannot long sustain concord'.[10] This sense of *amicitia* would in turn allow and encourage the virtuous to make the Commonwealth's institutions of government function well: for example, *Veritas* claims that by setting aside their private interests senators would swiftly be able to agree a joint *Votum* or recommendation to each new Sejm, and would be able to win over the Sejm envoys to support their recommendation not through powerful oratory or clever arguments, but through the *amicitia* between the estates. Virtuous Sejms could thus decide collectively on the common good, while thanks to the discord that *Veritas* considered inevitable among evil men, the unvirtuous would not be able to disrupt the government.

Lubomirski's *De Vanitate Consiliorum* can thus be read as an appeal to the mass of the szlachta, and to the senators in particular, to put aside their differences and come together in an atmosphere of mutual trust. As a solution to the Commonwealth's political problems in the late seventeenth and early eighteenth centuries, this proposal is of course open to the criticism of being unrealistic, indeed even naïve.[11] In particular, *De Vanitate Consiliorum* offers no advice on how this revival of public virtue might be brought about, or how once restored virtue might be maintained, given Lubomirski's arguments about the tendency of individuals to become corrupt and his premise that the Commonwealth's troubles stemmed from just such a degeneration in its szlachta citizens. The claim that a union of virtuous men would, if somehow created, be able to govern the Commonwealth also fails to deal with the objection that the *liberum veto* could allow even a single unvirtuous Sejm envoy to disrupt the government: a significant omission given the widespread szlachta claims that

---

[9] 'Perniciosissimum virtutis & securitatis venenum', Lubomirski, *De Vanitate Consiliorum*, p. 129.

[10] 'Boni diu discordes; Mali diu concordes esse non possunt', Lubomirski, *De Vanitate Consiliorum*, p. 12.

[11] See Lukowski, *Disorderly Liberty*, pp. 34–5.

the misuse of the *liberum veto* (rather than its existence per se) lay behind the Commonwealth's political dysfunction.

To defend Lubomirski against the charge of naïvety or lack of realism, however, it should first be acknowledged that he had deep and extensive experience of the Commonwealth's politics from the inside, both as a leading member of one of the Commonwealth's greatest magnate families, and as a man whose political career had taken him to the very highest level of public office. Lubomirski should, therefore, have been in a prime position to assess what was and was not realistic within a political system he knew so well. From that perspective, Lubomirski may have concluded that before the middle of the seventeenth century, the Commonwealth's regular institutions of government had been able to function, more or less effectively at different times, but without succumbing to the paralysis of the late seventeenth and early eighteenth centuries. If to Lubomirski the dysfunction of the Sejm appeared as a relatively recent phenomenon (not impossible, given that the first breaking of a Sejm by an individual envoy through the *liberum veto* had only occurred in 1652), the precedent of the preceding century may have encouraged him to believe that achieving consensus based on mutual trust and co-operation might be realistic.

As for how that trust could be fostered, Gierowski has noted that when *De Vanitate Consiliorum* was written, Lubomirski had had recent personal experience of mediating between rival factions. Following the disputed royal election of 1697, Lubomirski played a key role in brokering the compromise of Łowicz, in which the supporters of the defeated French candidate for the throne, the Prince de Conti, reconciled themselves to the election of King Augustus II and pulled back from violent opposition to the new king.[12] *De Vanitate Consiliorum* could, therefore, be seen as an expression of Lubomirski's hope that a similar grand bargain could be struck among the szlachta to restore order to the Commonwealth.

BROTHERHOOD IN ARMS

Lubomirski did not specify exactly how this bargain could be struck, or how the bond of *amicitia* among the szlachta that he saw as essential to restoring the Commonwealth's government could be created. One near

---

[12] Józef Gierowski, 'Stanisław Herakliusz Lubomirski jako polityk', in Wanda Roszkowska (ed.), *Stanisław Herakliusz Lubomirski: Pisarz—polityk—mecenas* (Wrocław, 1982), pp. 9–24 (p. 20).

contemporary of Lubomirski's did, however, offer a concrete proposal for rallying the szlachta to a common cause: war.

The anonymous 1709 pamphlet *Eclipsis Poloniae* called for a new crusade against the Ottoman Empire, arguing that 'war with the Turks . . . is absolutely essential for us'. The proposed war would both be justified as recapturing formerly Christian territories conquered by the Ottomans, and would win glory for those who fought, and the 'crown of martyrdom' for those who fell. It would also unite the szlachta, pacify the Commonwealth by putting an end to factional squabbles, and revive their patriotic virtue. In times of peace, the *Eclipsis Poloniae* claimed, the szlachta, 'sunk in leisure hatch lethal intrigues against the Fatherland'. 'War with the barbarians', however, would be 'more valuable, just as innocent bloodshed among Christians is more disgusting'. Once summoned for a new holy war the szlachta would no longer fight amongst themselves, but would instead be bound together and 'inclined to the glory of good deeds'.[13]

It is worth noting that the unity that the *Eclipsis Poloniae* argued would be forged in war had a confessional nature: the 'pernicious discord' (*perniciosis dissidiis*) that war was intended to overcome likely included religious disputes that were usually blamed on the 'dissenters' (i.e. non-Catholics). The *Eclipsis Poloniae* insisted that in future the Commonwealth's king should always be both a native and a Catholic, and apparently conceived of its crusading brotherhood as exclusively Catholic.[14] The proposed war with the Ottoman Empire also chimed well with the long-established (perhaps clichéd) description of the Commonwealth as the 'bulwark of Christendom'.[15] Nonetheless, the *Eclipsis Poloniae*'s call for war was out of tune with prevailing sentiment among the szlachta.

Around the turn of the seventeenth and eighteenth centuries, resolutions of the sejmiki repeatedly expressed war-weariness and called for peace to be maintained and international disputes to be settled by diplomatic means. For example, although many sejmiki were outraged in early 1701 by the coronation of Frederick III Elector of Brandenburg as King in Prussia (a move that technically violated the Commonwealth's vestigial overlordship over Ducal (East) Prussia), they nevertheless urged

---

[13] 'desides otio funesta parata in Patriam machinamenta', 'aestimatiori conflictu cum barbaris, quo foediori Christianos inter sanguinis innocui profusione', 'inclinatis tantum ad rectefactorum gloriam'. Candidus Veronensis [pseud.], *Eclipsis Poloniae* (1709), pp. 125–8.

[14] On the requirement for a native and Catholic king, Candidus Veronensis [pseud.], *Eclipsis Poloniae*, p. 136 (see also Chapter 4). For good measure, the pamphlet also advocated the expulsion of the Jews from the Commonwealth. Candidus Veronensis [pseud.], *Eclipsis Poloniae*, pp. 140–1.

[15] See Lukowski, *Disorderly Liberty*, pp. 55–75, and Henryk Olszewski, 'Ideologia Rzeczypospolitej—przedmurza chrześciaństwa', *Czasopismo Prawno-historyczne*, 35, 2 (1983), pp. 1–19.

that the matter be settled through exclusively peaceful means.[16] Similarly, the szlachta were also extremely reluctant to become involved in the Great Northern War, even when in December 1701 Charles XII of Sweden invaded the Grand Duchy of Lithuania. Faced with the Swedish invasion, the Sejm even offered to mediate between Charles XII and Augustus II, and only finally agreed to declare war in 1704.

Frost has even argued that the biggest military difference between the Commonwealth and its soon-to-be enemies on the eve of the Great Northern War was that in the years immediately preceding the outbreak of hostilities, the Commonwealth was preparing for peace, while others were preparing for war.[17] In particular, the szlachta were highly reluctant to support plans for wars of conquest hatched by kings such as Jan III Sobieski and Augustus II, fearing that the true purpose of such military adventures was to further the interests of the king, not those of the Commonwealth as a whole.[18]

On the other hand, the idea of the szlachta's innate warlike qualities had deep roots, in particular in the Sarmatian myth of the szlachta's descent from the warrior Sarmates. As Lukowski has shown, the supposed martial nature of the szlachta continued to be celebrated in szlachta literature throughout the eighteenth century. Accounts of the origins of szlachta liberty typically claimed that the various rights and privileges conceded to the nobility by past monarchs had been given in return for the szlachta's honourable service in war, while the szlachta's ancestors were 'sanctified' by the sacrifices of their own blood that they had allegedly made in the defence of

---

[16] See, for example, the resolutions of the sejmiki of Czersk, 19 May 1701, TP vol. 3, p. 26; Warsaw, 1 June 1701, TP vol. 32, p. 10; and Łęczyca, 10 November 1701, TP vol. 12, p. 53. Ducal Prussia had been a Hohenzollern possession since 1525, when following the dissolution of the Prussian branch of the crusading Teutonic Knights, the Order's Grand Master, Albert von Hohenzollern, a convert to Lutheranism, received the territory as a hereditary duchy, in vassalage from the Commonwealth. By 1701, all that remained of the Commonwealth's overlordship was a provision that the territory would revert to the Commonwealth in the event of the extinction of the Hohenzollern line.

[17] Robert Frost, *The Northern Wars: War, State and Society in Northeastern Europe, 1558–1721* (Harlow, 2000), pp. 266–8. See also Béla Király, 'War and Society in Western and East Central Europe in the Pre-Revolutionary Eighteenth Century', in Béla Király, Gunther Rothenberg, and Peter Sugar (eds.), *East Central European Society and War in the Pre-revolutionary Eighteenth Century* (New York, 1982), pp. 1–25. Note that until the 1699 Peace of Karlowitz, the Commonwealth was technically still a belligerent in the war of the Holy League against the Ottoman Empire, though by the time the peace was formally agreed Polish-Lithuanian armies had not been engaged in any high-intensity combat for a number of years.

[18] Benedict Wagner-Rundell, 'Holy War and Republican Pacifism in the Early-Eighteenth-Century Commonwealth of Poland-Lithuania', in David Onnekink and Gijs Rommelse (eds.), *Ideology and Foreign Policy in Early Modern Europe (1650–1750)* (Farnham, 2011), pp. 163–79.

the Commonwealth in ages past. Appealing to the example of these glorious ancestors, szlachta writers in the eighteenth century loudly proclaimed their own willingness to fight for the defence of their Commonwealth and the liberty it embodied. This readiness to defend liberty and fatherland 'to the last drop of blood' was particularly celebrated through the institution of the *pospolite ruszenie*, a mass levy of the szlachta which, despite its limited military value in the face of modern regular armies, was repeatedly exalted by szlachta writers as the epitome of szlachta virtue and the Commonwealth's ultimate bulwark. This attachment to martial values may explain why knightly academies in the Commonwealth continued to prioritize teaching military skills such as fencing and horsemanship, while similar institutions elsewhere in Europe gradually modernized their curricula to place more emphasis on 'courtly' subjects such as languages, dancing, and deportment.[19]

This emphasis on martial virtue thus provided the cultural context that allowed the *Eclipsis Poloniae* to advocate war as a way to unite the szlachta, despite the szlachta's war-weariness and suspicion of their kings' ambitions. Similarly, the continuing association in szlachta discourse between szlachta values and Catholicism may have made the Ottomans the enemy that the pamphlet's szlachta audience were least reluctant to fight. Yet the *Eclipsis Poloniae*'s call for a new crusade did not resonate among the szlachta, not least because by the time of its publication the Commonwealth had already been engulfed in a different war, against Sweden. In this context, it is perhaps unsurprising that the *Eclipsis Poloniae* did not succeed in resurrecting virtuous government in the Commonwealth by rallying the szlachta for a new crusade against the Ottoman Empire.

A GOVERNMENT OF WORTHY MEN

Even if the mass of the szlachta were not receptive to the *Eclipsis Poloniae*'s call for a holy war, however, the pamphlet's claims of a corrupt elite dominating the Commonwealth, and in particular monopolizing the fruits of royal patronage in their own private interests, certainly resonated with wider szlachta opinion. In particular in the period immediately following

---

[19] Irena Stasiewicz-Jasiukowa (ed.), *Wkład Pijarów do nauki i kultury w Polsce XVII–XIX wieku* (Warsaw, 1993). William Rose, *Stanislas Konarski: Reformer of Education in Eighteenth-Century Poland* (London, 1929). James Leith (ed.), *Facets of Education in the Eighteenth Century* (Oxford, 1977). Norbert Conrads, *Ritterakademien der frühen Neuzeit: Bildung als Standesprivileg im 16. und 17. Jahrhundert* (Göttingen, 1982). Mark Motley, *Becoming a French Aristocrat: The Education of the Court Nobility, 1580–1715* (Princeton, 1990).

the death of King Jan III Sobieski and the election of his successor, Augustus II, the szlachta through their regional sejmiki repeatedly called for this corrupt elite to be replaced with a new government of worthy men.

According to the Commonwealth's customary law, the king's power of appointment was limited by the requirement that he name only worthy ('*bene meritis*') szlachta to public offices, or to stewardship of portions of royal lands (*królewszczyzny* or *starostwa*).[20] This requirement was included in the *pacta conventa* (the terms upon which a newly elected king agreed to rule, which he was required to swear before his coronation) of all but one of the Commonwealth's kings since the extinction of the Jagiellonian dynasty in the sixteenth century.[21] Following the death of Jan III Sobieski in 1696, sejmiki across the Commonwealth instructed their envoys to the coming royal election to ensure that in future, offices were only given to *bene meritis* individuals. This demand was subsequently repeated in instructions to envoys to the first meetings of the Sejm under Augustus II.[22]

The emphasis by the sejmiki on the requirement that only the deserving should receive royal patronage implies a belief that hitherto this had not been the basis on which appointments had been made. Thus the sejmiki were implicitly endorsing the claim by both the *Eclipsis Poloniae* and in the previous century by Łukasz Opaliński, that the royal powers of appointment had been misused. Some sejmiki went further, and openly hinted at corruption. For example, the sejmik of Różan urged that appointments should be made 'without intrigues', while those of Proszowice, Łomża, and Nur urged that 'vacancies should not be given in return for payment' but instead to worthy and deserving men.[23]

---

[20] *Królewszczyzny* were crown estates, leased out for life. *Starostwa* were mediaeval offices: originally, a *starosta* had been the king's representative in a particular region, exercising executive and judicial functions. By the early modern period, these functions had largely disappeared, but in many cases a *starosta* remained the steward of royal estates in his region. In theory, a *starosta* was supposed to administer these estates on the king's behalf, paying to the central Treasury a predetermined revenue each year. But by the eighteenth century, lack of enforcement and failure to revalue the revenues of royal estates meant that the great bulk of the revenues from royal estates went to the *starosta*. Some *starostwa* were so high-yielding that their acquisition was a virtually guaranteed route to vast personal enrichment for their *starosta*.

[21] The relevant sections of the various *pacta conventa* can be found at: VL vol. 2, p. 152 (Stefan Bathory); VL vol. 3, p. 364 (Władysław IV); VL vol. 4, p. 95 (Jan Kazimierz); VL vol. 5, p. 14 (Michał); VL vol. 5, p. 143 (Jan III Sobieski); and VL vol. 6, p. 15 (Augustus II). Zygmunt III's *pacta conventa* contain no specific reference to the distribution of offices.

[22] See, for example, resolutions of the sejmiki of Lublin, 1 December 1701, TP vol. 16, p. 74; Nur, 25 April 1697, TP vol. 18, p. 132; and Warsaw, 17 July 1696, TP vol. 31, p. 430.

[23] 'Wakanse . . . oddawane były bez intryg', resolution of the sejmik of Różan, 13 May 1697, TP vol. 20, p. 351. 'Wakanse muneribus nabyte niebyły pieczentowane', Proszowice sejmik, 29 July 1696, Bibl. Czart. MS 2880 421–424 (422). 'Król JMsc przyszły wakanse . . . sine ullo premio dawał', Łomża sejmik, 2 May 1697, TP vol. 15, p. 153.

Perhaps unsurprisingly, the regional sejmiki picked out the king's immediate circle as a particular focus for corruption. After his death, Sobieski's queen was obliquely identified as a source of intrigue and corruption, with the sejmik of Zakroczym instructing its envoys to ensure that appointments were not made in accordance with the former queen's interest. At the same time, several other sejmiki called for Sobieski's widow and household, especially his son Jakub, to be excluded from the coming royal election.[24] After the election of Augustus II, suspicion of the court circle shifted its focus onto the new king's German advisers, brought with him from his Electorate of Saxony. Numerous sejmiki called on the king to dismiss these foreigners, or to appoint only szlachta to public office, with the king's promotion of his close confidant Jakob von Flemming to a senior position in the Commonwealth's army attracting particular criticism.

These attacks on corruption at court were accompanied by sustained criticism by the sejmiki of the activities of those close to the king, and in particular of their alleged collusion in 'private' government, contrary to the laws of the Commonwealth. The principal target was the Senate Council, which was repeatedly criticized for usurping the prerogatives of the Sejm. For example, the sejmik of Łęczyca protested in May 1699 that 'the Senate Council had, privately and in violation of positive law, usurped for itself the right to decide in private councils on matters that should depend upon the judgement and consent of the whole Commonwealth', and called for all such illegal decisions made by the Senate Council to be declared null and void. The sejmik of Sochaczew similarly insisted in 1701 that 'matters that affected the whole Commonwealth should not be decided by the Senate Council but should be left to the whole Commonwealth, and that whatever had been decided by the Senate Council without the consent of the whole Commonwealth should be annihilated'.[25] To prevent such 'private' government by the Senate Council in future, some sejmiki called for legal restrictions on its powers, or for its membership to include szlachta envoys as well as senators, to scrutinize its activities and ensure it

'wakanse rozdawane . . . non pretio vel meritis et virtutibus', Nur sejmik, 25 April 1697, TP vol. 18, p. 132.

[24] Resolutions of the sejmiki of Zakroczym, [January?] 1697, TP vol. 36, p. 221; Sieradz, 27 July 1696, TP vol. 26, p. 884; Warsaw, 17 July 1696, TP vol. 31, p. 430; and Wizna, 22 October 1696, TP vol. 33, p. 572.

[25] 'privata senatus consilia, violando positivas leges pozwalają sobie dispensare one i tak sobie uzurpują in privato consilio, co ad iudiciam całej Rzplitej et consensum tej należeć powinno'. Resolution of the sejmik of Łęczyca, 25 May 1699, TP vol. 11, pp. 954–5. 'Materye które tangunt totam Rempublicam aby in senatus consilio decydowane nie były, ale ad statum totum Reipublicae odedane y te którekolwiek sine consensu totius Reipublicae stanęł żeby były annihilowane'. Resolution of the sejmik of Sochaczew, 1701, TP vol. 30, p. 27.

stayed within the bounds set by law.[26] Other parts of the Commonwealth's central government were also singled out for criticism, with numerous sejmiki calling on the Treasurers to produce accounts of their management of public funds.[27]

The resolutions of the sejmiki at the turn of the eighteenth century thus echo the *Eclipsis Poloniae* (and Opaliński's squire) in expressing a profound suspicion of the Commonwealth's central government and of the corrupt elite that, the sejmiki implied, had captured that government for its own private interests rather than the common good. The sejmiki called upon the king to exercise his powers of patronage more wisely, and in future to appoint virtuous men to public office in place of this self-serving, corrupt elite.

Of course, not all political rhetoric is sincere, and the language of corruption has frequently been deployed merely as a polemical tool in factional conflicts, for example as a means for political 'outs' to attack the current 'ins' whom they seek to replace in positions of power of influence. Calls from the sejmiki for the appointment of worthy men to office cannot necessarily therefore be read uncritically. One particular example, from the sejmik of Lublin in 1701, illustrates this clearly. In May 1701, the Lublin sejmik joined many others in demanding that offices and honours be given only to worthy members of the szlachta. In a resolution of December 1701, however, the sejmik noted the egregious virtue of the Sieniawski family, and in particular of Adam Sieniawski, one of the Commonwealth's most powerful magnates, who would shortly thereafter rise to become Grand Hetman of the Crown. In view of his great virtue, the sejmik instructed its envoys to lobby the king to appoint Sieniawski to the *starostwo* of Mizaków.[28] In this case at least, those deemed deserving by the sejmiki could include a member of the Commonwealth's magnate elite.

It is possible, therefore, to read calls from the sejmiki for the appointment of worthy men as simply a rhetorical device deployed in the continual struggles between different magnate factions over power and

---

[26] Resolutions of the sejmiki of Warsaw, 15 June 1699, TP vol. 31, p. 482; Łęczyca, 18 April 1701, TP vol. 12, p. 13; Proszowice, 18 April 1701, Bibl. Czart. MS 2881 pp. 79–102 (86); Czersk, 9 June 1701, TP vol. 3, p. 36; and Sieradz, 8 June 1702, TP vol. 27, p. 111.

[27] Resolutions of the sejmiki of Czersk, 19 May 1701, TP vol. 3, p. 31; and Sandomierz, 18 April 1701, TP vol. 22, p. 22. Similar demands by sejmiki in the years after Augustus II's return to the Commonwealth: see resolutions of the sejmiki of Opatów, 23 February 1712, TP vol. 22, p. 408; and Łęczyca, 31 March 1712, TP vol. 12, p. 407. After the ravages of the Great Northern War had taken their toll on szlachta property, however, the focus of szlachta concerns about the activities of central officials shifted to the hetmans: see Chapters 5 and 6.

[28] Resolutions of the sejmik of Lublin, 18 May 1701, TP vol. 9, p. 21; and 1 December 1701, TP vol. 16, p. 77.

patronage, which some historians (most notably followers of the Kraków School) have seen as the central dynamic of the Commonwealth's politics. However, there are grounds for caution before such a negative, indeed cynical, interpretation is adopted. As is discussed in Chapter 3, the extent of magnate control over the mass of the szlachta and over the sejmiki is disputed by historians, and it cannot be assumed that sejmik resolutions were simply the expressions of different magnates' factional agendas. In this context, it is notable that calls for the appointment of worthy men feature in the resolutions of sejmiki not just in regions where land ownership was highly concentrated in the hands of a few families, where the case for magnate control is most plausible, but also in regions such as Masovia where large magnate estates never developed. It is also worth noting that although the language of corruption plainly could be used cynically, there are also historical examples in which it was the expression of a more genuine movement for political change. For example, Bailyn has shown how attacks on the corruption of the ruling elite of eighteenth-century Great Britain played an important role in rallying the population of Britain's American colonies to the cause of rebellion and independence.[29]

So although calls for deserving men to be appointed to office were no doubt occasionally useful to individual magnates seeking further advancement, such as Sieniawski, it is not clear that magnate politicking was all that lay behind these demands. It is also notable that even magnates lobbying for patronage found it necessary (or at least expedient) to use the language of virtue, and present themselves as *bene meritis* citizens, rather than making some other case for their personal advancement. That even the most powerful felt obliged to use the rhetoric of virtue and desert thus illustrates the centrality of the conceptual language of virtue in the Commonwealth's political discourse.

LIMITS TO CALLING FOR MORAL REVIVAL

Neither calling on the szlachta to embrace the common good, nor rallying them to a new crusade against the infidel, nor urging the king to promote virtue by appointing only worthy men to office, however, represented a structural solution to the Commonwealth's malaise. All assumed the maintenance of the Commonwealth's existing laws and institutions, and simply called on the citizens operating within those laws and institutions to behave better. Notwithstanding szlachta politicians' intimate

---

[29] Bernard Bailyn, *The Ideological Origins of the American Revolution* (enlarged edition, Cambridge, MA, 1992).

knowledge of their own political system, therefore, all of these responses could be characterized as naïve or unlikely ever to be effective.

But szlachta responses to the perceived turmoil of the Commonwealth and corruption of its government were not restricted just to calls for citizens, and kings, to become better people. Institutional changes were also advocated, proposed, and in some cases implemented—with the aim of restoring government in the common interest.

One such institutional response can be observed developing in the late seventeenth and early eighteenth centuries in the grassroots of szlachta politics, the sejmiki. For the same sejmiki who agitated for the appointment of worthy men to office at the centre were simultaneously building up local institutions of government, controlled by those the sejmiki deemed *bene meritis*, not by the corrupt elite at court. This growth of local government based on the sejmiki is the subject of Chapter 3.

3

Government of Local Worthies

THE ERA OF SEJMIK GOVERNMENT

Ever since the work of Adolf Pawiński in the nineteenth century, historians of the Commonwealth have characterized the late seventeenth and early eighteenth centuries as an 'era of sejmik government'. From at least the middle of the seventeenth century until the 'Silent Sejm' of 1717, sejmiki across the Commonwealth gradually expanded their functions in government, taking on more and more of the responsibilities previously discharged by central officials and institutions.[1]

Thus at the same time as attacking central government as corrupt, as discussed in Chapter 2, the sejmiki were steadily eroding its role. Similarly, alongside calling for virtuous nobles to be appointed to office in place of self-serving ministers and senators, the sejmiki were giving more power to worthy men at the local level. The expansion of sejmik government can

---

[1] There is a rich literature of studies of the growth of the powers and role of the sejmiki, most of it focusing on developments in particular regions. This historiography began with Adolf Pawiński, *Rządy sejmikowe w Polsce 1572–1795 na tle stosunków województw kujawskich* (1st edition 1888, 2nd edition ed. Henryk Olszewski, Warsaw, 1978), which focused on Kujawy. More recent studies include Józef Gierowski, *Sejmik generalny Księstwa Mazowieckiego na tle ustroju sejmikowego Mazowsza* (Wrocław, 1948); Adam Lityński, *Szlachecki samorząd gospodarczy w Małopolsce (1606–1717)* (Katowice, 1974) and various articles, for example 'Małopolskie sądy skarbowe do roku 1717', *Czasopismo Prawno-historyczne*, 24, 2 (1972), pp. 107–24 and 'Samorząd szlachecki w Polsce XVII–XVIII wieku', *Kwartalnik Historyczny*, 99, 4 (1992) 4, pp. 17–34; Kazimierz Przyboś, *Sejmik województwa krakowskiego w czasach saskich (1697–1763)* (Kraków, 1981); Wojciech Kriegseisen, *Sejmiki Rzeczypospolitej szlacheckiej w XVII i XVIII wieku* (Warsaw, 1991) and *Samorząd szlachecki w Małopolsce*; Jolanta Choińska-Mika, *Sejmiki mazowieckie w dobie Wasów* (Warsaw, 1998) and *Między społeczeństwem szlacheckim a władzą: problemy komunikacji społeczności lokalne władza w epoce Jana Kazimierza* (Warsaw, 2002); Andrzej Zakrzewski, *Sejmiki Wielkiego Księstwa Litewskiego XVI–XVIII w. Ustrój i funkcjonowanie: sejmik trocki* (Warsaw, 2000); see also Andrzej Rachuba, *Wielkie Księstwo Litewskie w systemie parlamentarnym Rzeczypospolitej w latach 1569–1763* (Warsaw, 2002). The 'era of sejmik government' has usually been dated as starting in the mid-seventeenth century: Kriegseisen has suggested 1648 as a start date. Lityński, however, has argued that signs of the expansion of sejmik power can be seen well before this date, even in the final decade of the sixteenth century.

thus be seen as an attempt to replace corrupt government at the centre with virtuous government in the regions.

Key areas in which local institutions expanded their powers and activities were taxation and security. Lityński has shown that starting from the early seventeenth century, the sejmiki of Małopolska began to establish local militias to defend szlachta property against bandits and roaming soldiers, in the absence of effective action from central government to guarantee security. In order to pay for local defence measures, the sejmiki began retaining a growing portion of the revenues from taxes raised in their localities, in particular those from the *czopowe* and *szelężne* alcohol taxes. Alongside this takeover of local tax revenues, the Małopolska sejmiki also assumed for themselves the right to appoint local tax-collectors. Previously appointed from the centre by the Treasurer, whom many sejmiki accused of corruption, these local officials began to be elected by the sejmiki at the same time as Sejm envoys and Tribunał deputies.[2]

Pawiński and Gierowski have described similar developments in Kujawy and Masovia, where over the course of the seventeenth century sejmiki gradually took over more responsibility for local security, including by organizing local militias, and for the administration of local taxes.[3] A parallel trend has also been observed in the Grand Duchy of Lithuania, where sejmiki also became more active during the seventeenth century in organizing local defence while retaining a greater share of local tax revenues. Rachuba has linked these developments to the 'republican' opposition to magnate power, noting that the election of local tax collectors may only have taken place in sejmiki dominated by 'republicans', who made a point of asserting their right to elect local officials and to raise local taxes.[4]

As well as taking on new functions, the sejmiki developed new local institutions through which to exercise them. The most important of these new institutions were local fiscal courts (*Sądy skarbowe*) and later województwo councils (*Rady wojewódzkie*). Fiscal courts were initially

---

[2] Lityński, *Szlachecki samorząd gospodarczy*, passim, esp. pp. 36–70.

[3] Pawiński, *Rządy sejmikowe w Polsce 1572–1795*, p. 473. Gierowski, *Sejmik generalny Księstwa Mazowieckiego*. Unlike other regions of the Commonwealth, Masovia had two tiers of local government: a General Sejmik covering the whole region (a remnant of the mediaeval Piast Duchy of Masovia's central representative body), as well as individual sejmiki for each of Masovia's ten districts, which elected envoys both to the General Sejmik and to the Sejm. The relationship between the two levels of sejmiki in Masovia was never precisely defined, and Gierowski has observed a move towards greater localism in this period within Masovia as well as between Masovia and the Commonwealth's central government, with the ten district sejmiki increasingly organizing militias and taking control of taxes at the district level, rather than leaving these functions to the General Sejmik. Gierowski, *Sejmik generalny Księstwa Mazowieckiego*, pp. 106–7 and 165–70.

[4] Zakrzewski, *Sejmiki Wielkiego Księstwa Litewskiego*, pp. 178–81. Rachuba, *Wielkie Księstwo Litewskie w systemie parlamentarnym Rzeczypospolitej*, pp. 206–12.

established to administer the collection of local taxation, but then took on responsibility for allocating tax quotas within their regions and for paying local militias, and by the end of seventeenth century evolved into a general executive arm of local government. They were supplemented at the beginning of the eighteenth century by województwo councils, typically established with broad mandates, perhaps because fiscal courts were felt to be too specialized to respond effectively to the new challenges posed by the outbreak of the Great Northern War and the threat to szlachta property from looting by soldiers of the various belligerent armies.[5] Local security was the primary focus of these new institutions, which continued to organize local militias to defend their regions and on occasion to call out the *ruszenie pospolite*, the mass levy of the local szlachta.[6] They also began to dispatch envoys to local commanders as well as to the hetmans, the king, and even foreign rulers such as Charles XII of Sweden and Peter I of Russia, to try and negotiate for army units to be withdrawn from their particular regions.[7]

Thus alongside taking over some of the fiscal responsibilities of the allegedly corrupt Treasurers, local government also increasingly attempted to take on the hetmans' task of protecting their regions, and szlachta property, against invading armies and their 'licentious' pillaging. As will be discussed in Chapters 5 and 6, in the 1710s, the hetmans would be bitterly criticized for failing to discharge their duty in this regard and to uphold the common good. While sejmiki and their envoys were attacking this apparent failure of virtue on the part of the hetmans, local institutions were also taking the initiative themselves, attempting to ensure the defence of the common interest in the immunity of property at the local level.

LEGITIMIZING LOCAL GOVERNMENT

The expansion of local government during the seventeenth and eighteenth centuries constituted a significant innovation in the Commonwealth's form of government. It was legitimized through the authority of the sejmiki, the Commonwealth's oldest public councils. It was by resolution

---

[5] Kriegseisen, *Samorząd szlachecki w Małopolsce*, pp. 81–96.
[6] See, for example, resolutions of the sejmiki of Lublin, 8 June 1702, TP vol. 16, p. 82; Opatów (the sejmik for the Województwo of Sandomierz), 8 June 1702, TP vol. 22, p. 36; Czersk, 22 June 1702, TP vol. 3, p. 60; and Liw, 27 February 1703, TP vol. 5, p. 296.
[7] For examples of sejmiki dispatching envoys in this way see resolutions of the sejmiki of Łęczyca, 18 March 1707, TP vol. 12, pp. 227ff.; Nur, 29 August 1707, TP vol. 18, pp. 140ff.; Dobrzyn, 2 August 1710, TP vol. 4, p. 336; and Różan, 8 August 1716, TP vol. 20, p. 455.

of the relevant sejmiki that institutions such as fiscal courts or wojew-ództwo councils were established in each region, and it was the sejmiki that set these bodies' remits and chose their membership. This can be seen as an evolution of the long-established role of the sejmiki in choos-ing envoys to the Sejm or deputies to the Tribunał, and giving formal instructions to their representatives to these central bodies. With the new institutions being based on the sejmiki and their authority in this way, Kriegseisen has even described fiscal courts and województwo councils as in effect standing sub-committees of the sejmiki that estab-lished them.[8] Rooting their existence, role, and powers in the authority of the sejmiki allowed the new developments in local government to be presented as an organic growth from the Commonwealth's established constitution, and hence legitimate acts of the Commonwealth's collec-tive sovereignty, serving the common good.

As well as legitimizing the establishment of new local institutions, the sejmiki were simultaneously expanding their own activities during this period. The most notable development was the increase from around the middle of the seventeenth century in the frequency of sejmik meetings, achieved through the adjournment of sejmik sessions, a practice known as the *limita*.[9]

According to the Commonwealth's traditional laws, legally constituted sejmiki could only meet if summoned by either the king (or during an interregnum, the Primate acting as interrex) or the Sejm. An assembly not formally summoned could not claim to be a sejmik, but was rather just a 'private' gathering, with no power to take decisions on public busi-ness.[10] However, in order to circumvent the requirement for a formal summons and to meet more regularly, from around the middle of the seventeenth century, sejmiki increasingly took to adjourning, rather than dissolving, their sessions. This, defenders of the practice argued, allowed them to reconvene at a time of their own choosing, while retaining the legal authority conferred by the original summons. The first *limita* for which records survive was that of the sejmik of Halicz in 1655.[11] Over

---

[8] Kriegseisen, *Samorząd szlachecki w Małopolsce*, p. 56.

[9] The *limita* was occasionally also used for the central Sejm, for example in 1712–13 (see Chapter 5), but was highly controversial, given fears that Sejm envoys might be cor-rupted by royal patronage. The *limita* was eventually banned by law for both the sejmiki (in 1717) and the Sejm (in 1726).

[10] Arguably, therefore, although the *szlachta* did enjoy the right to free assembly, this did not extend to a right of free *political* assembly. Adam Lityński, 'Problem szlacheckiego prawa zgrodadzeń ziemskich w Polsce w XVII i XVIII wieku', *Czasopismo Prawno-Historyczne*, 26, 1 (1974), pp. 175–83.

[11] Some earlier resolutions (the earliest from 1651) survive of Ukrainian sejmiki recon-vening after having previously been adjourned. However, no records of the original adjourn-ments in these earlier cases have survived.

the rest of the seventeenth century, the frequency of sejmik adjournments increased. By the reign of Jan III Sobieski, on average sejmiki were meeting approximately once per month. From Sobieski's death until 1717 (when the practice was outlawed by the 'Silent Sejm'), the frequency of sejmik meetings increased further: at some points during these years the sejmiki were assembling on average five or six times each month.[12]

More frequent meetings not only gave the sejmiki more opportunities to debate local needs and priorities, but also allowed a separation of local business from the priorities of the centre. When sejmiki were summoned by the king, for example to elect envoys to a coming Sejm, the summons was accompanied by an agenda set from the centre, which the sejmiki were called upon to discuss. The *limita*, however, permitted the sejmiki to reconvene the next day to discuss local business in addition to the matters on the summons agenda. These locally focused sejmik meetings came to be termed *sejmiki gospodarskie* or *sejmiki boni ordinis*, and it was from these sessions that fiscal courts and województwo councils developed. Separating local business from the 'high politics' of electing Sejm envoys in this way both gave the sejmiki more time to debate local matters, and made those discussions less vulnerable to disruption by centrally focused political controversies and rivalries. Kriegseisen has shown that whereas the Commonwealth's most powerful magnates, who were intensely interested in who was elected by each sejmik as Sejm envoys or Trybunał deputies, involved themselves closely with the first day of sejmik deliberations, they displayed almost no interest at all in the meetings of *sejmiki gospodarskie* and their discussions of purely local business. Probably as a result, locally focused sejmiki were far less likely to be broken up and finish inconclusively than electoral sejmiki.[13] The separation of local business from Commonwealth-wide politics thus allowed local government to become more effective during the late seventeenth and early eighteenth centuries.

In different ways, therefore, the *limita* was crucial to the expansion of local government in this period. Its legality, and the legitimacy of the sejmiki that met by virtue of the *limita*, were however strongly contested by the centre. From the 1650s, various kings protested that the practice was illegal, and Jan III Sobieski attempted to legislate to ban it (which may have been an implicit concession that the practice was not in fact contrary to any existing law), on the grounds that repeated sejmik meetings were

---

[12] Henryk Olszewski, 'Praktyka limitowania sejmików', *Czasopismo Prawno-Historyczne*, 13 (1961), pp. 33–55.
[13] Kriegseisen, *Sejmiki Rzeczypospolitej szlacheckiej*, p. 179, and *Samorząd szlachecki w Małopolsce*, p. 51.

both a waste of resources and a cause of internal disorder. In this, Sobieski failed: it was not until the 1717 'Silent Sejm' that the practice was eventually banned, on the grounds that 'private' assemblies had both led to disorder, and had prevented the taxes decreed by the Sejm from being fully collected.[14] After 1717, the *limita* disappeared almost completely.

Before 1717, however, supporters of local government vigorously defended the legality of the *limita*, advancing a variety of different arguments in its support. Some argued that since no law forbade the *limita*, it must be legal, and even asserted their right under the law to adjourn and reconvene without any summons by the king. Others argued that the sheer necessity of holding more frequent sejmik sessions justified the means by which this was achieved as serving the common interest.[15] One particularly vigorous defence of the *limita* in the 1710s was mounted by Stanisław Łętowski (1677–1735), a prominent local politician in Małopolska. Łętowski claimed that debate was essential to the health of the Commonwealth, arguing that 'forbidding a Free Nation to hold councils would be like God denying mankind free Will'. If the *limita* were not allowed, he warned, private assemblies would gather instead of sejmiki, leading to faction, contrary to the common good.[16]

LOCAL WORTHIES

To help maintain the claim that sejmiki returning from adjournment were still the original assemblies summoned in accordance with customary law (and not illegitimate 'private' gatherings), sejmiki typically kept the same marshals and other officials chosen at the start of their original sessions. Together with the growth of institutions such as fiscal courts and województwo councils, the *limita* thus helped to support the emergence of a body of local office-holders who regularly had responsibility for local administration. As with the growth of institutions, this was a gradual process, beginning in the mid-seventeenth century with some individuals serving repeatedly (but only for a day at a time) as sejmik officials, but

---

[14] VL vol. 6, pp. 148–9. Given that one of the central concerns of local government appears to have been ensuring local security, the claim that more frequent sejmiki led to disorder may have seemed somewhat rich to those participating in *sejmiki boni ordinis* and the institutions that grew out of them. But even they would have had to concede that the charge of having taken control over a portion of tax revenues was justified.

[15] Kriegseisen, *Samorząd szlachecki w Małopolsce*, pp. 44–7. Olszewski, 'Praktyka limitowania sejmików', pp. 42–5.

[16] 'ktoz broni Wolnemu ieszcze sobie radzie o sobie Narodowi,—wszak y sam Bog nie tąmie liberam Voluntatem człowiekowi y radzic pozwala o sobie'. Speech to the Proszowice sejmik, Bibl Ossol MS 701, pp. 70–1.

by the early eighteenth century leading to prominent local szlachta being members of permanent bodies such as województwo councils.

Participants in local government were typically moderately wealthy locally prominent landowners, who often held local offices but were generally not senators or members of great magnate families.[17] A few of the most prominent of these local political activists might on occasion serve as their sejmik's envoy to the Sejm, for example Stanisław Łętowski, three times Sejm envoy for Proszowice, or the political writer Stanisław Dunin Karwicki, a regular envoy for Opatów, the sejmik of the Sandomierz region. In truly exceptional circumstances, some could even rise to positions of significant power in the Commonwealth. One example was Stanisław Ledóchowski, a middling landowner from Volhynia who held a variety of local offices, and was envoy to the central council of the Sandomierz Confederation in 1707, before coming to Commonwealth-wide prominence in 1715 as Marshal of the General Confederation of Tarnogród. Such cases were far from representative, however, of the great majority of local government activists, who typically had little direct involvement with the politics of the centre.

It was this population of local officials who, through the development of local institutions established by the sejmiki, increasingly took over the responsibilities that had previously been discharged by the Commonwealth's central ministers whom the sejmiki criticized as corrupt and self-interested. In place of that allegedly self-serving elite, the sejmiki gradually substituted a cadre of local worthies, appointed to serve the common good.

By contrast, the Commonwealth's magnates had little direct involvement in the burgeoning local government in this period, for example rarely participating in *sejmiki gospodarskie* or other local institutions such as fiscal courts or województwo councils.[18] Some historians have nonetheless seen magnate power as the true driving force behind the growth of sejmik power. This interpretation has presented the rise of local government as an element of the progressive decentralization of the Commonwealth's government at the expense of its central institutions. Decentralization has in turn been associated with the emergence of the so-called 'magnate oligarchy' that supposedly appeared at the same time, and which was long blamed for preventing any positive reforms (and in particular any centralization) of

---

[17] Modern historians have often described such individuals as belonging to the 'middle szlachta', but for the problems with identifying a distinct 'middle' stratum of the szlachta, see footnote 30 to Chapter 1.

[18] Kriegseisen, *Samorząd szlachecki w Małopolsce*, p. 51. Przyboś, *Sejmik województwa krakowskiego*, p. 40.

Poland-Lithuania's government and hence for the Commonwealth's ultimate ruin. The link between the expansion of local government and the growth of a 'magnate oligarchy' in the Commonwealth was made explicitly by Olszewski, who argued that it was no accident that the development of the *limita* coincided with that of the 'dictatorship of the magnate oligarchy' in the second half of the seventeenth century.[19]

Given the lack of direct magnate participation in local government, the argument that the growth of local government was driven by a magnate agenda and served magnate interests requires that the local landowners and office-holders who played the leading role in the newly expanded local government were in fact loyal and obedient clients of magnate 'oligarchs'. The ability of great magnates to rally substantial numbers of less wealthy szlachta to their side, and thus build powerful factions to advance their own interests, has been generally acknowledged. Central to their ability to do so was magnates' use of patronage, either economic (for example appointing supporters as bailiffs or administrators of portions of the magnate's private estates) or political (magnates using their influence to have supporters appointed to public office at either local or central level).

Although magnates' power of patronage was clearly substantial, it is not clear that it gave them complete or lasting control over the mass of the szlachta in the Commonwealth's regions. Kriegseisen has argued that at the local level magnate power was always constrained by the need to take into account the opinions of the broader szlachta assembled at the sejmiki, and that magnates attempting to force their will on the sejmiki always faced the possibility of a backlash, possibly a violent one, if they disregarded the views of the local szlachta. Given that magnate estates were typically dispersed across the Commonwealth's territory, it was also rare for any particular region to be under the exclusive dominance of a single magnate. Competition between magnates and their factions could thus be a significant constraint on any magnates' ability to control a given area and its sejmiki.[20]

---

[19] Olszewski, 'Praktyka limitowania sejmików', p. 53. The association between the growth of sejmik power and general decentralization has been highlighted in Pawiński, *Rządy sejmikowe w Polsce 1572–1795*, and Gierowski, *Sejmik generalny Księstwa Mazowieckiego*. The classic exposition of the claim that a 'magnate oligarchy' emerged in the mid-seventeenth century is Władysław Czapliński, 'Rządy oligarchii w Polsce nowożytnej', in Czapliński, *O Polsce siedemnastowiecznej*, pp. 130–63. See also Frost, 'The Nobility of Poland-Lithuania'.

[20] Kriegseisen, *Sejmiki Rzeczypospolitej szlacheckiej*, pp. 119–20. This emphasis on competition between magnate factions is analogous to the characterization by Butterwick of the politics of the Commonwealth as a whole in the eighteenth century, in which 'it was magnate rivalry rather than oligarchy' that predominated. Butterwick, *Poland's Last King and English Culture*, p. 21.

The ability of less wealthy szlachta 'clients' to play different magnates off against one another in order to advance their own interests is illustrated by a study of patronage relationships in the Brześć region of Lithuania for a slightly later period in the eighteenth century by Zofia Zielińska. Zielińska examined the memoirs of Marcin Matuszewicz, a moderately wealthy local nobleman who eventually rose to the minor senatorial office of Castellan of Brześć. Matuszewicz was at one point the leader at the Brześć sejmik of the supporters of the mighty Radziwiłł family, and benefited substantially from Radziwiłł patronage. Yet over the course of his political career, Matuszewicz repeated switched his allegiance from the Radziwiłłs to their rivals (apparently without much regard for any policy differences between the different factions), whenever different factions appeared to offer greater prospects of promotion. The ability of other potential patrons to satisfy Matuszewicz's ambitions thus substantially limited the extent to which any individual magnate could count on his loyalty or obedience. Zielińska's study also revealed how amorphous an individual magnate's faction could be: the Radziwiłł faction consisted of only a few regular leaders who formed a core of support, but needed to gather support (competing with rival factions) ahead of each meeting of the local sejmik. From sejmik to sejmik, therefore, the bulk of the Radziwiłł faction was fluid in its membership.[21]

A further reason to doubt the extent of magnate control over the expanding local government in this period is that similar patterns of increasing frequency of sejmik meetings, the use of the *limita*, and the development of new local institutions have been observed both in regions of the Commonwealth that featured large magnate land-holdings, and those where magnate latifundia never developed, such as Masovia. As magnates' political influence derived largely from their economic power, and specifically from their ability to use their wealth and estates for patronage purposes, if the expansion of local government was part of a 'magnate programme', the expectation would be that regions such as Masovia should have lagged behind other parts of the Commonwealth. Yet Gierowski's research has shown that Masovia experienced a very similar process of local government development as that described by Lityński for Małopolska and Kriegseisen across the Commonwealth as a whole. Gierowski has also demonstrated that the most prominent figures in Masovia local government were very much the same sort of middling landowners and local office-holders who Lityński and Kriegseisen have shown led the expansion of local institutions elsewhere in the Commonwealth.[22]

---

[21] Zofia Zielińska, 'Mechanizm sejmikowy i klientela radziwiłłowska za Sasów', *Przegląd Historyczny*, 62 (1971), pp. 397–419.
[22] Gierowski, *Sejmik generalny Księstwa Mazowieckiego*, pp. 49–52.

As discussed in Chapter 2, these local politicians through the sejmiki sharply criticized the Commonwealth's central ruling elite for its alleged corruption and usurpation of the Commonwealth's laws. They must also have been the target audience for tracts such as the *Eclipsis Poloniae*, which similarly lambasted the magnate elite for its corruption (as in the seventeenth century had Opaliński's *Rozmowa plebana z ziemianinem*). In resolutions of the sejmiki, these local szlachta called upon the king to use his powers of patronage to open up the Commonwealth's government and replace the existing elite with a government of worthy (*bene meritis*) men. And it must be presumed that the worthy men they had in mind were broadly the same worthy men as were prominent in the sejmiki and the institutions of local government that grew out of the sejmiki from the mid-seventeenth century onwards.

Meanwhile, at the same time as these sejmik activists were urging the king to put the Commonwealth's government into the hands of men such as themselves, at the local level they were already taking control of an increasing share of government responsibilities. Similarly, as well as demanding greater accountability of central government, especially the Treasurers, to the wider szlachta, the sejmiki were taking direct control over a growing portion of central government powers and revenues. So alongside calling for the establishment of a government of worthy men from above, these local szlachta politicians were building a government of local worthies from below.

The expansion of local government in the Commonwealth during the late seventeenth and early eighteenth centuries can thus be seen as another aspect of the wider szlachta response to the perceived corruption of the Commonwealth and of its ruling elite. The efforts of local worthies to bypass that elite and take control of more and more of the Commonwealth's government from below were thus another attempt to purge corruption from the Commonwealth, and restore virtuous government in the common interest.

Some locally prominent szlachta politicians, however, went further than advocating a change in personnel from above and the establishment of a government of local worthies from below. In the early years of the eighteenth century, as the Commonwealth was thrown into turmoil by the shock of the Great Northern War, a small group of szlachta writers proposed more sweeping reforms of the Commonwealth's government. Central to these reform proposals was a drive to open up the Commonwealth's central elite by giving much greater power to the wider szlachta, in particular over appointment to high office and the distribution of royal lands. These proposals for more radical reform of the Commonwealth's constitution are discussed in Chapter 4.

4

Proposals for Radical Reform

THE RADICAL REFORMERS

At the beginning of the eighteenth century, during the turbulent years following the election of Augustus II and the outbreak of the Great Northern War, a small group of szlachta politicians put forward a set of proposals for truly radical reform of the Commonwealth's government. In common with the sejmiki, they diagnosed the Commonwealth's turmoil and political dysfunction as the product of corruption at the highest levels of government, which had been captured by private interests rather than serving the common good.

To restore virtuous government, they proposed a dramatic shift of power within the Commonwealth's collective government, away from the monarchy and the Senate to the mass of the szlachta citizenry. In particular, they proposed that the royal powers of patronage, prime source of the corruption threatening the Commonwealth, be substantially restricted or even abolished outright. Giving the power of appointment to the szlachta would, along with other reforms, empower the szlachta to take control of their polity and govern it according to the common good, that is virtuously. The fullest and most detailed of these reform proposals, that of Stanisław Dunin Karwicki (1640–1724), described this new form of government as an 'absolute commonwealth'.

Karwicki was a Calvinist and a prominent landowner and active politician from the Sandomierz region of Małopolska, where he held a number of local offices (eventually rising to become Chamberlain (*podkomorzy*) of the Sandomierz Województwo in 1713), as well as repeatedly being elected as his sejmik's envoy to the Sejm and to royal elections.[1] Karwicki

---

[1] Karwicki's political career in the Commonwealth began in the early 1660s, after his return from extensive travels in western Europe, and was interrupted for some years in the 1670s when Karwicki served in the Crown Army. He was chosen as an envoy for the Województwo of Sandomierz to the Convocation of 1668, the royal elections of 1669, 1674, and 1697. He also served as envoy to the Sejm six times between 1681 and 1720. Karwicki was particularly active at the Sejm of 1712–13: see Chapter 5. Karwicki's religion does not seem to have impeded his political career, despite the growing intolerance

set out his plans for reform of the Commonwealth in a treatise entitled *De Ordinanda Republica seu de corrigendis defectibus in statu Reipublicae Polonae*, which was completed in the first decade of the eighteenth century and circulated widely in manuscript, though it was not to be printed until after Karwicki's death.[2] In this treatise Karwicki set out a programme for sweeping reform of all the Commonwealth's institutions of government, whose central theme was the full political empowerment of the whole szlachta citizenry, at the expense of the Commonwealth's other two estates.

Similar, though less complete or detailed, proposals were made in two other major contemporary political treatises, the 1707 *Traktat o elekcyi królów polskich* by Jerzy Dzieduszycki (1670–1730) and the anonymous 1709 pamphlet, the *Eclipsis Poloniae* referred to in Chapters 2 and 3. Like Karwicki, Dzieduszycki was an active politician who served as envoy to various Sejms, being particularly prominent at the 1703 Sejm held, as a result of the Swedish invasion of the Commonwealth, in Lublin. At that time a supporter of king Augustus II and the General Confederation of Sandomierz that had been formed to defend the Commonwealth and Augustus II's throne against the invading Swedes, Dzieduszycki was appointed to command a cavalry regiment, and to serve on the *hiberna* commission responsible for army pay.[3] Along with the rest of the leadership of the Sandomierz Confederation, however, Dzieduszycki recognized Augustus II's abdication in 1706 (forced upon him by Charles XII of Sweden under the Treaty of Altranstädt): it was in the context of

---

of non-Catholics that many historians have noted during the late seventeenth and early eighteenth centuries. Due to paucity of sources beyond his political treatises and public records, little is known of Karwicki's life outside politics. For more biographical details, see Władysław Konopczyński, 'Stanisław Dunin Karwicki (1640–1724)', *Przegląd Historyczny*, 37 (1948), pp. 261–75 and the Introduction to the most recent edition of Karwicki's treatises (translated into Polish), Adam Przyboś and Kazimierz Przyboś (eds.), *Stanisław Dunin Karwicki: dzieła polityczne z początku XVIII wieku* (Wrocław, 1992).

  [2] The most recent edition of the *De Ordinanda Republica* is that in Przyboś and Przyboś (eds.), *Stanisław Dunin Karwicki: dzieła polityczne*: references here are all to this edition. An earlier Latin edition also exists, *De Ordinanda Republica* (ed. Stanisław Krzyżanowski, Kraków, 1871). *De Ordinanda Republica* was itself a revised version of an earlier treatise by Karwicki, entitled *Exorbitancye we wszystkich trzech stanach Rzeczypospolitej krótko zebrane* that Staszewski has dated to 1701. Staszewski, 'Pomysły reformatorskie', p. 741 (see also Władysław Konopczyński, *Polscy pisarze polityczni XVIII wieku (do Sejmu Czteroletniego)* (Warsaw, 1966), p. 36). A full discussion of the surviving sources for Karwicki's treatises and their relation to one another is given in the Introduction to Przyboś and Przyboś (eds.), *Stanisław Dunin Karwicki: dzieła polityczne*, pp. 12–19.

  [3] The *hiberna* was a supplementary tax levied on royal and ecclesiastical lands to support the Commonwealth's armies during winter months. The *hiberna* commission was appointed by the Sejm and its responsibilities included setting the tariffs that each particular portion of royal land was required to pay.

the interregnum following this abdication that he composed his *Traktat*, which he may have dedicated to Karwicki.[4]

Traditionally, the *Eclipsis Poloniae* has been attributed to Stanisław Szczuka (1652/4–1710), a noted Lithuanian politician who served as crown referendary and marshal of the 1699 Sejm before being promoted to the Senate as Lithuanian vice-chancellor in the same year. This attribution has been accepted by Konopczyński, Gierowski, and Olszewski. Staszewski, however, has challenged it, arguing first that little firm evidence for Szczuka's authorship exists, and second that on a number of issues the views put forward by the *Eclipsis Poloniae* were either contrary to Szczuka's known opinions or else incompatible with his position as a senator.[5] The authorship of the *Eclipsis Poloniae* is therefore uncertain.

The programme for reform of the Commonwealth's government set out in these three works involved a radical shift in power away from the monarchy and the Senate, and the empowerment and enfranchisement of the szlachta as a whole in order to deliver government in the common good. It consisted of three main elements: reform of the Sejm; restriction of the royal powers of patronage; and election by the szlachta for all public offices in the Commonwealth.

REFORMING THE SEJM

Empowering the szlachta required reform of the Sejm, the central body in which they were represented, to make it an effective, permanent institution of government. Under the Commonwealth's customary laws, the Sejm was an occasional and short-lived event. According to the *pacta conventa* sworn by all newly elected kings, the king was only required to summon the Sejm for a six-week session once every two years. In between, the king was free to call additional 'extraordinary' Sejms, but these lasted for only two weeks. Sejm sessions could only be extended by unanimous agreement of the Sejm's envoys.

Karwicki argued that such short, infrequent Sejms posed a danger to szlachta liberty, as they left open space (and/or created the need) for the Commonwealth's kings to develop alternative institutions of government during the long gaps between Sejms. These new councils would, Karwicki argued, be dependent solely on the will of the king, and so would

---

[4] The work is dedicated to 'my beloved lord and brother': its early twentieth-century editor identified this as Karwicki. Introduction to Jerzy Dzieduszycki, *Traktat o elekcyi królów polskich* (1707, ed. Teodor Wierzbowski, Warsaw, 1906), p. 3.
[5] Staszewski, 'Pomysły reformatorskie', pp. 746–7.

be a form of private government or *absolutum dominium*. According to Karwicki, the first king to seek to establish an alternative council through which to govern had been Zygmunt III in 1590. As noted in Chapter 3, around the time Karwicki was composing the *De Ordinanda Republica*, many sejmiki were protesting bitterly against the latest attempt by a king to set up a 'private' government, Augustus II's efforts to rule through the Senate Council. To deny kings the opportunity to establish alternative bodies to the Sejm, Karwicki therefore proposed that the Sejm be made permanent by in future holding annual sessions, each lasting for a whole year. This proposal was repeated in the *Eclipsis Poloniae*.

As well as making the Sejm annual, both Karwicki and the *Eclipsis Poloniae* also proposed that the Sejm be made unbreakable. In common with all contemporary mainstream szlachta politicians and commentators, both professed their support for the *liberum veto* and the requirement for legislation to be agreed unanimously, to ensure it was in accordance with the common good. Indeed, Karwicki defended the veto as the ultimate safeguard against the loss of szlachta liberty, even as he argued that the Commonwealth would truly be in a terrible state (and one that no patriot could ever hope to see) if a single envoy's veto was all that stood between it and *absolutum dominium*.[6]

Karwicki did, however, propose that the veto should in future apply only to individual pieces of legislation, but not to the entire proceedings of a Sejm. Echoing an opinion commonly aired by his contemporaries, Karwicki denounced the use of the veto to 'break' a Sejm as a dangerous recent innovation, indeed one that had only arisen in his own lifetime. The ability to break a Sejm derived from the twin customs that new legislation would only be formally enacted in a single package at the end of each Sejm session, and that Sejm sessions could only be extended (usually by a single day at a time) with the unanimous agreement of the envoys. The Sejm had first been broken in 1652 by an envoy named Władysław Siciński, who had refused his consent to an extension of a Sejm session, and then left Warsaw immediately after using his veto, denying his fellow envoys an opportunity to persuade him to change his mind.[7] The Sejm was thus unable to reach agreement on new laws, and had to end inconclusively. Following this precedent, subsequent Sejms were repeatedly 'broken' by the veto either at the end of their sessions or earlier in

---

[6] Karwicki did qualify his support for the *liberum veto* with the argument that as Sejm envoys were bound by the instructions of their sejmiki, they could only legitimately veto a proposal if specifically mandated to do so, and only if all the envoys from a given sejmik agreed. Karwicki, *De Ordinanda Republica*, pp. 122–3.

[7] Karwicki erroneously dated the first breaking of the Sejm to 1659, and claimed to have witnessed it himself. Karwicki, *De Ordinanda Republica*, p. 113.

their proceedings, if there was no prospect of an envoy using his veto being persuaded to withdraw it.[8]

By making Sejm sessions run for a full year, Karwicki hoped to create sufficient time for negotiations with any envoy who used his veto, or threatened to do so, before the Sejm ended. This would allow a compromise to be reached on the particular measure to which the envoy objected (or even for that measure to be dropped altogether) without imperilling the rest of the deliberations of the Sejm. The result would be that the veto was effectively restricted to individual pieces of legislation, rather than to the entire Sejm. The *Eclipsis Poloniae* similarly called for the veto to be retained for individual bills, but for the Sejm to be made annual and unbreakable.[9]

In addition to calling for continuous, unbreakable Sejm sessions, Karwicki also proposed sweeping reform of the Sejm's membership and organization. First, he proposed that the Sejm's membership be regularized and increased through reform of the means by which Sejm envoys were themselves elected by the sejmiki. Instead of having them elected unanimously at the same time as the rest of a sejmik's business was being transacted, he argued that envoys should be elected at the beginning of the sejmik session, before other business was addressed and other controversies potentially arose. Further, he proposed that envoys be elected by majority vote on a secret ballot, and that the ballot boxes should not be opened immediately after voting had finished. Thus the sejmiki would first choose their envoys and then, in ignorance of their identities, draw up their instructions and complete their other business, on a second day if necessary. Only after all other business had been carried out would the ballot boxes be opened by the senior senator present, and the sejmik's choice of envoys be known. This way, Karwicki claimed, arguments over the instructions that the sejmik wished to give its envoys would not prevent envoys being chosen, and indeed even if the sejmik were to be broken during the later debates, envoys would still have been elected.[10] This separation of the election of envoys from the wider business of the sejmiki in some ways mirrored the changes already taking place in sejmik proceedings, as discussed in Chapter 3, though Karwicki's focus was more on protecting the election of envoys from controversies arising from other business than vice versa.

Ensuring that all sejmiki successfully elected envoys would ensure each Sejm had its full complement of members.[11] The Sejm to which these envoys

---

[8] Konopczyński, *Liberum veto*. Lukowski, *Disorderly Liberty*, pp. 21–6.

[9] Karwicki, *De Ordinanda Republica*, pp. 114–15. Candidus Veronensis [pseud.], *Eclipsis Poloniae*, p. 121.

[10] Karwicki, *De Ordinanda Republica*, pp. 111–12.

[11] As a further measure to ensure Sejms were fully attended, and to support participation by poorer as well as richer szlachta, Karwicki also proposed that envoys be paid a salary,

were elected would then also be substantially reformed. Karwicki proposed that in addition to the existing Chamber of Envoys and Senate a third chamber, the Fiscal Chamber (*Izba Skarbowa*), should be created by merging into the Sejm the existing Fiscal Tribunal (*Trybunał Skarbowy*).[12] Next, he proposed radical changes to the membership of the reformed Sejm's three chambers. Citing past precedents of senators and envoys attending debates in each other's chambers in the past, Karwicki proposed that all envoys and senators should be evenly distributed between the three chambers. The youngest and least experienced third of the envoys and senators would be assigned by their sejmiki to the Fiscal Chamber, the oldest and wisest third to the Senate, and the middle cohort to the Chamber of Envoys. The marshals of the three chambers (interestingly, Karwicki did not explicitly state whether the king should continue to chair the Senate) would retain the ability to bring the three chambers together for occasional plenary sessions, and only such a full session of the Sejm would be able to enact new legislation.

As well as being distinguished by the age and experience of their members, the three chambers of Karwicki's reformed Sejm would also have different functions. He insisted that the Chamber of Envoys should remain the principal chamber, which would discuss general matters concerning the common good, before passing some items on to one of the other two chambers. The Chamber of Envoys would also be the forum for envoys' instructions from their sejmiki to be read, and the common interest of the entire Commonwealth considered. The Senate would be charged with deliberating on matters of foreign affairs and with conducting diplomacy with foreign powers. Also, occasionally the Senate could, Karwicki proposed, act as a Sejm court. Finally the Fiscal Chamber would be charged with all financial business. In particular, Karwicki proposed that in future the Fiscal Chamber of the Sejm, and not the king, should be responsible for the distribution and administration of royal lands.[13]

CURBING ROYAL PATRONAGE

Both Karwicki and the *Eclipsis Poloniae* repeated the charge made by other pamphleteers and by the sejmiki (discussed in chapters 2 and 3) that the

---

and given accommodation in publicly funded hostelries for the duration of Sejm sessions. Karwicki, *De Ordinanda Republica*, pp. 122–3.

[12] The Fiscal Tribunal, which met at Radom, was the central body responsible for overseeing the fiscal administration of the Commonwealth, assigning tax quotas to particular regions and adjudicating disputes over tax payments.

[13] Karwicki, *De Ordinanda Republica*, pp. 117–20.

Commonwealth's malaise was the result of the corruption of its ruling elite, largely through the misuse of the royal powers of patronage. Both complained that royal lands in particular had been monopolized by a narrow circle of the Commonwealth's wealthiest magnates, who had ceased to work for the common good but instead pursued only their private interests, especially their material interest in maintaining their exclusive grip on royal patronage. The intriguing of self-interested magnate factions had then created turmoil and dysfunction in the Commonwealth's government.[14] For both Karwicki and the *Eclipsis Poloniae*, therefore, curtailing the royal powers of patronage and transferring them to the Sejm instead was a key element of their reform proposals.

The *Eclipsis Poloniae* therefore proposed that in future royal lands should become the possession of the Commonwealth as a whole, not just the king. Royal (perhaps after the proposed reform 'public' would be a more appropriate term) estates should be administered not by *starostas* chosen for life by the king but by commissioners appointed each year by the Sejm. The revenues from these lands, which the *Eclipsis Poloniae* intended should be used to support the Commonwealth's armies, should be handed over to the Sejm, with commissioners being required to account for them each year.[15]

Karwicki proposed a similar system, which he set out at greater length. First he proposed that upon the death of every current holder of royal lands, these properties should revert to the Commonwealth. The king's power to redistribute royal estates was thus to be gradually abolished.[16] Instead of being leased to men chosen by the king, Karwicki proposed that in future royal lands be administered by officials appointed by the Fiscal Chamber of the Sejm, and responsible to that chamber. These men would be appointed publicly, on the basis of their peers' recognition of their merits, rather than owing their positions to court intrigues or private interests.

With administrators of public lands being appointed publicly in this manner, Karwicki anticipated that the court intrigues, factions, and corruption that competition for royal lands had stirred up would come to an end, as the incentive to win the favour of the king or

---

[14] Karwicki, *De Ordinanda Republica*, p. 125. Candidus Veronensis [pseud.], *Eclipsis Poloniae*, p. 118.

[15] Candidus Veronensis [pseud.], *Eclipsis Poloniae*, p. 120.

[16] So too was the so-called *ius communicativum*, a legal device according to which the holder of a portion of royal land could, with the approval of the king, transfer it to someone else. This device had previously been used to pass control over royal lands (and their revenues) down the generations within a single family, making them almost into hereditary possessions. Karwicki denounced this practice as one way that some families had been able to accumulate huge wealth through winning the favour of kings rather than through outstanding public service. Karwicki, *De Ordinanda Republica*, p. 130.

of an influential court faction would be removed. Rather, appointing administrators on the basis of merit would reward public service, encouraging all szlachta to behave more virtuously instead of engaging in factional intrigues. Thus harmony and public service would be nurtured throughout the Commonwealth, and order and stability restored to its government.

Putting better men in charge of administering public property would also mean that revenues would no longer be either lost through incompetent administration or embezzled by corrupt officials. The Commonwealth would thus be guaranteed a decent income, which would also grow over time, as more of the existing holders of royal lands died off and control of these estates reverted to the Commonwealth. This income, Karwicki argued, would be sufficient not only to pay for the cost of the Commonwealth's armies, but also to provide pensions for veterans and cover other government expenses, and all without having to oppress the peasantry with excessive burdens or to resort to additional taxation or dependence upon foreign subsidies.[17]

Tying the revenue from these estates to paying for the army also provided for Karwicki a further mechanism for promoting honest and competent administration. He proposed that individual army units should be attached to specified royal estates, on which they would be stationed in peacetime and from whose revenues they would draw their pay. The troops of each individual unit would thus have a permanent interest in the honest and efficient management of their 'home estate' and so could be counted upon to keep a close watch on the official responsible for it, making sure that he did not either divert or embezzle the revenues it produced or attempt to seize the property for himself. The virtuous men appointed to administer public lands would therefore be kept honest by the scrutiny of their activities exercised both by the Sejm and by the army.

Promoting honest service of the common interest was thus a central objective of Karwicki's and the *Eclipsis Poloniae*'s proposals for reform of the distribution and administration of royal lands. Achieving this involved breaking the alleged monopoly on royal lands of the existing magnate elite, as demanded by many contemporary sejmiki. Karwicki echoed this demand, arguing that it would be preferable to appoint less wealthy nobles as administrators of public estates, both on the grounds that they would be less likely to be distracted by their private interests, and in order to

---

[17] Karwicki, *De Ordinanda Republica*, pp. 131–3. Note that paying for the army accounted for the lion's share of the Commonwealth's total budget throughout the early modern period. Lukowski, *Liberty's Folly*, p. 111.

offer greater opportunities for poorer szlachta to pursue careers in public service.[18]

ELECTING HIGH OFFICIALS

The radical reformers took a similar approach to the question of appointment to high public office. They argued that just as leases on royal estates were being distributed corruptly, so too appointments to ministerial and senatorial office were being made according to private interests, encouraging men to flatter the king or serve a magnate faction, rather than working for the common good. As with royal lands, the solution they proposed was to give the power to choose public officials to the szlachta.

Karwicki proposed that in future all ministers (that is the marshals, chancellors, treasurers, court treasurers, and hetmans of both Poland and Lithuania) should no longer be appointed by the king, but elected by the Sejm. Consistent with his proposals for the election of Sejm envoys by the sejmiki, Karwicki called for election of ministers by secret ballot.[19] Dzieduszycki agreed, arguing that it would ensure that ministers would no longer be chosen as a result of intrigues or personal influence at court, but instead 'the free nation would elect [ministers] . . . by a secret calculation, seeing [the candidates'] virtues and their vices'. Ministers chosen in this way, being 'dependent on the Commonwealth [not the king], will be better custodians of the laws rather than intriguers'.[20]

Karwicki also called for the term of office of the hetmans, commanders of the Commonwealth's armies and arguably the most powerful of all ministers, to be reduced from life tenure to a fixed term of three years. This proposal was echoed by the *Eclipsis Poloniae*, which also called for greater power for the Sejm over the hetmans. The *Eclipsis Poloniae* proposed that although the king should retain the power to appoint hetmans, they should only be reappointed to a further term with the consent of the Sejm. This effectively gave the Sejm the power to remove a hetman from office upon the expiry of his term.[21] In the years following the Great Northern War, the questions of restraining the powers of the hetmans, of

---

[18] Karwicki, *De Ordinanda Republica*, pp. 131–2. Interestingly, Karwicki did not discuss the counter-argument that those of lesser private means might be more tempted (or driven) towards corruption or embezzlement than their wealthier fellow szlachta.

[19] Karwicki, *De Ordinanda Republica*, p. 135.

[20] 'per secretum calculum, widząc bona malaque sua, . . . wolny obierze naród'; 'Rzeczypospolitej obligowani, lepsi będą custodes legum, aniżeli antekamery.' Dzieduszycki, *Traktat o elekcyi królów polskich*, pp. 22–3.

[21] Candidus Veronensis [pseud.], *Eclipsis Poloniae*, pp. 123–4.

subjecting them to greater oversight by the szlachta, and of providing for the dismissal of hetmans deemed to have acted against the common interest were topics of intense debate, as discussed in Chapters 5 and 6.

These reform proposals were intended to make the Commonwealth's ministers more dependent on the Sejm not the king, with the objective of ensuring that more virtuous men would in future occupy these offices. Karwicki went further still, arguing that not just ministers but almost all senators should be elected rather than appointed, the great majority of them elected directly by the szlachta in the sejmiki. He proposed that wojewodas and castellans, who made up the majority of the Senate,[22] be elected by secret ballot at their respective regional sejmiki, in the same way as Sejm envoys and local officials.

So under Karwicki's reform plan virtually all senators would be elected by the szlachta either directly or indirectly and would thus be dependent on the Commonwealth's szlachta citizenry and not the king. At the same time, it is important to remember that following Karwicki's proposed reorganization of the Sejm, those holding senatorial office and those sitting in the Senate would not be the same people. Rather, with senators and envoys distributed across all three of Karwicki's proposed chambers, only the wisest and most experienced senators would sit in the Senate for debates, while the remainder sat in the Chamber of Envoys and the Fiscal Chamber. So although Karwicki anticipated that senators would continue to perform dignified ceremonial functions, such as presiding over elections at the sejmiki, under his reform proposals the separate political role of the 'senatorial order' would disappear.

The proposals of these radical reformers thus amounted to a very significant shift in power away from the Commonwealth's existing senatorial and magnate elite, and towards the mass of the szlachta, who would in future elect, supervise, and potentially dismiss holders of the highest offices. Election by the szlachta to office would promote service to the common good rather than intriguing or subservience to the will of the king, and

---

[22] The Senate had 146 members: 10 ministers (a Grand Marshal, Vice-Marshal, Grand Chancellor, Vice-Chancellor, and Treasurer for each of Poland and Lithuania), 17 Roman Catholic Bishops, 33 Wojewodas, 85 Castellans, plus the Starosta of Żmudź. Hetmans did not sit *ex officio* in the Senate (though they invariably held other senatorial posts as well as the hetmanship), and Karwicki was firmly opposed to making the hetmanship a senatorial office. Interestingly, in the earlier version of reform proposals, the *Exorbitacje*, Karwicki had proposed that the 17 Bishops also be elected, by their cathedral chapters. (See Przyboś and Przyboś (eds.), *Stanisław Dunin Karwicki: dzieła polityczne*, p. 47.) Karwicki dropped this proposal from the *De Ordinanda Republica*: perhaps feeling that as a Calvinist it was wiser to avoid making recommendations concerning the internal organization of the Catholic Church.

thus the Commonwealth's corrupt ruling elite would be swept away, and replaced by a virtuous government of worthy szlachta.

REFORMING ROYAL ELECTIONS

The highest office-holder of all in the Commonwealth, and the one most frequently attacked by sejmiki and by szlachta polemicists in this period for failing to uphold the common good, was the king. A particular priority for Karwicki and his fellow radicals was to ensure that in future only suitably worthy men were elected to the throne, and to this end they proposed thorough reform of the royal election process.

First of all, the radicals insisted that only natives of the Commonwealth (termed 'Piasts') should be eligible for the throne.[23] They argued that foreign princes should be excluded because, having been brought up in other countries and under different laws and customs, they could never know and love the Commonwealth, its laws and liberties sufficiently well to be whole-hearted servants of the Commonwealth and the common good.

This argument was made most fully by Dzieduszycki. Dzieduszycki argued that personal virtue, and above all a love of liberty, was essential for kings if they were not to degenerate into tyrants, an argument, rooted in classical philosophy, that had been part of mainstream szlachta political thought since at least the time of Modrzewski. If the szlachta wanted to live in freedom and happiness, Dzieduszycki claimed, it was essential that they choose as their king a man of virtue, on the model of the Roman emperors Augustus, Trajan, and Marcus Aurelius, or the semi-legendary ancient Polish king Piast. The szlachta could not, however, hope to find such a man outside the Commonwealth, for in other lands it was absolute monarchy rather than liberty that prevailed. Dzieduszycki presented the contrast between the free Commonwealth and the despotic monarchies that he claimed dominated the rest of the world in the starkest terms:

> Here, [there is] reasonable, there servile obedience, here, long Sejms that are sometimes distasteful and are prevented by licence from finishing their deliberations, there instant subservience, naked as to the law, with [the ruler's] will serving as reason, with opposition a sinful act, with sometimes the slightest expression of discontent, the smallest suspicion about a decree [being seen] as a crime, any mistake in the service of the state [being] a step towards death, [and with] a flighty change in favours ending in imprisonment.

---

[23] The term 'Piast' derived from the first historical royal dynasty of the Kingdom of Poland, who reigned until 1370. The Piast dynasty in turn took its name from the semi-legendary ancient king Piast.

Princes raised in these absolutist conditions abroad could never love, or even truly understand, szlachta liberty, Dzieduszycki claimed, so foreign-born kings would inevitably be absolutists at heart, and would seek to win for themselves similar power over the szlachta as their foreign fellow-monarchs enjoyed over their unfortunate subjects.[24]

Given this, Dzieduszycki argued that it was little wonder that in the past the Commonwealth's foreign-born kings had failed to uphold its laws and liberties, but had rather sought only to use the Commonwealth's resources for their own ends, such as the Swedish-born Zygmunt III's attempts to win back his Swedish crown, or more recently Augustus II's attempts at dynastic aggrandizement. The example of Augustus II was particular resonant for Dzieduszycki, as his tract appeared shortly after Augustus II's abdication in the 1706 Treaty of Altranstädt, and the specific example he chose of a foreign absolute monarchy was Augustus II's electorate of Saxony. It is also notable both that Dzieduszycki's description of the Saxon monarchy quoted above significantly over-played the extent of the prince-elector's powers, and failed to draw any distinction between monarchies outside the Commonwealth or to acknowledge that by no means all foreign kings enjoyed such unbridled power as he claimed.

Nevertheless, on the basis of his comparison between the free Commonwealth and the near-tyrannical monarchies that he claimed prevailed elsewhere, Dzieduszycki concluded that only a native Piast, brought up under the Commonwealth's laws and customs, as an equal to his brother nobles, could possibly be expected to love and preserve those laws and the szlachta's treasured liberty. So only a native Piast could possibly be sufficiently virtuous to be trusted with the crown.[25]

Both Karwicki and the *Eclipsis Poloniae* similarly proposed that foreigners be barred from the Commonwealth's throne. Karwicki briefly discussed the standard argument against electing a Piast king, namely that a native king would favour his own relatives and connections when making appointments to office, which would encourage factions and stir up discord. Karwicki dismissed this argument by noting that, following his proposed reform (or abolition) of the royal powers of patronage, this threat would no longer exist. Piast kings were therefore safe for the

---

[24] 'Tu rationabile, tam servile obsequium; to długie sejmów częstokroć niesmaczne et licentia obostrzone ad resolvenda deliberacye, tam promptido posłuszeństwa, nutus za prawo, ratio pro voluntate, sprzeciwienie się pro piaculo, chimeryczna czasem dysplicencya pro crimine, suspicya najmniejsza na dekret, zmylony cokolwiek w usłudze status krok śmiercią, płocha faworów odmiana kończy się więzieniem.' Dzieduszycki, *Traktat o elekcyi królów polskich*, p. 16.

[25] Dzieduszycki, *Traktat o elekcyi królów polskich*, pp. 9 and 15.

Commonwealth, as well as necessary if its laws and liberties were to be preserved.[26]

Having excluded foreigners from the throne, the next issue was how future Piast kings should be chosen. The radical reformers were determined to maintain the principle of an elective monarchy, and a central objective of their proposals was to empower the szlachta more fully to elect their kings. This is despite some modern historians' identification of support for the elective monarchy as characteristic of a conservative 'magnate' political agenda, rather than a reformist 'republican' one.[27]

The most detailed proposals were those of Karwicki, who sought to permit greater participation in the royal election by the mass of the szlachta, while at the same time keeping as short as possible the interregnum that followed the death of a king, and which Karwicki recognized as an exceptionally dangerous time for the Commonwealth. He therefore proposed that the length of an interregnum be fixed at eight weeks, during which time a three-stage election could be held. The first stage of this process was the selection of eligible candidates. Karwicki proposed that as soon as the old king had died, the Primate, acting as Interrex, should convene a special council of senators and Sejm envoys tasked with drawing up a shortlist of candidates for the throne. These candidates would all be worthy Piasts who had already distinguished themselves by service to the common good, and who had experience of holding the highest offices in the Commonwealth. Members of the old king's family would be ineligible, to prevent the crown passing from father to son as if a hereditary possession.[28]

Having drawn up a shortlist of candidates, Karwicki proposed that the Primate should then summon special województwo sejmiki[29] for the next stage of the royal election. These sejmiki were to meet four weeks after the death of the old king, and at each sejmik the szlachta of each region would vote for a new king from among the shortlisted candidates. Voting would be by secret ballot, with votes being counted three days after polling, in

---

[26] Candidus Veronensis [pseud.], *Eclipsis Poloniae*, p. 136. Karwicki, *De Ordinanda Republica*, p. 181.

[27] For example, Gierowski, *Między saskim absolutyzmem a złotą wolnością*, p. 99 and Staszewski, 'Pomysły reformatorskie', p. 759. For a fuller discussion of the problems that attempts to distinguish 'magnate' and 'republican' political agendas have encountered, see the Introduction to this book.

[28] Karwicki claimed that the election of repeated members of the Vasa dynasty in the seventeenth century had encouraged corruption and the build-up of a Vasa faction. He therefore proposed that members of the same family should only be eligible for election to the throne every fourth interregnum. Karwicki, *De Ordinanda Republica*, pp. 129 and 182–8.

[29] With no powiat or ziemia sejmiki being convened, so the szlachta of Masovia, for example, would all assemble together at the Masovia General Sejmik, rather than in the region's ten district sejmiki.

the presence of the województwo's senior senator. Whichever candidate had received the most votes (Karwicki did not propose that an absolute majority was required) would be declared as that region's choice as king. After counting votes, each sejmik would then elect envoys to a Coronation Sejm, where the third and final stage of the royal election would take place.

Karwicki proposed that the Coronation Sejm meet eight weeks after the old king's death (thus a further four weeks after the sejmiki had voted), in Kraków. At the Coronation Sejm, the senior senators from each województwo would assemble and form an electoral college where each would cast a block-vote on behalf of his region for that region's favoured candidate. These block-votes would be weighted in proportion to the amount of hearth tax paid by each województwo. The candidate receiving the most votes (again, no absolute majority being required) would be proclaimed king and, after swearing his *pacta conventa*, crowned.[30]

Karwicki argued that this reformed process for royal elections would yield three key advantages. First, both by keeping interregna short and by excluding foreign candidates, it would minimize the opportunities for outside powers to use interregna and royal elections to interfere in the Commonwealth's affairs. Second, holding the first round of voting in the sejmiki would give the whole szlachta a chance to participate, unlike the existing system in which kings were elected directly by szlachta assembled at the 'election field' at Wola, just outside Warsaw. Karwicki noted that szlachta from the Commonwealth's outlying regions (and especially poorer szlachta from these parts) were rarely able to make the journey to Wola to vote: they were thus effectively disenfranchised. Third, having the Primate present to the szlachta a shortlist of candidates at the beginning of the interregnum would ensure that all szlachta citizens would have an opportunity to weigh the merits of the different candidates before voting. As candidates for the throne would all be men who had already been elected to high office, their virtues would already be known to and recognized by the szlachta. The entire szlachta would thus be able to make an informed choice over who should be their next king.[31]

Dzieduszycki and the *Eclipsis Poloniae* also endorsed the proposal that the szlachta should be empowered to make informed decisions over their future kings, as well as on wider matters. Dzieduszycki particularly condemned the practice of 'hiding' candidates for the throne from the szlachta

---

[30] Karwicki, *De Ordinanda Republica*, pp. 185–8.
[31] Karwicki, *De Ordinanda Republica*, pp. 180–8. Karwicki also noted that weighting the block-votes of each województwo at the Coronation Sejm in proportion to the amount of hearth tax they paid would encourage the regions to pay their full quota of tax, helping to protect the Commonwealth's revenues.

by only announcing their candidacy at the last possible moment: this he claimed was an unfair magnate stratagem to keep the mass of the szlachta in a state of ignorance in order to manipulate them and thus fix the outcome of royal elections in accordance with the magnates' private interests. He therefore proposed that as early as possible before an election (perhaps even while the old king was still alive, but at the very least by the time of the pre-election sejmiki) the names of the various candidates should be made known to the entire szlachta 'by public instruments' in order 'to prevent the secret intrigues of the great families'.[32] Knowing the identities of the candidates in advance would allow the szlachta to make an informed choice, and so the result of the election would reflect the citizens' judgement of the common good, rather than the private interests of magnate factions.

The radicals' faith in the capacity of the szlachta as a whole to discern and then follow the common good is striking, and was taken further still in a proposal in the *Eclipsis Poloniae*. This pamphlet called for the ordinary szlachta to be properly informed in order to take public decisions, not just at the time of interregna and royal elections, but continually, through the establishment at public expense of a system of gazettes to supply the szlachta with accurate information on the affairs of both the Commonwealth and the wider world. In every major town in the Commonwealth, the *Eclipsis Poloniae* urged, there should be a postmaster employed to distribute among the local szlachta weekly bulletins of 'news from the kingdom [i.e. Poland] and all the others in the whole world, and especially of the kingdoms and provinces of Europe, in the vernacular . . . free of charge'.[33] In addition, the *Eclipsis Poloniae* called for reform of public education, urging that geography and history be taught in all the schools of the Commonwealth, in order to teach the szlachta to be virtuous by holding up examples of good men from the past. Further, the pamphlet also proposed that the Commonwealth's schools should teach szlachta students all about the size, position, and constitutions of all the countries of the world in order that they might thus learn the art of government, 'the science that, among all others, is the most useful'.[34] As a result of the political education that would be provided both initially by these reformed schools and then continually by the postmasters' weekly

---

[32] 'per publica instrumenta . . . praescindere sekretne wielkich domów intrygi'. Dzieduszycki, *Traktat o elekcyi królów polskich*, p. 15.

[33] 'novitates e Regno, tum omnibus aliis Orbis & praecipue Europae Imperiis Regnis & Provinciis, native lingua typis impressas, . . . absque ulla mercede'. Candidus Veronensis [pseud.], *Eclipsis Poloniae*, pp. 128–9.

[34] 'Quia Scientia illa est perquam inter omnes alias utilissima'. Candidus Veronensis [pseud.], *Eclipsis Poloniae*, p. 129.

bulletins, the *Eclipsis Poloniae* claimed that the ordinary szlachta 'will give little credence to the representations of the magnates (which they use for their own advancement and to demonstrate their power)'. Instead, properly informed about public affairs, 'our people . . . will through general debate, by the most mature judgement, correct Counsel and spirit be borne towards the Common good'.[35] Liberated from magnate intrigue, the szlachta would thus be able to restore virtuous government to the Commonwealth.

THE 'ABSOLUTE COMMONWEALTH'

The radicals thus proposed a substantial shift in power away from the Commonwealth's first and second estates (the monarchy and the senate) in favour of the third, the szlachta. Under all three of the radical reform proposals the king and senate would have become much more dependent upon, and responsible to, the szlachta as a whole. Indeed, the most far-reaching of them, Karwicki's proposal, would have left the Commonwealth's monarchical and aristocratic elements with little more than ceremonial functions.[36]

Given that, according to traditional analyses of the Commonwealth's government, the szlachta estate was the 'democratic' element of the constitution, the radicals' proposed system of government might be described as a 'noble democracy'. The term 'noble democracy' has been used by modern scholars to describe the szlachta state, and in particular the Commonwealth's government during the sixteenth century when the szlachta as a whole are often thought to have played a greater role in government, before yielding power to the magnates in the seventeenth and eighteenth centuries. 'Noble democracy' has thus been contrasted positively with the 'magnate oligarchy' into which it mutated (or perhaps degenerated).[37]

---

[35] 'Eadem Magnatum relationibus, (quibus augmenta sui, & ostentamen potentiae procurare solent) minime Credet' 'gens nostra . . . maturrimo judicio, Cuncta disentiens, recto Consilio & animo in bonum Commune feretur'. Candidus Veronensis [pseud.], *Eclipsis Poloniae*, p. 130.

[36] Note that as discussed above, Karwicki did still envisage a distinct role in government for the Senate as a chamber of the Sejm. However, the majority of its members would be envoys elected by the sejmiki, rather than holders of senatorial office (ministers, wojewodas, castellans etc., who would themselves also be elected by the sejmiki or the Sejm). So those sitting in the Senate would not be the same as those holding senatorial office, who would participate in government as individual magistrates, but not as a distinct estate.

[37] Antoni Mączak, *Rządzący i rządzeni: Władza i społeczeństwo w Europie wczesnonowożytnej* (Warsaw, 1986).

The term 'noble democracy' was not, however, one used by the radical reformers or by contemporaries: it was first used only later in the eighteenth century, by Antoni Popławski in 1774.[38] Interestingly, the radicals also did not refer explicitly to the Commonwealth's experience in the sixteenth century, or to the sixteenth-century Movement for the Execution of the Laws, a political movement that sought to defend the power of the Chamber of Envoys against the pretensions of the Senate and magnates, as a precedent for their own reform proposals.

Instead of 'noble democracy', Karwicki called his proposed new constitution an 'absolute commonwealth' (*absolutna rzeczpospolita*). The choice of this term is significant for two reasons. First, Karwicki opposed the absolute commonwealth to an absolute monarchy, in which there could be no liberty as all matters depended solely on the will of the king. In contrast, under the absolute commonwealth everything would depend on the collective will. This included in particular appointments to high office, over which Karwicki claimed the king currently enjoyed 'absolute' power. In the 'absolute commonwealth', therefore, sovereignty would be properly collective.

This implied not just a rejection of absolute monarchy, but also of democracy as understood in classical political theory as the sole or exclusive rule of the many. According to this definition, a 'noble democracy' would be a constitution in which all power resided with the szlachta estate, while neither king nor senate played any part at all. This would be a rejection of the *forma mixta* identified by classical philosophers, as well as by szlachta writers since the sixteenth century, as the best possible constitution on the grounds that it was most likely to ensure government according to the common good.[39] Although they did not specifically refer to the *forma mixta* in their works, the radical reformers were not prepared to break completely with this model. Hence none of them advocated the abolition of either the monarchy or the senate, even if Karwicki proposed that in practice the Commonwealth's monarchical and aristocratic elements would have virtually no actual power.

The need to address the threat of corruption thus drove the radical reformers to propose a rebalancing of the *forma mixta* in favour of its 'democratic' element, the szlachta. The objective of ensuring collective government in pursuit of the common good, however, required that the

---

[38] Lukowski, *Disorderly Liberty*, p. 6.

[39] Note also that for classical political philosophers, the term 'democracy' generally denoted a corrupt form of government (serving the interests of the masses not the common good), although the early seventeenth-century Polish translator of Aristotle, Sebastian Petrycy, had applied '*demokracja*' to the pure form of the rule of the many. Petrycy, *Przydatki do Polityki Arystotelesowej*, vol. 2, pp. 141 and 223–6.

forma mixta be retained, albeit in Karwicki's proposal stretched to its very limit.

A similar tension between the desire for collective government on the one hand and the mixed constitution on the other has been noted by Pocock in the context of the Florentine republic. Pocock has described how in the classical political philosophy that underpinned Florentine republicanism, virtue could only be exercised and developed through active engagement by each citizen in public life, in pursuit of the common good. To test his virtue and keep it from degenerating, each citizen required constant competition and comparison with his peers. By offering fewer opportunities for citizens to participate in public life, monarchies and aristocracies restricted the extent to which citizens could exercise and maintain their virtue, and it was for this reason that these forms of government were so susceptible to corruption. A state wishing to encourage virtue therefore had to allow, or even require, as many of its citizens as possible to participate in public life, both to exercise their own virtue and to spur on their fellow-citizens. The very purpose for which political society existed, therefore, required that citizens be given scope to participate in government, and hence required the constitution to include a popular element.

The *forma mixta*, however, also included aristocratic (and monarchical) elements, from which at least a portion of the citizenry had, by definition, to be excluded. The exclusion of the mass of the citizens from these elements of government posed a double threat to virtue: it denied most citizens a chance to exercise their own virtue through participating in the aristocratic (and monarchical) elements' functions in the government, and it narrowed the competition to which members of the aristocratic (and monarchical) elements were themselves exposed, increasing the risk of their virtue degenerating. Renaissance Italian political thinkers attempted to solve this paradox by arguing that the mass of the citizenry and the elite possessed distinct virtues that suited them to different roles: the elite's superior wisdom and prudence fitting them for high office, while the superior collective (but not individual) judgement of the masses qualified them to elect magistrates.[40]

In the traditional szlachta understanding of the Commonwealth, the existence of the Senate and the senatorial estate despite the principle of szlachta equality was justified in a similar way. Senators were appointed to the exclusive 'aristocratic' element of the Commonwealth's government in recognition of their individual virtues (with the king being supposed only

---

[40] Pocock, *The Machiavellian Moment*, pp. 88–91 and 117–55.

to appoint *bene meritis* men to high office, as noted in Chapter 3). Thus while fundamentally equal to their fellow szlachta (an oft-repeated szlachta rhyme asserted that 'a nobleman on his garden patch was any Wojewoda's match', '*szlachcic na zagrodzie równy wojewodzie*'), senators were understood to have earned their elevation. This position, at once equal to yet elevated above the mass of the szlachta, was traditionally encapsulated in the description of senators as the 'elder brothers' of the szlachta.

The claim that the Commonwealth's senatorial elite had earned their status by their virtues was, however, incompatible with the claim that that elite had become corrupt and owed its position to court intrigues or factional politicking. Rather than displaying special virtue, according to this argument the elite were characterized by their vice, and could no longer be trusted with a distinct, independent role in government. The old balance of the Commonwealth's *forma mixta* thus became unsustainable, and only the 'absolute commonwealth' could deliver virtuous government.

A PERSUASIVE VISION OF REFORM?

Historians' judgements of the radicals' reform proposals, and their contribution to restoring effective government (and perhaps thus enabling the Commonwealth to resist the incursions of its neighbours) have been mixed. A positive view has been offered by Gierowski and Staszewski, who praised the radicals for their commitment to reviving the Commonwealth's central government, against the decentralizing drive of 'magnate oligarchs' determined to defend their privileges against any interference from the centre.[41]

Although reforms of central institutions, above all the Sejm, were a key part of their proposals, characterizing the radical reformers simply as supporters of greater centralization overlooks the extent to which their reform proposals left local institutions such as the sejmiki with very substantial powers, and in some places actually increased those powers. The most striking area in which the radicals proposed to enhance the power and role of local institutions is in the election of high officials. As noted above, Karwicki proposed that all local officials including castellans and wojewodas be elected by their regional sejmiki, rather than appointed from the centre. The great majority of senators would thus be elected locally, with the central Sejm choosing only ten ministers out of a total of 147. In a similar vein, Karwicki, Dzieduszycki, and the *Eclipsis Poloniae* all sought

---

[41] Gierowski, *Między saskim absolutyzmem a złotą wolnością*, p. 100. Staszewski, 'Pomysły reformatorskie'.

to increase the influence of the sejmiki in royal elections, with Karwicki proposing that the first round of voting be held in the sejmiki.

A strong element of localism was also included in the reformers' proposals for the management of royal (or public) lands. Both Karwicki and the *Eclipsis Poloniae* proposed that the power to appoint administrators of royal estates be retained at the centre, transferred from the king to the Sejm. The Sejm should also have responsibility for monitoring the management of those estates, and holding their administrators to account. But Karwicki also proposed that the revenues from each portion of royal land should be assigned to a particular army unit, which would in peacetime be stationed on that same estate. This would involve military officers in each województwo (województwo colonels) collecting the soldiers' pay directly from the administrators of local royal estates, and then passing this money on to the relevant army units. Only the (presumably small) remainder of the revenues from public lands would therefore be sent to the Commonwealth's central treasury, and only in exceptional circumstances (such as when an army unit's home region was too devastated to provide enough pay) would the soldiers' wages be met out of centrally collected funds such as tariffs or the revenues from salt mines, described by Karwicki as 'a treasure given to us by God'. [42] In line with the distrust of the central Treasury expressed in sejmik resolutions discussed in Chapter 3, Karwicki thus proposed that the bulk of the Commonwealth's revenues be managed locally, not at the centre. Thus the radical reformers were not unambiguous centralizers, despite their desire to restore the effectiveness of the Sejm.

More negative interpretations of the radicals' programme have tended to focus on their proposals for the Sejm, and in particular the *liberum veto*. Konopczyński and Lukowski have both condemned the radicals' failure to reject the principle of unanimity, arguing that without the abandonment of the veto there was no prospect of making the Sejm an effective institution of government. According to this view, the radicals' proposal to restrict the veto to single items of legislation (preventing the breaking of an entire Sejm) was both half-hearted and unrealistic. [43]

The radicals' apparent belief that the *liberum veto* could be made compatible with orderly government was, however, rooted in their optimism about the nature of the szlachta. Their proposal to restore virtuous government by empowering the mass of the szlachta depended on the assumption that the szlachta would act virtuously, once freed from the corrupting influences of royal patronage and factional intrigues. In particular the

---

[42] 'skarb od Boga nam dany'. Karwicki, *De Ordinanda Republica*, pp. 149–50 and 167.
[43] Konopczyński, *Polscy pisarze polityczni XVIII wieku*, pp. 39–42. Lukowski, *Disorderly Liberty*, pp. 45–8.

argument that election to high office would result in a government of worthy men being elected assumed that sufficient worthy men were available to be elected by their fellow nobles (just as calls from the sejmiki for the king to appoint more worthy men, discussed in Chapter 2, assumed that such men were available to be appointed).

Karwicki also argued that his proposed reforms would serve to promote greater virtue among the szlachta. If individuals could attain honour and office only through their peers' recognition of their virtues, rather than through winning the personal favour of the king or some mighty magnate, he argued, they would compete in virtue, not in intrigues. This would apply at all levels of public office, with even the most senior ministers or senators competing to further the common interest in the knowledge that, if sufficiently worthy, they might even be eligible for the highest honour of all, the crown. Competition among the szlachta to serve the common good would thus create a mutually reinforcing virtuous circle of better government and better citizens.[44]

This optimism about the szlachta's potential for virtue, combined with the belief that abuse of the *liberum veto*, and indeed the Commonwealth's political dysfunction more generally, was a relatively recent phenomenon, pointed to the conclusion that if only modern sources of corruption could be overcome, the szlachta would be able to act together for the common good: a conclusion made explicitly by the *Eclipsis Poloniae*, as discussed above. In that case, the *liberum veto* would not pose much of a barrier to effective government.

The radical reformers thus shared the optimistic view of the szlachta adopted by activists in the sejmiki and by Lubomirski. This optimism could fairly be criticized as utopian or even naïve, though the fact that it was espoused by politicians with extensive personal experience of the Commonwealth's system of government points to a degree of caution in this regard. That the assumption that the szlachta were essentially virtuous lay behind the radicals' sweeping proposals for reform, however, demonstrates that this perspective was not an exclusively conservative one.

The impact of the radicals' reform proposals was, however, mixed. Karwicki's ideas were clearly influential on later programmes for reform, such as the *Głos wolny* perhaps written by the exiled former pretender to the throne Stanisław Leszczyński in the 1740s. Exactly how widely his treatise, the *Eclipsis Poloniae*, or Dzieduszycki's *Traktat*, were read by contemporaries is, however, uncertain.[45] Although the prospect of a greater

---

[44] Karwicki, *De Ordinanda Republica*, pp. 137 and 180–1.
[45] Karwicki's *De Ordinanda Republica* only appeared in print in 1746, but did circulate in manuscript during the 1700s. For the impact of the radicals' proposals on reformers later in the eighteenth century, see this book's Conclusion.

role in government must presumably have had some appeal for the mass of the szlachta, there is little evidence of substantial support for the radical programme as a whole. In particular, the radicals' proposals for reform of the Sejm and for the election by the szlachta of ministers, senators, and holders of royal lands do not appear to have commanded significant support—perhaps surprisingly, given the widespread attacks by the sejmiki on the corruption allegedly caused by royal patronage.

Some elements of the radicals' programme do, however, appear to have resonated in the years following the end of the Great Northern War in the Commonwealth and the return of Augustus II to the throne in 1710. In particular, the radicals' proposals for ministers to be made accountable to the szlachta were taken up by first the envoys to the Sejm of 1712–13 (who included both Karwicki and Dzieduszycki among their number), and after them the leadership of the General Confederation of Tarnogród in 1715–16. Focusing primarily on the hetmans, widely condemned for having failed to protect szlachta property during the war years, szlachta politicians pressed for a 'circumscription' of ministerial offices, designed to hold high officials to account for their actions and punish them for any failure to act according to the common good. These attempts to enact reform at the centre are discussed in Chapters 5 and 6.

5

The Sejm of 1712–13

RESTORING SECURITY OR VIRTUOUS GOVERNMENT?

At the Sejm of 1712–13, the szlachta envoys agitated for a set of reforms intended to curb 'licentious' behaviour, and restore virtuous government to the Commonwealth. In line with the proposals of the radical reformers, the envoys (who included both Stanisław Dunin Karwicki and Jerzy Dzieduszycki) sought to make the Commonwealth's ministers, in particular the hetmans, accountable for their conduct to the szlachta citizenry, to ensure that they only acted in accordance with the common good. Although ultimately unsuccessful, the envoys' programme thus both illustrates the centrality of virtue to szlachta politicians' analysis of the Commonwealth and its condition, and shows how this moral approach did not preclude consideration of changes to the Commonwealth's government, but could rather inspire attempts at significant constitutional reform.

The Sejm of 1712–13 was summoned by Augustus II to restore order to the Commonwealth by recognizing him as the legitimate king, and ratifying a package of fiscal and military reforms designed to ensure 'internal and external security'. Augustus II had only returned to the Commonwealth in the autumn 1709, having previously been forced by King Charles XII of Sweden to abdicate at the treaty of Altranstädt in 1706, following Charles XII's invasions of first the Commonwealth and then Saxony. It was only after Charles XII had suffered a crushing defeat at the battle of Poltava in July 1709, and Swedish power in the Commonwealth had subsequently collapsed, that Augustus II was able to return and attempt to reclaim his throne.

Following his return, in 1710 Augustus II had convened the General Council of Warsaw (*walna rada warszawska*), a hybrid quasi-parliamentary body comprising the ruling council of the General Confederation of Sandomierz,[1] the Senate, and envoys elected by the szlachta, to recognize

---

[1] The General Confederation of Sandomierz was the emergency government proclaimed in May 1704 in defence of the Commonwealth against the Swedish invasion and of Augustus II against Charles XII's demands for his dethronement.

him as king and to consolidate his position on the throne. The General Council confirmed Augustus II's as the Commonwealth's legitimate king, rejecting his forced (and technically illegal) abdication and the claim of his Swedish-backed rival, Stanisław Leszczyński.[2] To restore order and security, it also agreed a set of fiscal and military reforms, notably the establishment of a new enlarged (36,000-strong) standing army paid for by permanent taxes (not dependent on renewal by future Sejms), administered centrally by the Commonwealth's Treasurers. These measures significantly strengthened the Commonwealth's central government, and arguably could have provided the foundations for further centralization and the emergence of a more powerful monarchy.[3] As an irregular institution, and crucially one whose decisions were not subject to the *liberum veto*, the General Council's authority was not accepted by many sejmiki or their envoys, who insisted that the power to make permanent legislation belonged to the Sejm alone. They therefore insisted that the General Council's resolutions be valid only for two years, unless ratified by a Sejm.[4]

To secure his position on the throne, and the reforms agreed at the General Council, Augustus II was therefore obliged to call a Sejm, which he summoned to convene on 5 April 1712. The Sejm was originally summoned as an extraordinary Sejm, to meet for two weeks. This was itself controversial. According to the Henrician Articles, part of the oath sworn by every newly elected king, the king was obliged to summon a six-week

---

[2] Abdication was technically illegal in the Commonwealth, having been banned by law following the abdication of King Jan Kazimierz in 1668.

[3] For the resolutions of the General Council of Warsaw see VL vol. 6, pp. 69–106. Józef Gierowski, noting that the establishment of standing armies and centralized fiscal and administrative structures played a key role in the development of absolutist monarchy elsewhere in early modern Europe, even went so far as to suggest that these reforms could have been the first step towards the establishment by Augustus II of an absolutist monarchy in Poland-Lithuania. Gierowski, *Między saskim absolutyzmem a złotą wolnością*, p. 156. See also Gierowski, 'Rzeczpospolita szlachecka wobec absolutystycznej Europy', in Antoni Mączak (ed.), *Pamiętnik X Powszechnego Zjazdu Historyków Polskich w Lublinie 9–13 września 1969r. Referaty i dyskusja III Referaty Plenarne sekcje I–IV* (Warsaw, 1971), pp. 99–126, and Gierowski 'Centralization and Autonomy in the Polish-Saxon Union', *Harvard Ukrainian Studies*, 3/4 (1979–80), pt. 1, pp. 271–84. Note, however, that even under the reforms agreed at the General Council, important barriers to further centralization and to the development of a stronger monarchy remained. In particular, the new army remained under the command of the hetmans, who were largely independent of the king. Also, the fiscal administration supporting the new army remained to some extent decentralized, with army units being paid for by the revenues from particular portions of royal land (on which they were stationed), and tax collectors being in the first instance elected by the sejmiki.

[4] Many sejmiki went even further in rejecting the legitimacy of the General Council of Warsaw, and refused to collect the taxes that its resolutions established. Olszewski, *Doktryny prawno-ustrojowe*, pp. 124–7.

ordinary Sejm once every two years, and was free to summon a two-week extraordinary Sejm whenever the need arose. Since in the chaos of the Great Northern War, no Sejm had been summoned since the Lublin Sejm of 1703, many sejmiki rejected the claim that the coming Sejm could be considered extraordinary, and argued that the Sejm should have been summoned for a full six-week term. Some even called for the Sejm to be summoned as a 'Pacification Sejm' (*sejm pacyfikacyjny*), the term used for a Sejm held to reunite the Commonwealth after a period of internal strife, such as a disputed royal election.[5] In the event, the Sejm convened for two weeks in April 1712, but was unable to conclude its business in that time, so an adjournment (*limita*) was agreed, with the Sejm to reconvene on 31 December 1712. The Sejm's second session lasted until the Sejm was broken on 18 February 1713. Although the *limita* was well-established for sejmiki (see Chapter 3), its application to the Sejm was much more recent (the first Sejm to be adjourned was that of 1701–2) and very controversial, given fears that the king might suborn Sejm envoys through patronage. The practice was eventually to be banned by the Sejm of 1726.[6]

After opening formalities, and the election of Stanisław Denhoff (1673–1728), Field Hetman of Lithuania and a prominent supporter of Augustus II, as Marshal of the Chamber of Envoys, the substantive business of the Sejm began on 9 April 1712.[7] At a plenary session, the Crown Grand Chancellor, Jan Szembek (d. 1731) set out the king's programme in an address to the Sejm 'from the throne'. Szembek, another key supporter of Augustus II, argued that order had to be restored and reforms agreed to ensure 'internal and external security' for the Commonwealth. To secure internal order, Szembek called on the Sejm to recognize Augustus II as the Commonwealth's legitimate king, to reject the rival claim of Leszczyński, and to establish a special tribunal to try supporters of Sweden (known as the Swedish 'Adherents' (*Adherenci*)) as traitors. To protect the Commonwealth against external enemies, Szembek urged the establishment of a standing army, as agreed at the General Council of Warsaw, paid for by permanent taxation. Only once the Commonwealth had the ability to defend itself, he argued, would it be able to dispense with the foreign 'auxiliary' armies of its allies Saxony and Russia. Only if regular army pay were provided could military discipline be ensured, szlachta property

---

[5] Gierowski, *Między saskim absolutyzmem a złotą wolnością*, p. 122.
[6] Olszewski, *Sejm Rzeczypospolitej epoki oligarchii*, pp. 426–34.
[7] Two copies of a diary of the first session of the Sejm survive in APG MS 300.29.208, one in German (pp. 120–36) and one in Polish (pp. 144–54). For the second session of the Sejm, one full diary (in Polish) exists in APG MS 300, R/Ff, 1, pp. 3–63. In addition, a diary of the first few days of January 1713 survives in AGAD Arch. Radz. II, 45, pp. 57–9, as well as a 'Dyaryusz Proiektow Seymowych 1712' in Bibl. Ossol. MS 233, pp. 1241–9.

protected, and the law upheld. Szembek thus argued that the measures he proposed would restore both the independence of the Commonwealth and the authority of the Sejm.[8]

The Sejm envoys were, as will be discussed below, sympathetic to many of Szembek's proposals. Following Poltava, support for Sweden and Leszczyński had collapsed, and Augustus II was widely acknowledged as the rightful king. After several years in which szlachta property had suffered from pillaging and the levying of 'contributions' (which included requisitioning of supplies and collection of informal taxes) by both the Commonwealth's and foreign armies, many envoys and sejmiki sought the withdrawal of foreign 'auxiliaries' and the imposition of military discipline. Many also accepted the case for the establishment of a new standing army.

Despite this, however, the envoys brought to the Sejm a very different analysis to Szembek's of the problems facing the Commonwealth, and hence very different objectives for the Sejm. The envoys' top priority was to protect szlachta property against the levying of 'contributions' by foreign auxiliaries or the Commonwealth's own armies. Arguably, this goal was consistent with Szembek's agenda of ensuring 'internal security'. Yet whereas Szembek presented 'contributions' as the result of structural problems, such as the breakdown of central authority or the absence of regular army pay, the envoys described them in explicitly moral terms. The plundering of szlachta estates and the levying of 'contributions' were repeatedly denounced as acts of 'licence' (variously *swawola, licencya,* and *licentia*) on the part of soldiers and their commanders, above all the hetmans. In this the envoys followed their sejmiki, many of whom in their instructions condemned the soldiers' 'licence' and demanded recompense for damage caused to szlachta property. They similarly complained at the 'arbitrary' power wielded by the armies.[9]

Following the sejmiki, the envoys thus presented 'contributions' as the product of moral failings not structural flaws, and as evidence not of disorder or anarchy but of excessive power unrestrained by law and exercised contrary to the common interest. Rather than focusing on structural reforms such as those proposed by Szembek, the envoys therefore instead prioritized reasserting the sovereignty of the Commonwealth and the law in the face of arbitrary power, and restoring virtuous government

---

[8] APG MS 300.29.208, p. 146.
[9] See, for example, speeches made on 4 January, 20 January, and 9 February 1713, APG MS 300, R/Ff, 1, pp. 6, 20, and 45. See also the resolutions of the sejmiki of Różan, 30 January 1710, TP vol. 20, p. 427; Sandomierz, 23 February 1712, TP vol. 22, p. 411; and Lublin, 26 April 1713, TP vol. 9, p. 72.

by holding to account those guilty of 'licentious' conduct. This moral perspective informed both their response to the measures sought by the king, and their own proposals for reform.

WITHDRAWAL OF FOREIGN 'AUXILIARIES'

With the 'licentious' conduct of the troops as the prime concern, the envoys agreed whole-heartedly with the objective set out by Chancellor Szembek of having foreign 'auxiliary' forces withdraw from the Commonwealth. Numerous sejmiki had instructed their envoys to secure the withdrawal of foreign armies, and during April 1712 envoys repeatedly raised this demand, with some even calling for the *pospolite ruszenie*, the general levy of the szlachta, to be summoned if foreign 'auxiliaries' refused to leave the Commonwealth.[10]

Among the foreign forces that they wanted withdrawn, the envoys included the king's Saxon army, units of which had re-entered the Commonwealth following the king's return in 1710. Particularly during the Sejm's second session, envoys from across the Commonwealth called for the Saxons' immediate withdrawal, interrupting debates on other issues to repeat this demand, and denouncing the Saxon army as a 'private' force inimical to the common interest that had acted 'licentiously' and imposed 'arbitrary' rule on the szlachta.[11] Virtue therefore demanded that the Saxons be withdrawn.

The envoys' calls for the removal of the king's 'private' army from the Commonwealth was consistent with long-running opposition among the szlachta to the presence of the Saxon army. Ever since his election in 1697, Augustus II had sought to maintain a substantial number of Saxon troops in the Commonwealth, but sejmiki and szlachta pamphleteers had strongly objected to this army, responsible only to the king, within the Commonwealth's borders. The 1699 Sejm had passed legislation requiring the Saxons' withdrawal, and anger at their continued presence contributed to the breaking of the Sejm of 1701–2. Even the Lublin Sejm of 1703, summoned in the face of the Swedish invasion of the Commonwealth,

---

[10] For sejmik instructions, see, for example, the resolutions of the sejmiki of Opatów, 23 February 1712, TP vol. 22, p. 407; Czersk, 31 March 1712, TP vol. 3, pp. 134f.; and Liw, 31 March 1712, TP vol. 5, p. 357. For the debates at the Sejm, see APG MS 300.29.208, pp. 145–9.

[11] APG MS 300, R/Ff, 1, pp. 14–26. According to the Sejm diary, a speech on 26 January 1713 by Rosnowski, envoy for Przemyśl, calling for the Saxon army to be withdrawn was particularly well received by the Chamber. APG MS 300, R/Ff, 1, p. 23.

had made the withdrawal of Augustus II's Saxon army a condition of its agreeing to declare war on the invading Swedes.[12]

Opposition among the envoys to the presence of the Saxons was especially vocal during debates on the size (*komput*) of the proposed new standing army, which took place during the Sejm's second session, in January 1713. The envoys accepted in principle the case for a new standing army, though there were differences among them over whether the Commonwealth could sustain an army *komput* as large as the 36,000 men agreed at the General Council of Warsaw, with some envoys arguing for a lower figure. The envoys were adamant, however, that whatever the new *komput*, it should not include any units of the Saxon army who although notionally subject to the authority of the hetmans might owe their true loyalty to the king alone. The very first speech on the new *komput* called upon the Sejm to ban by law the incorporation of any Saxon troops into the Commonwealth's armies, and throughout the debate numerous envoys repeated this demand. Some envoys even argued for a smaller total army *komput* on the basis that this would give the king less scope to incorporate his Saxon army.[13] At no point did any envoy defend the presence of the Saxons in the Commonwealth, or express support for their incorporation into the *komput*.[14]

The Sejm envoys thus repeated the opposition of the sejmiki and previous Sejms to the presence in the Commonwealth of an army dependent solely upon the king, and instead asserted the sovereignty of the law and the Sejm. Both the presence of a 'private' army and its 'arbitrary' levying of contributions on szlachta property were condemned as 'licentious'. The envoys therefore demanded the withdrawal of the Saxons in order to preserve collective government and the pursuit of the common good.

---

[12] For the response of the sejmiki, see, for example, the resolutions of the sejmiki of Ciechanów, 5 May 1699, TP vol. 1, p. 96; Łęczyca, 25 May 1699, TP vol. 11, p. 947; and Sieradz, 18 April 1701, TP vol. 27, p. 49. For opposition at the Sejm, see Bogusław Dybaś, *Sejm pacyfikacyjny 1699r.* (Toruń, 1991), Przemysław Smolarek (ed.), *Diariusz Sejmu Walnego 1701–1702r.* (Warsaw, 1962), and Lukowski, *Liberty's Folly*, p. 133.

[13] According to the Sejm diary, debate over the right figure for the *komput* dominated the discussions of the Wielkopolska Provincial Session held between 19 and 26 January 1713, with envoys from Poznań arguing strongly for a *komput* of 30,000 rather than the 36,000 proposed by the Chancellor, including on the basis that the lower figure would pose a barrier to the incorporation of Saxon troops. APG MS 300, R/Ff, 1, pp. 20–2. Provincial sessions were separate meetings of all the envoys (plus some senators) from each of the Commonwealth's three provinces of Wielkopolska, Małopolska, and the Grand Duchy of Lithuania. Gierowski, *Między saskim absolutyzmem a złotą wolnością*, p. 153.

[14] APG MS 300, R/Ff, 1, pp. 14–26. During the Sejm's first session, the envoys had also agreed a bill banning the use of foreign ranks including '*Kriegskommissar*' in the Lithuanian army, possibly intended as a further barrier to the incorporation of German officers and their troops into the Lithuanian army. VL vol. 6, p. 111.

IMMUNITY AND ACCOUNTABILITY

The envoys similarly sought to uphold the legal rights of the szlachta, in particular their immunity against taxation without their consent, against the 'licentious' and 'arbitrary' actions of the Commonwealth's own armies. As noted above, the particular incidence of 'licence' on which the envoys focused was the levying of forced 'contributions' on szlachta property. Despite the szlachta's legal immunity to taxation without the consent of the Sejm, during the war years, szlachta estates had suffered gravely from the levying of 'contributions' by both foreign and especially the Commonwealth's own armies, as the hetmans supported and supplied their troops through 'contributions' in the absence of regular pay.[15] In the years leading up to the 1712–13 Sejm, sejmiki across the Commonwealth had repeatedly protested against 'contributions' as illegal, 'arbitrary', and 'licentious', and many had dispatched envoys to plead directly with the hetmans or other local military commanders to restrain their troops and respect szlachta property. The sejmiki summoned to elect envoys to the Sejm continued these protests (one, melodramatically, even claimed that 'contributions' had left the local szlachta 'barely able to breathe' (*vix spirante*)), and many instructed their envoys to the coming Sejm to ensure that all 'contributions' cease immediately and be forbidden in the future.[16]

In line with these instructions, the envoys made tackling the problem of 'contributions' their highest priority for the Sejm. One argued that the immunity of szlachta property was the foundation 'on which all Security depended';[17] another that legislation banning 'contributions' was essential in order to restrain the 'arbitrary' power of the soldiers and to ensure that 'the Commonwealth should have Power and Dominion over the Army, not the Army over the Commonwealth'.[18] The priority that the envoys ascribed to this issue can be seen from the fact that they insisted that the question of immunity be addressed before the Sejm debated the programme set out by Chancellor Szembek. Discussion of immunity, and

---

[15] The szlachta's immunity from taxation except by their own consent dated to the fifteenth-century privilege of Nieszawa. During the Great Northern War, the levying of contributions had been used not only as a means of supporting armies in the field, but also as a political weapon, through the targeted pillaging of the property of political opponents.

[16] Resolution of the sejmik of Łęczyca, 31 March 1712, TP vol. 12, p. 402. See also resolutions of the sejmiki of Liw, 5 June 1708, TP vol. 5, p. 310; Sieradz, 7 January 1710, TP vol. 27, pp. 393–9; and Lublin, 26 March 1711, TP vol. 9, pp. 37–9. See also Kriegseisen, *Samorząd szlachecki*, pp. 81–96.

[17] 'od ktorey omnis dependet Securitas'. Unnamed envoy, 1 February 1713, APG MS 300, R/Ff, 1, p. 32.

[18] 'aby Rzepplta nad Woyskami nie Woysko nad Rzeppltą miało Potestatem et Dominium'. Unnamed envoy from Lwów, 1 February 1713, APG MS 300, R/Ff, p. 33.

measures intended to guarantee it, dominated both the whole two weeks of the Sejm's first session,[19] and much of the second session, after the Sejm returned from adjournment.

As the envoy from Lwów made clear, the envoys' objective was to reassert the sovereignty of the Commonwealth against the 'arbitrary' power of the armies, and to end 'licentious' behaviour: that is, to restore collective sovereignty and government according to the common good, not the private interest of the army or the hetmans. As the Sejm's initial two-week session neared its end, the envoys therefore pressured Denhoff to seek a proclamation from the king reaffirming the immunity of szlachta property and banning 'contributions'. Although a proclamation to this effect was indeed produced, the envoys pressed on, successfully demanding that the Sejm pass legislation as well. A law on Military Discipline was therefore adopted, which reaffirmed the immunity of szlachta property and banned the levying of contributions. Originally, this bill also contained provisions harshly censuring the hetmans and requiring them to pay compensation for the damage to szlachta property, but these were dropped during debate.[20]

Despite their focus on the moral transgressions of the armies and their commanders, the envoys did recognize that part of the solution to the problem of 'contributions' was ensuring that the soldiers were properly paid and stationed away from szlachta estates. The first session of the Sejm therefore also agreed to legislate six months' pay for the armies, and passed a law on the Condition of the Lithuanian Army. This provided for the Lithuanian army to be supported from the proceeds of alcohol taxes in the Grand Duchy, and for the troops to be billeted on royal estates.[21]

However, the envoys spent only a relatively small amount of time discussing such 'structural' measures to prevent the levying of 'contributions' and guarantee the immunity of szlachta property. In contrast, they devoted much more of their time to debating proposals for a limitation, or 'circumscription', of the hetmanship. This 'circumscription' did not involve a limitation of the hetmans' control over the Commonwealth's armies, or a reduction in their independence from the throne.[22] Rather, the main thrust of the envoys' 'circumscription' was to make the hetmans accountable to the szlachta for any breaches of the law. This focus on

---

[19] That is, the whole of the period for which the Sejm had originally been summoned.

[20] The debates are described at APG MS 300.29.208, pp. 150–2. The text of the law on Military Discipline is at VL vol. 6, p. 108.

[21] VL vol. 6, p. 111. The provision of pay for just six months helped to ensure that the Sejm had to be recalled from its adjournment (*limita*).

[22] Unlike proposals for reform of the hetmanship considered by allies of the king, as discussed below.

holding individuals to account for misbehaviour, or 'licence', rather than on correcting structural flaws or poor incentives illustrates how the envoys (like contemporary szlachta commentators and local government activists) analysed the problems facing the Commonwealth primarily in moral rather than structural terms, as the failure of individuals not of institutions. In line with this analysis, the envoys sought to ensure that in future individuals would behave virtuously and would uphold the law and the common good. This moral perspective did not, however, preclude institutional change, and so during the course of the Sejm the envoys considered a range of measures intended to ensure that the hetmans were accountable for any licentious conduct.

Although the objective (ensuring accountability for any 'licentious' conduct) remained constant, the envoys' proposals for a 'circumscription' of the hetmanship evolved over the course of the Sejm. The first proposals debated formed part of the law on the Condition of the Lithuanian Army agreed during the Sejm's first session. This law provided that 'whatever violent exactions take place on the orders or through the Commissariat of the Grand Hetman, for them their Lordships the Hetmans of the Grand Duchy of Lithuania will have to answer in whatever court and will have to repay any money taken'.[23] The provision that the hetmans be responsible 'in whatever court' (*in quovis foro*) made them liable for any 'contributions' levied in civilian, rather than just military courts. The law thus followed a similar approach to the resolutions of the General Council of Warsaw, which had declared the hetmans to be accountable to the Crown and Lithuanian Tribunals.[24]

The legislation agreed at the Sejm's first session did not, however, successfully tackle the problem of 'contributions', which continued to be levied by both the Crown and Lithuanian armies during the rest of 1712. Sejmiki continued to protest at this violation of the immunity of szlachta property, and in their supplementary instructions to their envoys ahead of the Sejm's second session, many once again called for legislation guaranteeing immunity, or an investigation into the conduct of the hetmans.[25]

---

[23] 'cokolwiek pokaże się exakcyi wiolencyi, za ordynansem, lub Kommissoryatem Wiel. Hetmana, tedy sami Wielmożni Hetmani W. X. L. in quovis foro respondere, et praevia deductione refundere powinni będą'. VL vol. 6, p. 111. This provision mirrored that originally included in the Military Discipline law, but dropped during the debate for lack of agreement. APG MS 300.29.208, pp. 151–2.

[24] Previously, all cases involving the army had been heard in separate military courts, presided over by senior army commanders, up to the hetmans themselves, so the army and its commanders were not accountable in civilian courts. Bardach (ed.), *Historia państwa i prawa Polski*, vol. 2, p. 268. For the relevant resolution of the General Council of Warsaw, see VL vol. 6, pp. 90–1.

[25] See, for example, the instructions of the sejmiki of Dobrzyn, 13 September 1712, Franciszek Kluczycki (ed.), *Lauda Sejmików Ziemi Dobrzyńskiej* (Kraków, 1887), p. 182;

Protests from the envoys at the continued levying of 'contributions' resumed as soon as the Sejm reconvened. Indeed, the Sejm diary records that these protests began even before the Sejm had come into formal session, and briefly held up proceedings entirely, as some envoys demanded that the issue of immunity be addressed even before the session had formally begun.[26] As at the first session, envoys repeatedly called for a bill guaranteeing the immunity of szlachta property. Envoys also demanded legislation 'on military discipline and the circumscription of the Hetmanship' (*de disciplina militari et circumscriptione Buławy*),[27] with the focus once again being on holding the hetmans to account for the 'licentious' conduct of their troops and forcing them to pay compensation (*satysfakcya*) for damage caused to szlachta property.

Debate on the 'circumscription' began in earnest on 27 January 1713, and dominated the rest of the Sejm's proceedings, up to the breaking of the Sejm on 18 February by supporters of the Lithuanian Grand Hetman Ludwik Pociej. It began with a proposal from one of the envoys from Halicz (unnamed in the diary), that the hetmans be liable to be sued in the Commonwealth's civil courts for compensation for the damage caused by 'contributions'.[28] This proposal followed the precedents of the resolutions of the General Council of Warsaw and the Lithuanian army bill agreed at the Sejm's first session. Some envoys objected, in particular a Lithuanian supporter of hetman Pociej, Krzysztof Puzyna, who argued that the legislation on the immunity of szlachta property already agreed at the Sejm's first session made further measures unnecessary. Another defender of the hetmans, Michał Puzyna, envoy from Wizna, also claimed that there was no need to legislate to require the hetmans to pay compensation, as they had already agreed to do so of their own accord.[29]

The bulk of the envoys, however, were not persuaded by these objections, and instead pressed ahead with proposals for a 'circumscription'. On 1 February, Stanisław Dunin Karwicki suggested that military commanders should be made responsible to the Tribunals, following the model of the resolutions of the General Council of Warsaw. The proposal commanded widespread support, and on 6 February a new bill on the

Liw, 11 October 1712, TP vol. 5, p. 368; Różan, 29 November 1712, TP vol. 20, p. 448; Sochaczew, 15 December 1712, TP vol. 30, pp. 181–2. The sejmiki did not need to elect new envoys to the Sejm's second session, as the existing envoys continued to serve when the Sejm returned from its adjournment. The sejmiki could, however, give their envoys fresh instructions ahead of the Sejm's second session.

[26] APG MS 300, R/Ff, 1, pp. 3–8. See also AGAD Arch Radz II, 45, pp. 57–8.
[27] AGAD Arch. Radz. II, 45, p. 58.   [28] APG MS 300, R/Ff, 1, p. 25.
[29] APG MS 300, R/Ff, p. 27. It is not clear whether, or how, the two envoys named Puzyna were related.

immunity of szlachta property was read to the chamber, which made the hetmans accountable to the Tribunal for any illegal actions.[30]

This satisfied many of the envoys, including the envoy from Halicz whose intervention had begun the debate, and who now proclaimed that the 'circumscription' had been achieved.[31] Other envoys, however, pushed to go further. In particular, they argued for a more decentralized model for holding the hetmans to account, which would have given the szlachta of the Commonwealth's regions, who may not have been able to travel to make their case before the central Tribunal, an opportunity to sue the hetmans for compensation. Even before the bill containing Karwicki's proposal had been read, on 3 February, Paweł Jaroszewski, envoy from Płock, argued that 'the Hetman should be accountable not just in whatever court [*in quovis foro*, the form of words used in the Lithuanian army bill agreed at the Sejm's first session], but also in the district' where damage was done.[32] On 7 February, an envoy from Bełz proposed another alternative model. This envoy (unnamed in the diary) complained bitterly against the levying of 'contributions' by the Lithuanian army in the region of Podlasie, and attacked hetman Pociej for permitting it. He then proposed that the Sejm establish a special commission of inquiry into the levying of 'contributions' by the Lithuanian army.[33]

This idea was not immediately supported by the other envoys. Some envoys from Kalisz and Lwów questioned whether providing for the hetmans to be accountable to the Tribunal as already agreed made any additional commission unnecessary. Others from Sieradz warned that it might be unfair to establish a commission just to investigate the conduct of the Lithuanian army without the agreement of the Lithuanian envoys to the Sejm.[34] The idea of a special commission of inquiry gathered increasing support, however, especially after Rosnowski, the envoy from Przemyśl, proposed that it should be established not just to investigate 'contributions' levied by the Lithuanian army in Podlasie, but to conduct a general inquiry into damage caused to szlachta property anywhere in

---

[30] Karwicki's intervention on 1 February 1713, APG MS 300, R/Ff, p. 33. The introduction of the new bill APG MS 300, R/Ff, p. 38.

[31] The Marshal of the Chamber of Envoys, Stanisław Denhoff, also attempted to move the debate on to the issue of regular army pay (a key part of the king's programme outlined by Szembek) at this point. APG MS 300, R/Ff, 1, p. 35.

[32] 'aby in quovis Foro nietylko respondeat Hetman, ale tez in districtu', APG MS 300, R/Ff, 1, p. 35.

[33] APG MS 300, R/Ff, 1, p. 38.

[34] APG MS 300, R/Ff, 1, p. 38. A sense that the Lithuanian army (and its hetman Pociej) were being unfairly targeted in the debate on the 'circumscription' may have fostered some sympathy among the Lithuanian envoys for the breaking of the Sejm by supporters of Pociej later in February 1713: see below.

the Commonwealth by both the Crown and Lithuanian armies. Another envoy followed this up by proposing that levying and pillaging by foreign 'auxiliary armies' should also be brought within the commission's remit. These proposals appear to have commanded substantial support among the envoys, and on 7 February the marshal, Denhoff, brought forward amendments to the bill read the previous day that established a commission of inquiry that would investigate claims of damage caused by the Commonwealth's armies to szlachta property and force those responsible to pay compensation.[35]

Discussion then turned to how the new commission should be organized. One key question was whether the commission should be a singular, central body or should be established on a more decentralized model. Perhaps persuaded by the arguments made a few days previously by Jaroszewski, the majority of the envoys who spoke supported a decentralized structure, in which each województwo would have its own local commission of inquiry. Reflecting this view, on 8 February further amendments to the Immunity bill were read to the chamber, establishing the new Województwo Commissions for Injuries. These were to be grafted onto existing structures of local government, with commissioners appointed by the sejmiki, and using (on Karwicki's suggestion) the records of the local (*gród*) courts to establish whether any injury had been suffered, and if so the appropriate level of compensation.

The extended debate over 'circumscription' thus saw the envoys shift from agreeing a centralized model under which the hetmans would be answerable to the Tribunal, to a more decentralized one involving the establishment of judicial commissions in each województwo. Throughout, however, the envoys' central objective remained the same: to ensure that the hetmans could be held to account for their actions and punished for any 'licentious' conduct. The envoys' 'circumscription' was thus primarily focused on upholding existing legal rights (in particular the immunity of szlachta property) rather than on creating new structures or laws. This suggests that the envoys saw the problem of 'contributions' primarily as one of individual conduct, not one of flawed institutions.

The envoys were, however, well aware that their proposed mechanism for curbing 'licentious' behaviour (the establishment of Województwo Commissions) was itself a constitutional innovation. Some expressed unease at this novelty: on 7 February, a Lwów envoy named Łos argued against the new commissions, on the traditional grounds that no new legislation was necessary, as the Commonwealth's existing laws (which

[35] APG MS 300, R/Ff, p. 39.

he claimed already guaranteed the immunity of szlachta property) were perfectly adequate. He also warned that the proposed new commissions would have powers greater than the Tribunal and so might constitute a 'new dictatorship'.[36]

Łoś's intervention prompted a significant response from another envoy, Adam Śmigielski, the Starosta of Gniezno. Śmigielski first offered reassurance about the new commissions and their powers, in particular to allies of the hetmans. As the current hetmans, he argued, were lovers of justice who would of their own accord compensate any szlachta who had suffered injury at the hands of their troops, the proposed commissions would not need to force them to do so. Indeed, Województwo Commissions were really only needed to guard against bad hetmans in the future, rather than to deal with the present ones. Having attempted to reassure the envoys about the commissions, and how they might use their powers, however, Śmigielski then confronted head on the claim that the commissions were a novelty. He acknowledged that this was true, but argued that the innovation was justified, as 'New Circumstances produce New Laws.'[37] Śmigielski's arguments appear to have been broadly accepted by the envoys. The next envoy to speak, Michał Czacki, echoed his argument when he said that although he believed the laws the szlachta had inherited from their ancestors were excellent, nevertheless he supported the establishment of the new Województwo Commissions to ensure the immunity of szlachta property. No other envoy objected to this argument, and after Czacki's intervention, the Chamber accepted the amended Immunity bill.[38]

So on the issue that they considered the top priority for the Sejm, the envoys openly accepted a degree of constitutional innovation in order to secure the traditional principles of the sovereignty of the Commonwealth over 'arbitrary' power, and the imperative for the common good to trump 'licentious' behaviour according to private interests. The envoys' approach to the issues of the immunity of szlachta property and the 'circumscription' of the hetmanship thus not only demonstrates that their approach to the problems facing the Commonwealth was a moral one. It also shows that this moral perspective did not preclude institutional change: rather, as with the radical reformers discussed in Chapter 4 (albeit on a more limited scale), this moral approach could inspire proposals for reform of the Commonwealth's government.

---

[36] 'Nowa to dictatura', APG MS 300, R/Ff, p. 40. It is not clear from the diary whether Łoś was the same envoy from Lwów who had previously argued against the original narrower proposal for a commission to investigate the activities of the Lithuanian army in Podlasie, but this seems likely.

[37] 'Novi Casus dant Novas Leges', APG MS 300, R/Ff, p. 40.

[38] APG MS 300, R/Ff, p. 41.

TRYING THE 'ADHERENTS'

Both the envoys' willingness to accept some institutional innovation, and their opposition to 'arbitrary' power were similarly displayed in their response to proposals from the throne for the establishment of a special tribunal to try as traitors and rebels the supporters of Augustus II's Swedish-backed rival for the throne, Stanisław Leszczyński, the so-called 'Adherents'. As noted above, this was presented by Szembek as a key step to secure Augustus II's claim to the throne and restore 'internal security' to the Commonwealth.

Recognizing Augustus II as the legitimate king was largely uncontroversial. Following Charles XII's defeat at Poltava, both Swedish power in the Commonwealth and support for Leszczyński among the szlachta had collapsed.[39] Augustus II's abdication was technically illegal, while Leszczyński was widely seen by the szlachta as owing his throne solely to Swedish military power (indeed, one pamphleteer of 1702 mocked him as king only 'by the grace of Sweden' (*z Szwedzkiey Laski*) not by the grace of God).[40] The Sejm therefore acknowledged Augustus II as the Commonwealth's rightful king during its first session without any significant argument.[41]

The envoys were much more wary, however, of the proposal for a special tribunal, a bill on which was introduced by the Marshal, Stanisław Denhoff, on 9 January 1713. Following Szembek, Denhoff argued that the special court was necessary for internal security, both to uphold Augustus II's legitimate claim to the throne and more generally in the interests of justice, 'through which Kingdoms stand'.[42]

The bill did not gain immediate support among the envoys. Some argued that the Commonwealth's existing laws and courts were already adequate to deal with traitors, so a new tribunal for the 'Adherents' was unnecessary. In a similar vein, others argued that it would be better for the 'Adherents' to be united with the rest of the szlachta than judged and punished, and several urged the king to show clemency.[43]

A particular concern voiced by the envoys was that the new special tribunal might be used not just to prosecute genuine rebels, but also to

---

[39] Gierowski, *Między saskim absolutyzmem a złotą wolnością*, p. 91.
[40] Bibl. Czart. MS 2447, pp. 141–50. This rejection of Leszczyński was despite his potential attraction as a 'Piast' king, brought up in a free and virtuous Commonwealth. That Leszczyński's election (and the earlier dethronement of Augustus II by the pro-Swedish Warsaw Confederation) had occurred under Swedish guns meant that a majority of the szlachta never accepted him as their legitimate king, and indeed regarded his election as an impingement upon their liberty. Poraziński, *Epiphania Poloniae*.
[41] VL vol. 6, p. 107.   [42] 'per quam Stant Regna', APG MS 300, R/Ff, p. 8.
[43] APG MS 300, R/Ff, pp. 10–14. This position was consistent with earlier calls for a Pacification Sejm to reconcile the entire Commonwealth after its recent internal conflicts.

persecute political opponents of the king. This raised the risk of the tribunal being not a means for asserting the sovereignty of the Commonwealth as Szembek had claimed, but a tool for advancing the king's private interests. To address this risk, the envoys pressed for safeguards to be added to the bill. The first was a limited amnesty for any 'Adherents' who surrendered themselves within a set period of time. An amnesty of this sort had been agreed at the General Council of Warsaw, which had proclaimed as traitors any who did not acknowledge Augustus II as the rightful king within six months.[44] The Sejm envoys repeatedly pressed for similar provisions to be added to Denhoff's proposed bill, and such was the support among them for an amnesty that on 13 January the marshal conceded, and brought forward an amended bill that provided for a six-month amnesty, with only those 'Adherents' still refusing to acknowledge Augustus II's claim to the throne after that period being liable for trial.[45]

As a further safeguard against the special tribunal becoming a tool to advance the king's private interest, Rosnowski, the envoy from Przemyśl, proposed that it should consist not of elected deputies but of 'the whole Commonwealth' (*cała Rzeczpospolita*), presumably meaning the Sejm, and other envoys echoed his call for the tribunal to be a 'universal court'.[46] Faced with these objections, Denhoff was obliged to reassure the envoys that the special tribunal would indeed depend on the whole Commonwealth and not just the king, as it would be established by the Sejm, which would select half of its judges (with only the other half being nominated by the king). Only when offered this reassurance were the envoys willing to agree to the establishment of the new court, and to accept Denhoff's bill late on the evening of 14 January 1713.[47]

The envoys' cautious reception of the proposal for a tribunal to try the 'Adherents' thus shows that while they were prepared to recognize Augustus II as the Commonwealth's legitimate king, they nonetheless continued to oppose any measures that might give the king 'arbitrary' power to pursue his private interests. The envoys thus remained determined to preserve the collective sovereignty of the Commonwealth as a whole, and to ensure that power was only exercised in pursuit of the common good, that is, virtuously.

---

[44] VL vol. 6, p. 70.

[45] In a similar vein to calls for an amnesty, some envoys suggested that the court's hearing be postponed until the next Sejm, while others also proposed a 'sunset' provision making the special court's authority subject to a time limit (one envoy suggested a limit of just three months). These ideas did not, however, command widespread support and were not included in the bill eventually agreed by the envoys. APG MS 300, R/Ff, pp. 10–18.

[46] APG MS 300, R/Ff, pp. 15–16.   [47] APG MS 300, R/Ff, p. 18.

THE BREAKING OF THE SEJM: A MISSED OPPORTUNITY?

The special court for the 'Adherents' that the envoys eventually agreed did not, however, come into existence. Nor did Województwo Commissions, a new army *komput*, or regular army pay, as the Sejm was broken by the *liberum veto* in mid-February 1713. The veto was exercised by two Lithuanian envoys, Krzysztof Puzyna and Jan Nestorowicz, who were both supporters of Lithuanian Grand Hetman Ludwik Pociej, and most likely acting on his instructions.

Puzyna and Nestorowicz began to disrupt the proceedings of the Sejm on 8 February, after the Immunity bill had been read to the Chamber. They started by denouncing the levying of 'contributions' by the Saxon army in Lithuania, complaining that the Sejm had failed to ensure the immunity of szlachta property. On 9 February, they began to raise procedural objections, alleging that the Sejm's session should have concluded the previous day, and that the marshal, Denhoff, had failed to secure the consent of all the envoys for an extension. This led to a protracted and heated procedural argument, in which the vetoers accused Denhoff of 'oppressing' szlachta liberty by failing to follow the will of the envoys, while other envoys (including Karwicki) responded that liberty depended on the Sejm being allowed to continue, and pleaded with the vetoers to withdraw their objections. After several interruptions, on 11 February the discussion returned to the substantive issues of the immunity of szlachta property, and proposals for holding to hetmans to account for the levying of 'contributions'. Puzyna and Nestorowicz objected to the establishment of Województwo Commissions in Lithuania, and to the provision of Lithuanian army bill agreed at the Sejm's first session that the Lithuanian hetmans should be accountable '*in quovis foro*' for any 'contributions'. On 16 February, they left the Chamber, refusing to return until their demands were met. Attempts by Denhoff to reach a compromise the next day were unsuccessful, and on 18 February the rest of the envoys agreed to disperse, bringing the Sejm to an inconclusive end.[48]

The Lithuanians' final demand suggested that in breaking the Sejm they were acting in the interests (and likely on the instructions) of hetman Pociej, who had been repeatedly and bitterly attacked by the sejmiki and many Sejm envoys for the 'contributions' levied by his troops, and would no doubt have been a prime target for investigation by the new Województwo Commissions. Pociej may also have feared that the commissions would be

---

[48] APG MS 300, R/Ff, pp. 56–62.

used as a means to attack him by political opponents within Lithuania, as part of ongoing conflict between supporters and opponents of the Sapieha clan.[49] Alternatively, he may have seen the establishment of the commissions as an attack on his position by Denhoff, who as well as being Marshal of the Sejm was also Lithuanian Field Hetman, notionally Pociej's subordinate but during this period a rival for power and influence. This personal rivalry may well have accounted for some of the bitterness of the exchanges between Pociej's supporters and defenders of the marshal at the end of the Sejm, when the two groups traded accusations of 'oppressing' szlachta liberty.[50]

Whether there was any substantive basis for Puzyna and Nestorowicz's veto is less clear. From the diary, it is plain that their claim that the Sejm session was being extended without the consent of the chamber was not accepted by their fellow envoys, as every one who spoke in response to the Lithuanians argued in favour of the Sejm session continuing. Their objection to the Lithuanian army law's provision that the Lithuanian hetmans be accountable '*in quovis foro*' may have had some substance, if it implied that Lithuanian cases could be heard in Crown (i.e. Polish) courts, contrary to the separation of the Crown and Lithuanian judicial systems. There may have been some sympathy among the envoys for an argument based on the particular rights of the Grand Duchy: the diary records that earlier in the second session, when the Sejm first began to debate damage caused by the Crown and Lithuanian armies, and how the hetmans should be held to account, some Polish envoys cautioned their fellows against legislating on Lithuanian matters without the consent of the envoys from the Grand Duchy.[51] The diary does not record whether Puzyna and Nestorowicz argued along these lines when objecting to the

---

[49] During the 1690s, Lithuania had descended into civil war between the powerful Sapieha family and their opponents. Aided by the patronage of King Jan III Sobieski, the Sapiehas had risen to a position of near total hegemony in the Grand Duchy during the 1690s, but were bitterly opposed by so-called 'republicans' who first sought to curb Sapieha power through a 'coequalization' (*koekwacja*) of the laws of Lithuania with Poland, before launching an armed uprising against the Sapiehas in 1699. The Lithuanian internal conflict became subsumed into the wider struggle of the Great Northern War, with the Sapiehas becoming allies of Charles XII of Sweden while their 'republican' opponents, among whom Pociej was prominent, looked to Russia for support.

[50] APG MS 300, R/Ff, pp. 43–7. The memoirs of another Lithuanian envoy to the Sejm, Krzysztof Zawisza (who was elected as envoy by the sejmik of Minsk, but only attended the Sejm's first session, sending his son to attend the second session in his place), record that the Sejm was broken amid arguments between the Lithuanian hetmans. Krzysztof Zawisza, *Pamiętniki Krzysztofa Zawiszy, Wojewody Mińskiego (1661–1721)* (ed. Julian Bartoszewicz, Warsaw, 1862), p. 303. See also Gierowski, *Między saskim absolutyzmem a złotą wolnością*, pp. 150–1.

[51] APG MS 300, R/Ff, p. 38.

'*in quovis foro*' provision. If they did, however, their argument would have been vulnerable to the objection that this provision had already been accepted (apparently without any Lithuanian objections) by the Sejm's first session in 1712.

Whatever the merits of the two Lithuanians' position, Puzyna and Nestorowicz persisted with their veto, and the Sejm was broken. In his 1953 analysis of the 1712–13 Sejm (the most comprehensive study of the Sejm published to date),[52] Józef Gierowski argued that the breaking of the Sejm represented a significant missed opportunity for reform of the Commonwealth. Gierowski argued that the conditions existed at the 1712–13 Sejm for an alliance between the king and the envoys, led by 'republicans' such as Karwicki, and that together king and envoys could have enacted reforms that would have restored a functioning, effective central government to the Commonwealth. Indeed, Gierowski even suggested that these reforms could have strengthened the Commonwealth's central government so far as to give Augustus II 'the start towards absolutism that he could not have achieved on his own'.[53]

The basis for this putative alliance would have been the significant alignment of interests between Augustus II and the envoys (and the wider szlachta they represented) over the need for military and fiscal reform. As Gierowski noted, the envoys accepted the need for a new army *komput* and for regular army pay to ensure military discipline, both key objectives of the king. The envoys recognized Augustus II's claim to the throne and were willing to endorse some (albeit limited) action against his internal opponents, the 'Adherents'. The envoys also sought restrictions on the hetmans, whose powers Augustus II's closest advisers (correctly) identified as a very significant barrier to the development of a stronger monarchy. Gierowski argued that sufficient common ground thus existed for co-operation between the king and the envoys. He blamed the fact that this was not achieved on Augustus II's unwillingness to drop his unpopular 'magnate' ministers in favour of an alliance with the envoys and the so-called 'middle szlachta'.[54]

---

[52] But see also Benedict Wagner-Rundell, 'A Missed Opportunity? Conflicting Programmes for Reform at the Sejm of 1712–13', *Central Europe*, 6, 1 (2008), pp. 3–16.

[53] Gierowski, *Między saskim absolutyzmem a złotą wolnością*, p. 156.

[54] This analysis was endorsed by both Olszewski and Rostworowski. Olszewski, *Doktryny prawno-ustrojowe*, p. 138, Emanuel Rostworowski, 'Czasy Saskie i Oświecenie', in Janusz Tazbir (ed.), *Zarys Historii Polski* (Warsaw, 1980), pp. 295–370 (p. 300). Revisionists such as Staszewski and Frost, however, have questioned whether an alliance between the monarchy and the wider szlachta was in fact feasible, noting both the financial dependence of even a king possessing outside resources such as Augustus II could draw from Saxony, and the king's isolation from the mass of the szlachta. They have therefore argued that kings had little option but to co-operate closely with magnates. Staszewski, *August II Mocny*, p. 75. Frost, *After the Deluge*, pp. 139–41. Poraziński, however, has argued that Augustus II was able to

Considering the envoys' approach to the issues of immunity and to trying the 'Adherents', it is not, however, clear that the objectives of the envoys and the king were in fact sufficiently compatible to support a meaningful alliance between them. As noted above, Augustus II's goals for the Sejm were to consolidate his position on the throne, including by implementing a package of reforms intended to strengthen central government, led by the king. Some of these reforms, in particular the establishment of regular army pay and permanent taxation, would also have lessened the central government's dependence on the Sejm.[55] The envoys, however, attempted to reassert the sovereignty of the Sejm, and the principle of collective government in the common good, rather than government according to a single, 'private' will. The envoys plainly suspected the king of seeking to further his private interest at the expense of the common good: hence their cautious response to the proposed special court to try the 'Adherents'. In this context, is it also worth noting that at the Sejm a number of the envoys voiced other long-running szlachta complaints against the Commonwealth's central government. For example, in January 1713 numerous envoys complained at the Senate Council's ability to 'decide and formulate [policy] concerning us but without our participation', echoing earlier protests against the Senate Council, and called for the Council's records to be made public.[56] A few went further, and called for a 'Delegation' of envoys to be added to the Senate Council.[57] Other envoys complained at the behaviour of the Treasurers, and called for an audit of their accounts, which was eventually agreed on 14 January 1713.[58] Given

reach out directly to the wider szlachta via sejmiki and ad hoc regional 'general councils' when looking to rally support against the Swedish invasion of 1701. Poraziński, *Epiphania Poloniae*, pp. 14–50.

[55] In this context, Staszewski has noted that Augustus II was simultaneously working to increase the independence of his government in Saxony from the Saxon estates. Staszewski, *August II Mocny*, pp. 199–200.

[56] 'de Nobis sine Nobis formuią y postanawiaią', envoy from Ruthenia, APG MS 300, R/ Ff, 1, p. 10. This protest was echoed by envoys from Grodno, Kraków, Wyszogród, Podlasie, and Sandomierz (the Sandomierz envoy in question was Stanisław Dunin Karwicki). APG MS 300, R/Ff, 1, pp. 12, 18, 19, 20, and 24.

[57] Rosnowski, envoy from Przemyśl, and Boguszewski, envoy from Płock, APG MS 300, R/Ff, 1, pp. 32 and 41. This too echoed a proposal that had occasionally been made by the sejmiki, for example that of Sieradz. Resolution of the sejmik of Sieradz, 8 June 1702, TP vol. 27, p. 111.

[58] One envoy alleged that although the Sejm's first session had agreed six months of pay for the army, the Treasurers had paid the soldiers 'with paper, not with money' ('Papierami nie Pieniędzmi'), implying that the Treasurers had embezzled the actual cash. When the audit of the Treasury was established, one envoy from Słonim gloomily predicted that the audit was doomed to fail, as the Treasurers would not be willing to produce their accounts. Given that the Sejm diary makes no mention of the audit being completed, his pessimism may have been justified. APG MS 300, R/Ff, 1, pp. 10, 18, and 21.

this suspicion of the king and his ministers, it is not clear that the envoys would have supported further strengthening of the power of the throne, as Gierowski suggested.

The particular policy on which Gierowski argued an alliance between the king and the envoys (in particular 'republicans' such as Karwicki) could have been based was a restriction on the powers of the hetmans. It is important to emphasize, however, that the envoys' plans for a 'circumscription' of the hetmanship were very different from those circulating among supporters of the king around this time, and were not obviously aligned with the interests of the throne. Royalist proposals for a limitation of the hetmanship focused above all on reducing the independence of the hetmans from the throne. For example, one court-inspired pamphlet of 1710 entitled *Propozycje na sejmiki i walną radę warszawską* ('Proposals for the sejmiki and the General Council of Warsaw') proposed the establishment of a Council of War to supervise the army and its commanders, the hetmans. This Council should be royally appointed, and both its members and the hetmans themselves should be dismissible by the king. Two years later, Augustus II's diplomatic representative in Berlin, Ernst Christoph von Manteuffel, wrote to suggest that the king seek to abolish the hetmans' life-long tenure in office, and replace it with a fixed term of three years.[59] Either proposal would have significantly reduced the hetmans' independence from the king, giving the king much greater control over the Commonwealth's armies, and potentially much greater scope to impose his will upon the szlachta.

There is no evidence, however, that the envoys were prepared to support any such extension of royal control over the hetmans. On the contrary, their proposals for making the hetmans accountable to the szlachta were intended to ensure that 'the Commonwealth [NB *not* the king] should have Power and Dominion over the Army'.[60] Power for the Commonwealth would allow government according to the common good, whereas greater power for the throne would serve only the king's private interest, contrary to the virtuous government that the envoys sought to restore and preserve. So it is not clear that the envoys' objectives for a 'circumscription' of the hetmans were aligned with those of the king, or that co-operation on a 'circumscription' was a realistic prospect.[61]

---

[59] Józef Feldman, 'Geneza konfederacji tarnogrodzkiej', *Kwartalnik Historyczny*, 42 (1928), pp. 493–531 (p. 509). Gierowski, *Między saskim absolutyzmem a złotą wolnością*, p. 104.

[60] 'aby Rzepplta nad Woyskami . . . miało Potestatem et Dominium', APG MS 300, R/Ff, p. 33.

[61] It could be argued that the Województwo Commissions agreed by the envoys could have been made to serve the interests of the throne, if a king had been able to win sufficient support among the mass of the szlachta to use the commissions to attack a hetman the king

That the king had little interest in the envoys' 'circumscription' is also illustrated by the events of the last days of the Sejm. Following the withdrawal of the Lithuanian envoys Puzyna and Nestorowicz from the Chamber, supporters of Augustus II, in particular Chancellor Szembek and Marshal Denhoff, attempted to find a compromise that would persuade the Lithuanians to return and allow the Sejm to complete the task of ratifying the measures sought by the king. During these negotiations, the Sejm diary records that Denhoff offered to concede to the Lithuanians' demand that the provision that the Lithuanian hetmans be accountable '*in quovis foro*' for 'contributions' be dropped. Denhoff was thus prepared to sacrifice the principle of accountability in order to achieve the programme of legislation sought by the king, prioritizing structural reforms over the individual, moral approach favoured by the envoys. His proposed compromise failed, however, on both fronts. Despite Denhoff's offer to meet their demands, the Lithuanian envoys still refused to return to the Chamber. Meanwhile the other envoys were outraged at Denhoff's proposal to concede the measures to curb 'licence' and hold the hetmans to account that had been their top priority for the Sejm. The envoys therefore concluded that no acceptable compromise could be reached that would allow the Sejm to continue, and so decided to bid the king farewell and disperse on 18 February 1713, formally bringing the Sejm to its inconclusive end.[62]

In the final days of the Sejm, the gap between the objectives of the king and of the envoys thus proved unbridgeable. Rather than a missed opportunity for a reformist alliance, the Sejm of 1712–13 (and its failure) is perhaps better characterized as a collision between two incompatible programmes for political reform, one aiming at strengthening the monarchy, the other seeking to preserve collective government in the common interest. The 1712–13 Sejm thus displayed in microcosm the tension throughout the early eighteenth century between the ambitions of the monarchy (and especially Augustus II) and the attempts by szlachta activists to resist 'arbitrary', 'private' power and restore virtuous government to the Commonwealth.[63]

The failure of 1712–13 Sejm left both groups frustrated: Augustus II failed to secure the fiscal and military reforms he had pushed since his return from abdication, while the envoys failed to put an end to 'contributions' or tackle the 'licentious' conduct of the Commonwealth's armies. In

---

wanted to undermine (or remove). But it is questionable whether a strategy along these lines would have been feasible given the isolation of the king from the bulk of the szlachta noted by Staszewski, as well as the widespread szlachta mistrust of the king's motives.

[62] APG MS 300, R/Ff, 1, pp. 60–2.

[63] Wagner-Rundell, 'A Missed Opportunity?'

the following years, the king attempted to break this deadlock by force, and impose his will on the Commonwealth using his Saxon army. By doing so, he provoked a mass uprising among the szlachta that came to form the General Confederation of Tarnogród. Formed to resist 'arbitrary' power, the Tarnogród Confederation again sought to restore virtuous collective government, including by implementing reforms that can be seen as a continuation of those supported by the envoys to the 1712–13 Sejm. This attempt by the Tarnogród Confederation to reform the Commonwealth in order to restore the traditional principles of the szlachta state will be the subject of Chapter 6.

6

The Confederation of Tarnogród

RISING UP FOR VIRTUE

The failure of the 1712–13 Sejm was followed by a chain of events that led to a mass uprising of the szlachta against Augustus II and his Saxon army, which the king brought back into the Commonwealth over the winter of 1713–14. This uprising took the form of the General Confederation of Tarnogród, proclaimed in defence of the Commonwealth's 'ancient laws and liberties' against oppression by the Saxon army.[1]

Central to the political programme of the Tarnogród Confederation was restoring collective sovereignty and government in the common interest, that is, virtuous government. This involved first of all resisting the 'arbitrary' power of the 'invading' Saxon army. Beyond this, the confederate programme called for institutional reform to prevent 'licentious' actions by the Commonwealth's ministers, in particular the hetmans, and to punish unvirtuous conduct.

The problems that the 1712–13 Sejm had sought to address were left unresolved by the Sejm's failure. For Augustus II, the task of consolidating his position on the throne was incomplete (even though his rival, Stanisław Leszczyński, finally gave up his claim in December 1712). Meanwhile, in the absence of regular army pay, the levying of 'contributions' on szlachta property continued. This prompted repeated protests from sejmiki, and widespread anger among the szlachta at the 'licentious' conduct of the soldiers and their commanders.[2]

---

[1] Proclamation of the General Confederation of Tarnogród, 27 [*sic*] November 1715, Bibl. Czart. MS 202, pp. 487–520. Another copy survives in Bibl. Czart. MS 546, pp. 398–413. A diary of the formation of the Tarnogród Confederation also survives in AGAD Arch. Radz. dz. VI. MS II-52, pp. 1–13.

[2] See, for example, the resolutions of the sejmiki of Lublin, 26 April 1713, TP vol. 9, pp. 71f.; Dobrzyn, 1 September 1713, Kluczycki (ed.), *Lauda Sejmików Ziemi Dobrzyńskiej*, p. 241; Czersk, 4 September 1713, TP vol. 3, p. 147; Łęczyca, 27 July 1714, TP vol. 12, p. 535; and Halicz, 29 October 1714, Wojciech Hejnosz (ed.), *Akta Grodzkie i Ziemskie z Archiwum Państwowego we Lwowie* (vol. 25, Lwów, 1935), p. 213. See also Gierowski, *Między saskim absolutyzmem a złotą wolnością*, pp. 184–215.

As in 1710 and 1712, many among the szlachta looked to a Sejm to resolve this situation and pacify the Commonwealth. Following the collapse of the 1712–13 Sejm, several sejmiki urged the king to summon a fresh Sejm at once, to try again to tackle the problems facing the Commonwealth and to guarantee the immunity of szlachta property. In this, they echoed calls from some envoys during the final days of the 1712–13 Sejm (one envoy, from Wschowa, even suggested that the king summon a Mounted Sejm, a mass gathering of the whole szlachta) as well as proposals made by some sejmiki before the 1712–13 Sejm had even met.[3]

Augustus II, however, demurred and in the late summer of 1713 departed the Commonwealth for Saxony, where he turned his attention to securing international recognition for his return to the Commonwealth's throne, and negotiations over the impending conversion of his son and heir (the future King Augustus III of Poland-Lithuania) to Catholicism.[4] During the winter of 1713–14, Augustus II then moved some 25,000 troops of his Saxon army into the Commonwealth, where they supported themselves by levying further 'contributions' on szlachta property, organized through an efficient commissariat. This prompted further protests from the sejmiki, as well as the allegation by contemporary pamphleteers that the king was using his Saxon army to mount a coup d'état to crush szlachta liberty and impose absolute monarchy on the Commonwealth.[5]

Historians have debated the king's intentions at this juncture. Writing in the 1920s, Józef Feldman argued against the proposition of an absolutist coup. He argued that Peter I of Russia would never have permitted the establishment by force of a strong monarchy in the Commonwealth, and that Augustus II was enough of a realist in international affairs to have understood this. So although earlier in his reign Augustus II had entertained ideas of a coup, by 1713 any such plans had been discarded as unfeasible. Feldman argued that Augustus

---

[3] Resolutions of the sejmiki of Proszowice, 23 February 1712, APKr Castr. Crac. MS 761, pp. 226–64 (p. 237); Dobrzyn, 20 November 1713, Kluczycki (ed.), *Lauda Sejmików Ziemi Dobrzyńskiej*, p. 243; and Halicz, 12 December 1714, Hejnosz (ed.), *Akta Grodzkie i Ziemskie*, p. 218. For suggestions from Sejm envoys from a fresh Sejm, see APG MS 300, R/Ff, 1, pp. 50, 54, and 62. See also Gierowski, *Między saskim absolutyzmem a złotą wolnością*, pp. 124 and 173.

[4] Staszewski, *August II Mocny*, pp. 187ff.

[5] *Consilium polityczne z pewnym dworzaninem krolewskim* (1713/14), Bibl. Czart. MS 1679, pp. 145–8. *Przestroga generalna stanów Rzeczypospolitej z docieczonej na zgubę wolności u dowru rad* (1713/14), reproduced in Gierowski, *Rzeczpospolita w dobie upadku*, pp. 197–210.

II moved his Saxon troops into the Commonwealth simply because Saxony itself had been too badly ravaged during the Great Northern War to sustain the large army that Augustus felt necessary in order to maintain his position within the Holy Roman Empire relative to his northern rival, Brandenburg-Prussia.[6]

Using archival material that had been unavailable to Feldman, however, Gierowski showed in his 1953 study that during the winter of 1713–14, Augustus II and his closest advisers discussed several plans for a coup d'état. Pietro Taparelli, count of Lagnasco, urged Augustus II to use his Saxon army to sweep aside the Commonwealth's constitution, and impose a wholly new government based on the king alone. Jakob von Flemming similarly suggested that the Saxons be brought into the Commonwealth to provoke a szlachta rebellion, which they could then crush.[7] Gierowski subsequently argued, however, that Saxon plans for a coup depended on external support (noting that plans for a coup were developed in the context of negotiations with Prussia for military backing for a coup in return for the ceding of parts of the Commonwealth's territory), suggesting that Augustus II recognized that he lacked the strength to carry out a successful coup on his own.[8]

Staszewski, however, has emphasized that alongside these international negotiations, several of the king's closest advisers prepared plans for a forcible alteration of the Commonwealth's form of government, including a proposal by Konstanty Szaniawski, Bishop of Kujawy, that the king retain institutions such as the Sejm but in practice bypass them through the establishment of a new governing council, centred on the king and backed up by Saxon force. Staszewski has also suggested that Augustus II may have hoped to capitalize on szlachta anger over 'contributions' and hostility to the hetmans, to rally support for the monarchy against the hetmans among the wider szlachta.[9]

---

[6] Feldman, 'Geneza konfederacji tarnogrodzkiej'.

[7] Gierowski, *Między saskim absolutyzmem a złotą wolnością*, pp. 103–4. See also Gierowski, 'Centralization and Autonomy', p. 277 and Olszewski, *Doktryny prawno-ustrojowe*, p. 146. Note that Flemming and Lagnasco were relative outsiders to the political culture of not only the Commonwealth but also Saxony itself. Hence, perhaps, their lesser attachment to either state's traditional political institutions, and their greater willingness to recommend simply sweeping them aside. By contrast, Augustus II's diplomat and adviser the Pomeranian nobleman Ernst Christoph von Manteuffel proposed that the powers of the monarchy be increased by constitutional means.

[8] Józef Gierowski, 'Pruskie i saskie projekty zamachu stanu w Polsce w 1715 r.', *Przegląd Historyczny*, 50 (1959), pp. 753–67.

[9] Staszewski, *August II Mocny*, pp. 187 and 195–6. For more on szlachta attitudes towards the hetmans (and other ministers), see below.

SAXONS OUT!

Precisely which (if any) of these plans Augustus II was in fact attempting to implement, and whether his objectives extended as far as the establishment of full-blown absolutism is unclear.[10] The szlachta, however, immediately identified the arrival of the Saxon army as an 'invasion' and an imposition of *absolutum dominium* on the Commonwealth. Sejmik resolutions denounced the Saxons for exercising 'arbitrary' and 'absolute' power in extracting 'contributions', and echoing the language of the 1712–13 Sejm envoys condemned the Saxons for acting 'licentiously' (*swawolnie, libidine*) and 'arbitrarily' (*pro libitu*). Pamphleteers alleged that the king was carrying out an absolutist coup d'état, a charge that the king's failure to summon a Sejm did nothing to refute.[11]

Beginning in 1714, a series of small-scale uprisings broke out, as sejmiki (particularly in Małopolska) formed local confederations and called out the *pospolite ruszenie* to defend their regions against the Saxons. These local confederations were typically led by the same local worthies who had been active in the expanding local governments during the preceding years, and as well as hostility to the Saxons showed a marked distrust for the Commonwealth's magnate and ministerial elite. The Treasurers were in particular criticized for colluding with the king in his 'absolutist' plans, while the hetmans were attacked both for failing to resist the Saxon 'invasion' and for the levying of 'contributions' on szlachta property by their own troops. The hetmans did not help themselves by appearing

---

[10] Some of the options for a coup discussed in negotiations with Prussia did go as far as including the abolition of the sejmiki and the abeyance of the Sejm and Senate Council, along with the conversion of the Polish-Lithuanian throne into a hereditary possession of the Wettin dynasty. Gierowski, 'Pruskie i saskie projekty zamachu stanu', pp. 758–9.

[11] Resolutions of the sejmiki of Lublin, 26 April 1713, TP vol. 9, pp. 71–2, and 10 April 1714, TP vol. 9, p. 103; Łęczyca, 27 July 1714, TP vol. 12, p. 535; and of the Masovian General Sejmik, 20 October 1714, TP vol. 17, pp. 282–3. 'Consilium polityczne z pewnym dworzaninem krolewskim' (1716), Bibl. Czart. MS 1679, pp. 145–8, and 'Przestroga generalna stanów Rzeczypospolitej z dociczonej na zgubę wolności u dowru rad' (1716), reproduced in Gierowski, *Rzeczpospolita w dobie upadku*, pp. 197–210. Gierowski has also noted that envoys of the szlachta of Małopolska to Berlin seeking Prussian support against the Saxon army claimed that the failure to summon a Sejm, along with the presence of the Saxon army, amounted to '*despotico imperio*' on the part of the king. Gierowski, 'Pruskie i saskie projekty zamachu stanu', p. 757. As noted above, the Henrician Articles required the king to summon the Sejm at least every two years. The Sejm of 1712–13 had originally been summoned as a short extraordinary Sejm, implying that a full ordinary Sejm was due the next year. As the 1712–13 Sejm returned from adjournment for a second session lasting just over six weeks (the customary length of an ordinary Sejm), arguably this might have counted as the requisite ordinary Sejm (though no record of any debate on this question survives in the available sources). If so, the next Sejm would have been due by the spring of 1715. If not, the next Sejm would have been due in 1714.

to equivocate in the face of these local uprisings. Crown Grand Hetman Adam Sieniawski first encouraged the Małopolska confederations, but then failed to support them, and instead tried to act as a mediator between the local szlachta and the king. Similarly Lithuanian Grand Hetman Ludwik Pociej offered only lukewarm support, while keeping his own lines of communication open with the king.[12]

The primary objective of these local confederations was to expel the Saxon army and protect their regions (and the Commonwealth as a whole) against the Saxons' 'arbitrary' rule. They were thus seeking to defend the szlachta state's traditional model of collective government for the common good against 'absolute' rule according to the private interest of the king.

Over the course of 1715, the various local confederations slowly coalesced. In October of that year, they were joined by a confederation proclaimed by the soldiers of the Crown (Polish) army in defence of 'ancient laws and liberties', which promptly arrested Grand Hetman Sieniawski.[13] In late November 1715, a General Confederation was proclaimed at Tarnogród in the Lublin region of Małopolska. As Marshal, the Tarnogród confederates elected Stanisław Ledóchowski, a moderately wealthy local office-holder from Volhynia, and the confederation's ruling council was made up of the marshals of the various local confederations that it brought together. The Tarnogród Confederation was thus to a large extent led by local worthies, rather than any of the Commonwealth's great magnates.[14]

The General Confederation of Tarnogród styled itself a league of the entire Commonwealth, formed to defend szlachta liberty, as well as the Catholic faith, against the Saxon army that the confederates claimed was 'licentiously' levying 'contributions' 'in the heart of the kingdom for the oppression of our free nation' in order for the king 'to seize for himself absolute power'.[15] Over the winter of 1715–16, the General

---

[12] Gierowski, *Między saskim absolutyzmem a złotą wolnością*, pp. 288–92; Olszewski, *Doktryny*, p. 154.

[13] Proclamation of the Crown army confederation, 2 October 1715, Bibl. Czart. MS 202 pp. 259–63. For more on the confederates' attitude towards the hetmans, see below.

[14] Gierowski, *Między saskim absolutyzmem a złotą wolnością*, pp. 288–92. Wojciech Stanek has, however, noted the prominent role played by some senators in the establishment of the Tarnogród Confederation, highlighting in particular the support of the Wojewoda of Kraków, Janusz Wiśniowiecki, for Ledóchowski's election as marshal. Senators and members of magnate families were thus not entirely excluded from positions of influence in the Confederation. Wojciech Stanek, *Konfederacje generalne koronne w XVIII wieku* (Toruń, 1991), pp. 45–6.

[15] 'in viscera regni in oppressionem wolnego narodu naszego', 'appropriando sobie absoluta potestas'. Proclamation of the General Confederation of Tarnogród, 27 [*sic*] November 1715, Bibl. Czart. MS 202, pp. 487 and 496. Bishop Konstanty Szaniawski, a supporter of the king, would later take issue with the Tarnogród Confederation's claim to constitute the entire Commonwealth, on the grounds that the Confederation did not include the king, who was one of the Commonwealth's three estates. In the language of the eventual treaty

Confederation gradually established its authority over local confederations throughout Poland. It took some time for the authority of the General Confederation to be accepted: in early January 1716, leaders of the Małopolska local confederations negotiated a local treaty independently of the Tarnogród leadership with the local Saxon commander, General Goltz, under whose terms Goltz's troops would leave Małopolska in return for the dissolution of the local confederations. A few weeks later, this treaty was rejected by Ledóchowski, who insisted that a single treaty covering the whole Commonwealth be negotiated between the king and the General Confederation instead.[16] By the spring of 1716, the authority of the Tarnogród Confederation had been accepted across Poland, while in March 1716 a parallel General Confederation of the Grand Duchy of Lithuania was proclaimed with similar aims, which subsequently merged with the Tarnogród Confederation.[17] The Tarnogród Confederation thus presented itself as a collective act of resistance by the entire Commonwealth to 'arbitrary' power in the name of the common good: an uprising for virtuous government.

Although no decisive battle between the Saxon army and confederate forces took place, a series of skirmishes occurred over the winter of 1715 and into the spring of 1716. The Saxons enjoyed initial success, securing the territory west of the river Vistula before pushing south-east as far as Zamość. The confederates then counterattacked into Wielkopolska, seizing the city of Poznań in the summer of 1716. The stalemate was ended by the intervention of Peter I of Russia who, using Russian forces in the Commonwealth as leverage, forced the king and the confederates to negotiate, with the Russian diplomat Grigori Dolgoruki acting as mediator.[18]

Talks between plenipotentiaries of the king (led by Bishop Konstanty Szaniawski, and Jakob von Flemming) and commissioners appointed by the Tarnogród Confederation began in Lublin in June 1716. Negotiations broke down in July, following the confederate offensive into Wielkopolska, and an uprising by the soldiers of the Lithuanian army against the authority

with the king, the confederates described themselves as the 'Confederated Estates of the Crown and the Grand Duchy of Lithuania' (*Stanow Skonfederowanych Koronnych y WXLitt*) instead. Bibl. Czart. MS 548, pp. 419 and 470–1.

[16] Treaty of Rawa, BN MS 6654, pp. 5–9. Manifesto by Ledóchowski rejecting the Rawa treaty, 27 January 1716, Bibl. Czart. MS 203, pp. 37–40.

[17] Proclamation of the Lithuanian Confederation, 23 March 1716, *Konfederacya Generalna Nierozdzielnie Cały Prowincyey Wielkiego Księstwa Litewskiego z Woyskiem, zgodnie od Woiewodztw, Ziem, y Powiatow Uczyniona w Wilnie Anno Domini 1716. Mśca Marca dnia 23* (printed Wilno, 1716).

[18] On the diplomatic manoeuvrings that led to the acceptance of Russian mediation by the two sides see Józef Gierowski, 'Wokół mediacji w Traktacie Waszawskim 1716 roku', *Zeszyty naukowe Uniwersytetu Jagiellońskiego, Prace Historyczne*, 26 (1969), pp. 57–68.

of Grand Hetman Pociej, whom they attempted to arrest (Pociej escaped and fled to the Saxon camp near Lublin).[19] Under further Russian pressure, talks eventually resumed in September 1716 in Kazimierz Dolny, before moving to Praga (across the river Vistula from Warsaw) later that month. The talks concluded with the agreement in November 1716 of the Treaty of Warsaw, which along with attendant legislation was ratified by the specially convened one-day 'Silent Sejm' of 1 February 1717.[20]

In line with their founding proclamation, the confederates' first demand was the immediate withdrawal from the Commonwealth of the Saxon army, and an end to 'arbitrary' rule. They demanded the restoration of the Commonwealth's traditional form of government, including the Sejm, the *liberum veto*, the elective monarchy, and restrictions on the prerogatives of the king. Augustus II's representatives eventually agreed,[21] and the Treaty of Warsaw provided that virtually all of the Saxon army was to be withdrawn immediately and that 'Sejms, Sejmiki, the Chamber of Envoys, the freedom to speak and to veto . . . are to be returned to their accustomed form'.[22] Further restrictions were imposed on the ability of the king to act independently of these institutions (in his private interest): the king was forbidden to appoint more than six ministers of foreign origin, and permitted a foreign bodyguard of just 1,200 men; the king was permitted to spend only six months every two years outside the Commonwealth, and required to be physically present within the Commonwealth's borders to sign acts relating to it.[23] The king's compliance with these (and other existing) restrictions was to be monitored by resident senators.

[19] See below on the confederates' attitudes towards the hetmans.
[20] A diary of the negotiations survives in Bibl. Czart. MS 548, pp. 414–1218. The Treaty of Warsaw and attached legislation are in VL vol. 6, pp. 113–201.
[21] After much discussion over the timing of the Saxon withdrawal and the dissolution (*exvinculatio*) of the Confederation. The king's negotiators pushed for the Confederation to be dissolved before the Saxon withdrawal, and before a Sejm was summoned to ratify the treaty. The confederates refused, wary that this could allow Augustus II scope to renege on the terms of the treaty. They also argued that denying it the chance to complete the pacification of the Commonwealth would be a grave insult to the Confederation's honour. Eventually, the king's representatives conceded that the Saxons would withdraw within 30 days of the treaty being agreed, and that the Tarnogród Confederation itself should then form the ratifying Sejm, to be held under the marshalcy of Ledóchowski on 1 February 1717. Only once the Sejm had ratified the treaty and passed its attendant legislation would the Tarnogród Confederation, along with all other confederations, be dissolved. To ensure that the Sejm did ratify the treaty, the confederates accepted Bishop Szaniawski's proposal that it should meet for just one day, with no further discussion of the treaty, or any other speeches, permitted. Bibl. Czart. MS 548, pp. 549, 567, 638, 655, and 706–8.
[22] 'Seymy, Seymiki, Izbę Poselską, libertatem sentiendi, ius vetandi, . . . ad solitam cursum reducimus', VL vol. 6, p. 113.
[23] These restrictions effectively ruled out any possibility of the personal union between the Commonwealth and Saxony developing into an institutional union. Gierowski, 'Centralization and Autonomy'. Staszewski, *August II Mocny*, p. 198.

According to the treaty preamble, this 'return[ed] the form of government to the ancient status of a free Commonwealth'.[24] It also reaffirmed the collective sovereignty of the Commonwealth, which was to ensure government according to the common good, over 'arbitrary' power in pursuit of the private interest of the king.

THE CONFEDERATE PROGRAMME
FOR REFORM

The Tarnogród Confederation did not just seek to restore the Commonwealth's traditional constitution. The confederates also pressed for a series of reforms, some of which were accepted by the king and included in the treaty terms. In many respects, these reforms were a continuation of those pursued by the envoys to the 1712–13 Sejm, and aimed to ensure virtuous government by restraining and punishing ministers who acted 'licentiously' or in pursuit of private interests. These reforms fall under two main headings: fiscal and military reform, and a 'circumscription' of ministers.

Fiscal and military reform was largely uncontroversial. In line with the sejmiki over the preceding years and the envoys to the last Sejm, the confederates accepted that regular army pay was essential to maintain military discipline and bring an end to the levying of 'contributions'. There was therefore little argument of principle during the main negotiation between the king's representatives and the confederates, and the details were left to technical discussions held after the treaty had been agreed in November.[25]

The legislation that was agreed provided for a new standing army *komput*, and for 24,000 units of pay, which in practice allowed for a total army strength of around 12,000 men. The soldiers' pay was to be funded from regular taxation, with taxes collected by commissioners appointed by the sejmiki or, in the event of sejmiki being broken, by the Treasurer.[26] To prevent soldiers damaging szlachta property (and

---

[24] 'formam regiminis ad antiquam statum liberae Reipublicae przywracamy', VL vol. 6, p. 113.

[25] Discussions of fiscal and military reforms, alongside various other technical matters, ran from November 1716 to the middle of January 1717, Bibl. Czart. MS 548, pp. 1018–274.

[26] 24,000 *porcje* of pay equated to a smaller actual army strength as it was only rank-and-file infantry who were paid one *porcja* each: cavalrymen, hussars, and officers received multiple *porcje*, the number rising gradually with rank. The taxes agreed were a mix of direct and indirect: in Poland the revenues of the *pogłówne* poll tax were allocated, while Lithuanian soldiers' pay was funded by a combination of alcohol duties, the Jewish poll tax, and the hearth tax. VL vol. 6, pp. 137–9 and 164–201.

in line with the proposals of Karwicki), individual army units were to be stationed on specified plots of royal land, from which they would draw their winter subsistence. If, despite these measures, any szlachta did suffer harm to their property, they would have the right to sue army commanders in local or central courts. This last provision echoed those agreed by the envoys to the 1712–13 Sejm, and demonstrates how even though the Tarnogród Confederation did accept the case for some structural changes in order to address the problem of 'contributions', the confederates also saw preventing 'licentious' behaviour by individuals as essential to tackling the threats facing the szlachta state. Individual morality was central to the confederates' analysis of the Commonwealth and the internal turmoil it was experiencing.

'CIRCUMSCRIPTION' OF MINISTERS

In line with focus on the behaviour of individuals, the Tarnogród Confederation followed the 1712–13 Sejm envoys in pushing for a 'circumscription' of the Commonwealth's ministers. As at the Sejm, this 'circumscription' focused primarily on making ministers accountable to the szlachta for their actions, and punishing any found guilty of acting contrary to the common good. That the confederates' demands should be so similar to those of the 1712–13 Sejm envoys is unsurprising, given that several active figures in the Tarnogród Confederation had been envoys to that Sejm. Participants at the formation of the General Confederation included the brothers Antoni and Jakub Morsztyn, respectively envoys from Sandomierz and Kraków, as well as one Dramiński, envoy from Bełz and Rosnowski, the outspoken envoy from Przemyśl.[27] Prominent among the Lithuanian confederates were a certain Kamiński, envoy from Lida in 1712–13, and Krzysztof Zawisza, elected as the envoy from Minsk.[28]

In some important respects, however, the confederates' proposals for a 'circumscription' were more far-reaching than those discussed at the 1712–13 Sejm, as they both extended to other ministers as well as the hetmans (though their primary focus remained the hetmans), and included provision for errant ministers not just to be forced to pay compensation, but also to be removed from office. The confederate proposals for ensuring

---

[27] AGAD Arch. Radz. dz. VI. MS II-52, p. 6. Dramiński may have been the same envoy from Bełz who at the 1712–13 Sejm was sharply critical of Lithuanian Grand Hetman Ludwik Pociej.

[28] Zawisza, *Pamiętniki*, pp. 299–300 and 312. Zawisza only actually attended the first session of the 1712–13 Sejm, sending his son Ignacy to the second session in his place.

accountability for ministers can thus be described as an evolution of those of the 1712–13 Sejm envoys.

Confederate demands for a 'circumscription' were also highly controversial, and resisted by both the king's plenipotentiaries and the Russian mediator of the negotiations. Some steps towards accountability for ministers were agreed during the negotiations: as noted above, the military legislation provided that the hetmans could be sued for any damage caused to szlachta property by their troops. But the confederates' further proposals for putting the hetmans on trial for their actions, and for providing for regular accountability of all the Commonwealth's ministers to the szlachta, were not accepted during the treaty negotiations. Despite this, the confederates' proposals still illustrate the strength of their concern to prevent the Commonwealth's ministers from acting 'licentiously', and the importance of the concepts of virtue and licence in the confederates' analysis of the Commonwealth and its situation.

According to the memoirs of Lithuanian Confederation activist Krzysztof Zawisza, when the soldiers of the Lithuanian army rebelled against Grand Hetman Pociej in July 1716, they initially wanted to put the hetman to death as a traitor for failing to defend the Commonwealth against the Saxons. They were dissuaded (before Pociej's escape made the question moot) by the leaders of the Lithuanian Confederation, who proposed instead that Pociej should be put on trial.[29] That the hetmans be tried was a key demand of the Tarnogród Confederation, which the confederate negotiators repeatedly made at the treaty talks. The diary of the negotiations also suggests that the confederates considered acting unilaterally, and trying the hetmans under the auspices of the confederation for their failure to protect the Commonwealth.[30] The confederates also

---

[29] Zawisza, *Pamiętniki*, p. 333.

[30] Bibl. Czart. MS 548, pp. 578 and 732. Zawisza, *Pamiętniki*, p. 338. The confederates plainly considered both Grand Hetmans guilty of this charge. The Crown army confederation alleged that Sieniawski had not used his army to defend the Commonwealth against the 'invading' Saxons, Bibl. Czart. MS 202, p. 259, while Zawisza's memoirs record Ledóchowski remonstrating with Pociej in June 1716 for failing to deploy the Lithuanian army against the Saxons (Zawisza, *Pamiętniki*, p. 319). Rising up against Pociej in July 1716, the Lithuanian army confederation accused him of putting his army 'to private use' (*in privatos usus*), rather than defending the Commonwealth against Saxon 'oppression'. Bibl. Czart. MS 548, pp. 500–4. See also Józef Gierowski, '"Opisanie" urzędów centralnych przez konfederatów tarnogrodzkich', in Józef Gierowski, Adam Kersten, Jarema Maciszewski, and Zbigniew Wójcik (eds.), *O naprawę Rzeczypospolitej XVII–XVIII: Prace ofiarowane Władysławowi Czaplińskiemu w 60 rocznicę urodzin* (Warsaw, 1965), pp. 193–211 (p. 197). Given that both Sieniawski and Pociej were at various points in Augustus II's reign leaders of opposition to the king, and that their control over the army independent of the king was such a significant barrier to any expansion of the powers of the monarchy, the suggestion that they might have aided the establishment of absolutism in the Commonwealth was highly ironic.

pressed for the Crown Grand Hetman, Adam Sieniawski, to be summarily dismissed from office, and replaced by his Field Hetman, Stanisław Rzewuski.[31]

The confederates intended that holding the hetmans to account for their actions would in future ensure 'that [the hetmans] would be a help to the king and the Commonwealth . . . and never act against the Commonwealth', that is, that they would in future always behave virtuously.[32] The confederates also proposed that the principle of accountability for their conduct should be applied not just to the hetmans but to all the Commonwealth's ministers. In a paper drawn up in late 1716 entitled *Suffragium prowentów skarbowych*, alongside a set of plans for fiscal and military reform, the confederates proposed the establishment of a special tribunal for ministers. This tribunal would be convened at each Sejm, and would have 24 judges, of whom 18 (six from each province) would be elected by the szlachta, and six would be senators (one clerical and one lay from each province). The tribunal would examine ministers' conduct since the previous Sejm, looking in particular at their accounts. If ministers were found to have abused their office or failed to uphold the common good, then 'by virtue of [this court's] decree without any delay or postponement the Chamber of Envoys should have the power to declare these offices vacant and appoint new ministers'.[33] A variant of this proposal was put forward at the treaty negotiations by one of the Lithuanian negotiators, Jan Scypion. He proposed that a ten-member tribunal to judge ministers be set up at the forthcoming Sejm.[34]

In pushing for a 'circumscription' of ministers, the confederates' focus was thus on holding ministers to account for any 'licentious' conduct and removing corrupt ministers from office. This was consistent with an analysis that saw the root of the Commonwealth's troubles in bad men rather

---

[31] In turn, the confederates proposed that their marshal Stanisław Ledóchowski should take Rzewuski's place as Crown Field Hetman. Gierowski, ' "Opisanie" urzędów centralnych', p. 198.

[32] 'żeby mogli być pomocą królowi i rzeczypospolitej . . . a nigdy nie być przeciw rzeczypospolitej', Zawisza, *Pamiętniki*, p. 338.

[33] 'vigore cuius decreti bez zadnych dylacyi albo iakich prolongacyi Izba Poselska powinna będzie te urzędy podać pro vacantibus'. 'Suffragium proventów skarbowych', AGAD Arch. Radz. II-52, pp. 154–6 (p. 155). The sections of this paper relating to fiscal and military reform (but not the ministerial tribunal) are reproduced in Gierowski (ed.), *Rzeczpospolita w dobie upadku*, pp. 246–8. The demand for an examination of the Treasurers' accounts reflected long-running szlachta suspicion of the Treasurers, discussed earlier in Chapters 3 and 5. Note in particular that the 1712–13 Sejm had agreed to the creation of a special commission to audit the Treasurers' accounts. APG MS 300, R/Ff, 1, pp. 10, 18, and 21.

[34] Zawisza, *Pamiętniki*, p. 343. It is not entirely clear whether Scypion intended this tribunal to be a one-off measure for the current cadre of ministers, or a regular event to take place at every Sejm.

than bad institutions or laws. Indeed, the confederates barely seem to have considered the idea of constraining the powers of any ministers. Only once did one of the confederate negotiators (again, the Lithuanian Scypion) suggest that 'it would be well for the Hetmans to serve for just three years', and after this proposal was rejected by the king's representatives, the confederates did not raise it again.[35] So although the confederates did push for some institutional changes, their primary focus was on ensuring that good men held office, not framing laws or creating institutions that would function even if the men running them were corrupt. In this context, it is notable that the confederates also repeated the well-established demand from the sejmiki that only virtuous (*bene meritis*) szlachta be appointed to office, a provision that was included in the Treaty of Warsaw.[36]

The confederates' proposals to hold ministers to account for their conduct were, however, strongly opposed by both the king's representatives and the Russian mediator Dolgoruki. Dolgoruki in particular was adamantly opposed to any plans for a trial or 'circumscription' of the hetmans, reflecting the close alliance that had been formed during the Great Northern War between Peter I and both Sieniawski and Pociej. During the summer of 1716, Dolgoruki wrote twice to Ledóchowski making clear the tsar's opposition to any 'circumscription' of the hetmans, on the grounds that this would undermine their ability to prosecute the ongoing war with Sweden. Menacingly, Dolgoruki informed Ledóchowski that his co-operation on this matter would aid the progress of the treaty negotiations.[37] When Ledóchowski coolly replied that the question of the hetmanship

[35] 'dobrze było aby Hetmani bywali Triennales', Bibl. Czart. MS 548, p. 824. The confederates may well have been aware that simply reducing the length of the hetmans' term of office would have significantly increased the power of the king over the army. In which case it is remarkable both that Scypion should propose such a step, and that the king's negotiators should reject it. It is possible that Scypion also had in mind further changes, for example limitation over the king's ability to nominate new hetmans, but the diary contains no record of such proposals. It is also worth noting that throughout the negotiations Scypion appears to have taken a particularly tough line against the hetmans, and Pociej in particular. For example, when the confederates' proposal that the Grand Hetmans be dismissed was rejected by the king's representatives, Scypion pushed for at least Pociej to be dismissed, if not Sieniawski too. This was also rejected by the king's negotiators, who urged Scypion not to pursue a vendetta against one man (Bibl. Czart. MS 548, pp. 839–41). Scypion's particularly vehement opposition to Pociej may have reflected ongoing internal tensions within Lithuania, since the civil war in the 1690s between former supporters of the Sapieha clan and their opponents (who called themselves 'republicans'), among whom Pociej was prominent. Gierowski has suggested that many among the Lithuanian Confederation wanted Pociej to be replaced as Grand Hetman by Jan Kazimierz Sapieha. Gierowski, ' "Opisanie" urzędów centralnych', p. 197.

[36] Bibl. Czart. MS 548, p. 467. VL vol. 6, p. 114.

[37] Letters from Dolgoruki to Ledóchowski, 18 June and 9 August 1716. Bibl. Czart. MS 548, pp. 421–2 and 585.

'does not depend on anyone else, but is a purely domestic matter of ours', Dolgoruki responded furiously, claiming that the confederates' hostility to the hetmans showed they were not truly interested in peace, and accusing the confederates of negotiating in bad faith and (bizarrely) of aiding Augustus II in the establishment of absolute monarchy.[38] During the negotiations, Dolgoruki was similarly vehement, repeatedly insisting that the hetmans 'be maintained in their jurisdiction according to ancient usage'.[39]

The king's negotiators were similarly opposed to a 'circumscription', threatening to walk away from the talks during the summer of 1716 if the confederates took forward plans to put the hetmans on trial, and during the negotiations rejecting all suggestions that the hetmans be tried or removed from office.[40] The talks did indeed break down following the uprising of the Lithuanian army soldiers against Pociej, and their attempt to arrest him, which the king's representatives condemned as a breach of the armistice under which the negotiations were taking place.[41] This might seem a rather strange position for the king's representatives to take: given that the hetmans were at various times prominent opponents of Augustus II, and that their independent control over the army was a significant check on the powers of the monarchy,[42] an opportunity to be rid of the troublesome Sieniawski and Pociej must have had some appeal to Augustus II. On the other hand, the king may have been concerned at the precedent that a trial for the hetmans would set, and might have regarded the confederates' proposals for tribunals with the power to remove and replace 'licentious' ministers as too great an incursion on the royal power of appointment. The only restriction on the king's power of appointment that his negotiators would accept was a requirement that hetmans only be appointed at a

---

[38] 'nie do kogo innego należą, tylko do Nas iako domowa Sprawa', letter from Ledóchowski to Dolgoruki, 10 August 1716, Bibl. Czart. MS 548, p. 594. Ledóchowski was repeating a point made at the beginning of the negotiations by Frezer, secretary to the Tarnogród Confederation, who called on Dolgoruki to recognize that the tsar's mediation in the talks was being undertaken purely from neighbourly affection, and did not give him any right to interfere in the Commonwealth's internal affairs (13 June 1716, Bibl. Czart. MS 548, p. 418). Dolgoruki's response to Ledóchowski is at Bibl. Czart. MS 548, pp. 597–8. For good measure, Dolgoruki in his letter also accused the Tarnogród Confederation of using envoys in Vienna and Constantinople to stir up diplomatic trouble for the tsar.

[39] 'byli utrzymani circa antiquum Usum Jurysdykcyi Swoich', Bibl. Czart. MS 548, p. 832. See also Bibl. Czart. MS 548, pp. 578 and 732, AGAD, Arch. Radz. VI. MS II-52, p. 171 and Zawisza, *Pamiętniki*, pp. 338 and 341.

[40] Bibl. Czart. MS 548, pp. 423 and 753.

[41] Bibl. Czart. MS 548, pp. 508–10.

[42] Indeed, as noted in Chapter 5, some of Augustus II's closest advisers had in recent years considered plans to reduce the hetmans' powers or their independence from the king.

Sejm, a requirement that the confederates presumably hoped would allow the Sejm envoys to exert some influence on the king's choice.[43]

Faced with opposition from both Dolgoruki and the king, the confederates were forced to drop (most of) their proposals for holding ministers to account.[44] In place of trials and tribunals, the Treaty of Warsaw introduced a range of new legal duties for ministers. Thus the Marshals were required to ensure the king appointed no more than his permitted six foreigners as ministers and that his foreign bodyguard never exceeded the 1,200 men that the treaty allowed. The Chancellors were charged with ensuring that the king did not spend more than six months every two years outside the Commonwealth, and generally abided by the terms of his *pacta conventa*. Senators resident with the king were obliged to ensure that the king adhered to all the laws. The hetmans were required to maintain the *komput* set by the Sejm, to ensure military discipline, not to conduct any diplomacy with foreign powers, and to remain on the Commonwealth's borders during interregna. The treaty also imposed a general duty on the hetmans to defend the Commonwealth, not to oppress the szlachta. Finally, the existing hetmans were required to swear oaths of loyalty to the Commonwealth before being allowed to resume command over the armies.[45]

These requirements were all consistent with the confederates' goal of ensuring that ministers uphold the law and only act for the common good, rather than according to any private interest. The lack of any way to hold ministers to account for their actions, however, meant that the treaty lacked an enforcement mechanism for these new duties. As a result, they were always likely to prove ineffective in practice.[46]

A SUCCESSFUL DEFENCE OF VIRTUE?

Historians' judgements of the Tarnogród Confederation and the legislation of the 1717 'Silent Sejm' have been mixed. The traditional view of the

---

[43] In practice, however, this provision had a very different effect, incentivizing the breaking of Sejms in order to prevent the king from appointing a new hetman. This problem was particularly acute in the late 1720s when all four hetmanships fell vacant and opponents of Stanisław Poniatowski (father of the future king Stanisław August Poniatowski) attempted to block his appointment as hetman. Lukowski, *Disorderly Liberty*, pp. 37–8.

[44] With the exception of the provision that hetmans could be sued for damage caused by their troops.

[45] VL vol. 6, pp. 125–8. The hetmans found the requirement to swear oaths deeply insulting, and lobbied hard to have this provision removed from the treaty. Bibl. Czart. MS 548 pp. 1011, 1118–39, and 1177.

[46] Gierowski, '"Opisanie" urzędów centralnych', pp. 202–11. In the following years, for example, the hetmans would openly flout the ban on dealing with foreign powers.

1717 settlement was as a purely conservative one that failed to address the fundamental constitutional flaws of the szlachta state, not least the *liberum veto*. It did nothing to help the emergence of the effective central government that the Commonwealth needed, while at the same time opening the door to future Russian interference in Poland-Lithuania's internal affairs. It was thus an example of the szlachta placing the preservation of their particular privileges before the interests of the state. Lukowski has indeed noted how within 20 years the 1717 legislation came to be described as 'a hallowed "ancient custom"' that could not therefore be challenged or overturned.

More positive interpretations have recognized the albeit limited reforms that the 1717 settlement did achieve. Michał Nycz has emphasized the creation of a fiscal and military system that lasted for half a century, while acknowledging that the 1717 legislation failed to tackle the Commonwealth's long-term fiscal problems, thus storing up trouble for the future. In a similar vein, Olszewski argued that although the 'Silent Sejm' did take some steps towards strengthening the Commonwealth's central government, it did not go far enough and so ended up acting as a 'brake on further reform of the state'.[47]

In contrast with this image of the 1717 settlement as incomplete or piecemeal, Gierowski has noted that some contemporaries, especially in Berlin, saw the 1717 legislation as a major strengthening of the Commonwealth's central government, and a basis for further reform. Indeed, the Prussian diplomat in Warsaw Georg Lölhöwell even argued that the provision for a standing army paid for by permanent taxation laid solid foundations for the future development of absolute monarchy. Staszewski has similarly argued that the establishment of permanent taxes were a first step towards making the king independent of the Sejm.[48]

These assessments of the 1717 settlement, however, are based on a perspective that is rather different from that of the Tarnogród confederates themselves. The confederates showed little sign of analysing the Commonwealth's problems in institutional terms, as the product of defective laws or an ineffective central government. On the contrary, they described them primarily in moral terms, as the result of corrupt individuals (not least the king) pursuing their private interests ahead of the

---

[47] Konopczyński, *Dzieje Polski Nowożytnej*. Norman Davies, *God's Playground: A History of Poland* (2 vols., Oxford, 1981), vol. 1, pp. 497–503. Lukowski, *Disorderly Liberty*, p. 36. Michał Nycz, *Geneza reform skarbowych Sejmu Niemego: Studium z dziejów skarbowo-wojskowych z lat 1697–1717* (Poznań, 1938). Olszewski, *Doktryny prawno-ustrojowe*, p. 172.

[48] Józef Gierowski, *W cieniu ligi północnej* (Wrocław, 1971), p. 141 and *Rzeczpospolita w dobie złotej wolności*, p. 290. Staszewski, *August II Mocny*, pp. 198–9.

common good. Furthermore, from the perspective of szlachta whose king was apparently ignoring the law and whose supposedly inviolate property was being seized as 'contributions' by either domestic or foreign armies, the chief problem facing the Commonwealth was not a lack of central government, but an excess of 'arbitrary' power.

Hence the overarching objective of the Tarnogród Confederation was to restore collective government according to the law in place of 'arbitrary' or 'absolute' power, and the pursuit of the common good in place of private interests. Measured against this goal, the Tarnogród Confederation achieved a partial success. By forcing the withdrawal of the king's Saxon army, the confederates succeeded in repelling the immediate challenge from 'arbitrary' power in the hands of the king, and by restoring the Commonwealth's traditional constitution they reasserted collective government (supposed to ensure the pursuit of the common good) against the 'absolute' rule of a single will. By agreeing to a new army *komput* and regular pay for the soldiers, the confederates also tackled the problem of 'contributions', a second instance of 'arbitrary' power, about which the szlachta had been complaining since at least the end of the Great Northern War.

The Tarnogród Confederation failed, however, to implement measures that would force those in power to act in the common interest, that is, to behave virtuously. This was a central objective of the confederates, and had to be so, if the Commonwealth's basic problem was understood not as one of laws but of morals. The confederates attempted to achieve this objective by making the Commonwealth's ministers (especially the hetmans) accountable to the szlachta citizenry for their actions, and providing for the removal of any who failed to uphold the common good. Their proposals to do this, however, were consistently blocked by opposition from the king and the Russian mediator.[49] Thus as at the 1712–13 Sejm, reform proposals from the szlachta that were based on a moral analysis and focused on the need to make men behave well collided with an alternative programme supported by the king aimed at building up the power of the monarchy. The confederates' reform proposals were also confronted by the interests of Russia in protecting Peter I's chief allies in the Commonwealth. So although the settlement of 1716–17 did reaffirm the Commonwealth's traditional collective government, and did restore internal peace at least for a time, the double opposition from both the king and the Russian mediator successfully frustrated the Tarnogród Confederation's attempts to revive virtuous government in the Commonwealth.

---

[49] Gierowski, '"Opisanie" urzędów centralnych', pp. 197–200.

7

A Reforming Moment?

RESPONSES TO CRISIS

The first 20 years of the reign of Augustus II were a period of unprecedented crisis and turmoil for the Commonwealth. During this period, the szlachta state and its political system faced an unprecedented series of challenges, both internal and external. These included the conflict in Lithuania at the turn of the eighteenth century between supporters and opponents of the Sapieha family and their hegemony in the Grand Duchy; the determination of an energetic king, possessed of external resources far beyond those available to any previous monarch, to bend or break the constitutional limitations placed on the throne; nearly a decade of devastating external war and foreign occupation; bitter civil war between rival claimants to the Commonwealth's throne; and when that conflict was eventually resolved, an attempted coup by Augustus II that triggered renewed internal conflict and then foreign intervention.

It must be acknowledged that in many respects the Commonwealth failed to meet these unprecedented challenges. In particular, during the years of the Great Northern War and the Swedish occupation, the Commonwealth's central government more or less disintegrated, leaving power in the hands of local bodies and rival confederations and their hetmans. Absent effective government, the Commonwealth was unable to prevent foreign armies from occupying its territory. In addition, until the uprising that became the General Confederation of Tarnogród, the szlachta state largely failed to constrain the ambitions of its dynamic king to pursue unilateral policies on his own, especially in the field of foreign policy.

The szlachta's response to the extended crisis of this period can therefore be judged to have been inadequate. It was nevertheless revealing, because when faced with such severe challenges to their state, szlachta politicians and commentators had to fall back on fundamental ideas and assumptions about their polity and its government in order to try to respond. The turbulent early years of Augustus II's reign thus throw into sharp relief the core ideas and values of the szlachta political tradition.

This study has argued that one key feature of szlachta political thought revealed by these years of turmoil was a preoccupation with public virtue, and a belief in the necessity of virtue for good government, and indeed for the survival of the Commonwealth at all. Uniting all of the different szlachta responses to the crisis was the objective of restoring public virtue to the Commonwealth, whether by exhorting those in power to act in the interests of all, agitating for a government of worthy men, or reforming parts or all of the Commonwealth's constitution to make those holding high office more accountable to the szlachta citizenry and to reward virtuous, and punish vicious or licentious, conduct.

The range of different calls or proposals for reform that were produced in this period, from the moralizing of Lubomirski to the grassroots expansion of local government, to the attempts of Sejm envoys and confederates to institute ministerial accountability, to the more sweeping proposals of Karwicki and his fellow radicals, shows that a substantial proportion of the Commonwealth's szlachta citizens accepted that their polity was ailing and in need of urgent, and perhaps extensive, repair. Given the variety of reform efforts that were generated during this period, it should perhaps be seen not just as a time of great crisis for the Commonwealth, but also as a 'reforming moment', when the szlachta state exhibited considerable energy for reform as well as a wide range of different approaches to the common problem of restoring virtue and thus good government.

FAILURE TO REFORM

By 1717, however, the great majority of these attempts at reform had come to nothing, notwithstanding the limited changes to the Commonwealth's fiscal and military structures that were greeted with such foreboding by observers such as the Prussian diplomat Lölhöwell. To a large extent, the Commonwealth's early eighteenth-century 'reforming moment' failed to bear fruit, with the szlachta state's traditional constitution remaining in place virtually unchanged. The political deadlock between the monarchy and the szlachta citizenry persisted. As a result, at least in part, the Commonwealth was about to experience a generation of political paralysis and military weakness.

Why did these reform efforts fail so comprehensively? Typically, accounts of the Commonwealth's failure to reform itself throughout the eighteenth century have emphasized four main factors: the innate conservatism of the szlachta; institutional barriers, not least the *liberum veto*;

foreign (most notably Russian) intervention; and internal divisions among the szlachta themselves.[1] All four were highly significant in preventing successful reform of the Commonwealth throughout the eighteenth century, though the importance of each individual barrier to reform should not be overstated. During the early years of the reign of Augustus II, however, a further factor can also be identified that hindered efforts at reform, namely tensions between different, and in some ways incompatible reform agendas. The following pages will first briefly examine the impact of the four generally acknowledged impediments to successful reform of the Commonwealth's government, before discussing how a collision between incompatible rival reform programmes contributed to the failure of the early eighteenth-century reforming moment.

The first 'traditional' explanation for the failure of efforts to reform the Commonwealth, the pervasive conservatism of szlachta political culture, has been well documented by historians. The reverence of the great majority of the szlachta for the Commonwealth's traditional laws and institutions, and in particular the szlachta's supposedly ancestral liberty, no doubt helped to fuel suspicion of any proposals for substantial reform, and especially of reform involving a strengthening of the Commonwealth's central government. This culture of conservatism may also to some extent explain the failure of even proposals for the szlachta to have greater power in government, such as that of Stanisław Dunin Karwicki, to command widespread support.[2]

Yet a conservative political culture is not a sufficient explanation for the failure of reform in the eighteenth century. The szlachta were hardly unique among contemporary European elites in revering traditional laws and institutions, and in seeking to defend their existing liberties (or privileges) by reference to established precedent. Elsewhere in eighteenth-century Europe the conservatism of hereditary elites was overcome, not only by superior force on the part of reformist rulers, but also through successful arguments that reform was necessary, especially in the face of outside threats. The Commonwealth, however, arguably suffered from its good fortune of surviving through most of the seventeenth and eighteenth centuries with its territory more or less intact (but for a few devastating yet temporary episodes of foreign invasion and occupation). Until relatively late in the eighteenth century it was therefore possible for szlachta

---

[1] See, for example, Lukowski, *Liberty's Folly*.

[2] On the reception of Karwicki's reform proposal, see Chapter 4. It is particularly remarkable that his call for the abolition of the royal powers of patronage, and their replacement with a system of election to office by the szlachta, apparently did not resonate among his contemporaries.

commentators to argue that the Commonwealth was not greatly suffering from its admitted political dysfunction.[3]

The conservatism of szlachta political culture was also not so pervasive as to stifle any innovative political thinking. On the contrary, over the course of the seventeenth and eighteenth centuries, politicians and writers such as Fredro, Opaliński, and Lubomirski as well as radicals like Karwicki, showed themselves able to entertain proposals for fundamental change, even if in some cases only to argue against them. At the same time, the force of custom and precedent did not prevent some practical constitutional innovations, such as the use of adjournment (*limita*) by many sejmiki and the development of new institutions of local government, which were typically legitimated as rooted in traditional practices or established institutions. Not all innovation had to be justified by reference to precedent, however: witness the claim by Śmigielski, envoy to the 1712–13 Sejm, that 'New Circumstances produce New Laws.' Indeed, Śmigielski also advanced an even more forward-looking argument that even if present circumstances did not demand the new institutions (Województwo Commissions for Injuries) that he proposed, they should nevertheless be put in place, to guard against the possibility of future hetmans behaving illegally.[4]

The failure of Śmigielski's proposal, despite his apparently having convinced his fellow envoys to support it, illustrates the second major barrier to successful reform: the *liberum veto*, deployed in 1713 by supporters of Lithuanian Grand Hetman Ludwik Pociej, who stood to lose much from Śmigielski's Województwo Commissions. As this example illustrates, the veto gave potential losers from any change a powerful mechanism to block reform. At the same time, institutions such as the life tenure of high officials helped to create some significant vested interests in the status quo. Given that only the Sejm, subject to the veto, had the legitimacy in the eyes of the wider szlachta to enact reforms, it is clear that the veto constituted a formidable impediment. Later in the eighteenth century, during the reign of Stanisław August Poniatowski, the veto was to some extent circumvented by forming a Sejm into a Confederation, where decisions were taken by majority vote. In the early eighteenth century, however, the practice of 'confederating' the Sejm had not yet been developed. Arguably, the General Council of Warsaw, a hybrid parliamentary/confederate body, could be seen as a forerunner of the confederated Sejms of Poniatowski's

---

[3] Felix Czacki (1723–90) wrote in 1765 that under Augustus III, 'not one Sejm reached a successful conclusion . . . save that of 1736. But no particular harm followed.' Quoted in Lukowski, 'Political Ideas among the Polish Nobility', p. 11.

[4] See Chapter 5.

time: but as noted in Chapter 5, the legitimacy of the General Council to make laws was denied by much of the szlachta at the time.

Even under Augustus II, however, in some exceptional circumstances it was possible for the veto to be effectively over-ridden. For example, the legislation of 1717, painstakingly negotiated between representatives of the king and the Tarnogród confederates, was passed into law in defiance of both the veto and the szlachta's customary 'free voice': when the Crown Field Hetman Stanisław Rzewuski attempted to voice dissent at the so-called 'Silent Sejm', he was prevented from speaking, prompting the Primate Stanisław Szembek to storm out in protest. The Tarnogród confederates also very nearly succeeded in over-riding the life tenure of hetmans Sieniawski and Pociej, who owed their continuation in office (and perhaps their very lives) to the protection of Saxon and Russian forces.

The Tarnogród confederates' failure to enact a significant 'circumscription' of the hetmanship is a prime example of the third factor generally cited to explain the failure of reform: foreign intervention. This was not, of course, to be the last time in the eighteenth century when foreign powers, in particular Russia, intervened to block change in the Commonwealth. Over the course of the century, Poland-Lithuania's neighbours increasingly saw it to be in their interests to ensure the Commonwealth's government remained weak and passive, before finally opting for partition instead. It is less clear, however, that in the early eighteenth century any of the Commonwealth's neighbours had adopted a coherent strategy of blocking reform (or indeed had any coherent strategy towards the Commonwealth's internal affairs at all).[5] It could even be argued that during the Great Northern War the other combatants intervening in the Commonwealth's internal affairs sought to support, not undermine, effective central government (albeit on an authoritarian model), in order more efficiently to exploit the Commonwealth's resources for the war. The Swedish establishment of a commissariat to support their army through taxation and levies beneath the puppet-regime of Leszczyński, or Russian backing for the hetmans Pociej and Sieniawski could both be seen in this way.[6] Similarly, throughout the early years of his reign Augustus II sought to use his Saxon

---

[5] Robert Frost, "'Everyone understood what it meant': The Impact of the Battle of Poltava on the Polish-Lithuanian Commonwealth', in Serhii Plokhy (ed.), *Poltava 1709: The Battle and the Myth* (Cambridge, MA, 2012), pp. 159–76 (pp. 163–6). See also Gierowski, *W cieniu ligi północnej*.

[6] It is also noteworthy that when, following Augustus II's abdication in 1706, Peter I of Russia pressed Sieniawski to accept the throne, it was Sieniawski who insisted that the traditional checks on the strength of the monarchy be retained, not the Russian emperor. Józef Gierowski, 'Projekt układu Piotra I z Adamem Sieniawskim z 1707 roku', *Śląski Kwartalnik Historyczny Sobótka*, 51, 1–3 (1996), pp. 210–20.

resources, in particular the Saxon army, to strengthen his central government, including the creation in 1713–14 of a centralized bureaucracy for the extraction of 'contributions' to support the Saxon army in the Commonwealth.[7] It was perhaps only in 1716–17, reacting to the Tarnogród Confederation, that one of the Commonwealth's neighbours, Russia, began to intervene in order to prevent reform and the creation of a more effective central government.

As for the fourth acknowledged barrier to reform, internal divisions among the szlachta, these were a regular feature of the Commonwealth's politics, which could be turbulent and fractious at the best of times. Infighting between rival individuals and factions could not only contribute to the general paralysis and ineffectiveness of the Commonwealth's government (for example in the 1720s, when opponents of the Czartoryski family repeatedly engineered the breaking of the Sejm to block the nomination of Stanisław Poniatowski to the vacant Crown Grand Hetmanship), but also on occasion escalate into political violence. The late seventeenth and early eighteenth centuries saw particularly bitter divisions within the Grand Duchy of Lithuania, most notably the clash between the Sapieha family and their 'republican' opponents, that in 1700 erupted into outright civil war. As noted in Chapter 1, arguably republicanism in the Grand Duchy was not the political orthodoxy as among the Polish szlachta, but the ideology of a particular group, opposed to magnate power. To the extent that this was so, Lithuanian magnates had a clear private political interest in blocking their opponents' efforts at reform, such as the *koekwacja* of 1699 or the drive for ministerial accountability by the 1712–13 Sejm envoys and the Tarnogród confederates.

The politics of the Grand Duchy in this period also illustrate how the ambitions, and quarrels, of individual politicians could hinder efforts at reform in this period. A prime example would be the case of Ludwik Pociej, who had been prominent among the 'republican' opponents of Sapieha power calling for the *koekwacja* at the turn of the eighteenth century, but a dozen years later orchestrated the breaking of the 1712–13 Sejm in order to block legislation on ministerial accountability to the szlachta. In breaking the 1712–13 Sejm, Pociej was likely both protecting his own position as Grand Hetman of Lithuania, and pursuing a political quarrel with his fellow hetman and rival Stanisław Denhoff.[8]

---

[7] Gierowski, *Między saskim absolutyzmem a złotą wolnością*. Note also that in 1714 Augustus II came close to persuading the Prussian king Frederick I to intervene in support of a stronger, more monarchical, central government. Gierowski, 'Pruskie i saskie projekty zamachu stanu'.

[8] On the breaking of the 1712–13 Sejm, see Chapter 5. As discussed in Chapter 6, Pociej was also one of the main targets of the Tarnogród confederates (some of whom wanted him summarily executed in 1716). There may have been an element of score-settling by former

Even so, it was possible in some circumstances for these internal divisions to be overcome, and for an overwhelming consensus in favour of one set of demands to form. The obvious example from the early eighteenth century is the Confederation of Tarnogród, which united a broad swathe of the szlachta in defence of the traditional laws and liberties which all claimed to support, with any dissenters effectively browbeaten into silence. With adherence to traditional constitutional principles more or less obligatory in the Commonwealth's public life, a basis for at least occasional unity did thus exist.

Each of these four 'traditional' factors was thus clearly significant in hindering attempts to restore effective government during the early eighteenth-century reforming moment, yet none individually appears to have been insurmountable. In addition, a further barrier to successful reform can also be identified in this period: tensions between rival programmes for reform, both among those that emerged from the szlachta, and that pursued by Augustus II himself.

Among the different szlachta reform proposals, despite their common goal of restoring virtuous government in the service of the common good, two key divisions can be seen. The first was between those who argued only for a change in the behaviour of individuals (such as Lubomirski, or those among the sejmiki calling on the king to use his power of appointment more virtuously), and those who claimed that institutional and legal changes were also required. As Quentin Skinner has noted, the tension between the arguments on the one hand that good government depends on good laws, and on the other that 'if the men who control the institutions of government are corrupt, the best possible constitutions cannot be expected to restrain them, whereas if men are virtuous, the health of the institutions will be a matter of secondary importance', has a long history.[9] In the Commonwealth, claims that the szlachta's laws and liberties were a precious, even perfect, inheritance from a golden age powerfully reinforced the argument that the true problem lay with the vice of individuals, not flaws in laws or institutions. As noted above, this reverence for tradition and precedent no doubt restricted the willingness of szlachta politicians and commentators to consider or support changes to the Commonwealth's laws and institutions.

---

supporters of the Sapiehas in the particularly bitter opposition to Pociej among Lithuanian confederate activists such as Jan Scypion. If so, there is a certain fitting irony to supporters of former magnate hegemons using 'republican' means to attack Pociej the former 'republican' now seeking to defend his own hegemony in the Grand Duchy.

[9] Skinner, *The Foundations of Modern Political Thought*, vol. 1, pp. 44–5.

Beyond this fundamental dispute over whether institutional change was required at all, there were also tensions between different reform agendas. In particular, the attempt by sejmik activists to revive virtuous government by building up local institutions was not entirely compatible with the defence of the prerogatives of the Sejm, or with some proposals for restoring the effectiveness of central government. The tension between the competing claims of centre and periphery can be seen in reform efforts throughout this period. Karwicki, for example, proposed an elaborate compromise in which the role of the sejmiki in electing senators and kings was enhanced, but control over fiscal policy was given to the Sejm, over whose decisions the influence of the sejmiki was reduced. At the Sejm of 1712–13, the question of whether accountability for the hetmans should be institutionalized at the central or local level was debated at some length, before being settled in favour of the regions. The legislation of 1717, however, significantly curbed the role of the sejmiki by banning the practice of adjournment (*limita*) and providing for the central Treasurers to appoint local tax-collectors in the event of the failure of the sejmiki. But the 1717 settlement failed to ensure the effectiveness of the Sejm, which reduced the extent to which the balance of power was shifted back towards the centre. This ongoing tug-of-war between centre and periphery fragmented szlachta efforts at reform, and the failure of the szlachta to unite behind a single vision for effective collective government posed a significant challenge to the success of any of the different szlachta proposals for reform.

Finally, all of the different szlachta reform attempts during this period also had to compete with the very different reform programme pursued by Augustus II, who was also seeking to restore effective government to the Commonwealth. Unlike that of the szlachta, for whom collective government remained a key principle, the king's model of effective government was, of course, a monarchical and (whether or not he aimed for formal absolutism) authoritarian one, based on central institutions such as the Senate Council or on Saxon resources, through which the king might, to a greater or lesser degree, impose his will on the Commonwealth. One result of this monarchist challenge to the traditional order was that a significant proportion of szlachta politicians' energy had to be devoted merely to defending, rather than reforming, the Commonwealth's existing constitution. At the same time, in the face of the threat from the throne some features of the constitution that reformers saw as flawed or corrupting, such as the unaccountability and life tenure of officials such as the hetmans, could be presented instead as bulwarks of the szlachta's traditional liberties. Both effects may have served to blunt the impact of the various szlachta attempts at reform.

It is thus possible to see the outcomes of the failed Sejm of 1712–13, the Tarnogród Confederation, and the legislation of 1717 as a prolonged stalemate between opposing drives to reform the Commonwealth, one monarchist, the other republican. Both in the Sejm and on the battlefield, neither was able to achieve a decisive victory. The result was that the Commonwealth's traditional constitution was preserved—but so were its various flaws: from the monarchist perspective the restrictions on the throne, and the vulnerability of government to disruption by szlachta opposition and especially the *liberum veto*; from the republican perspective the lack of ministerial accountability to the szlachta, and the king's corrupting powers of patronage. The debilitating deadlock *inter majestatem ac libertatem* was thus left unbroken, and the Commonwealth's political dysfunction continued.

THE PATH NOT TAKEN:
A 'REPUBLICAN KING'?

It is worth considering whether an alternative outcome was possible. Specifically, instead of pursuing his own monarchist agenda, contrary to szlachta ideas of good government, was it open to Augustus II to work with his szlachta citizens to restore (or establish) an orderly, effective government in the Commonwealth? Might the king have been able to harness the widespread view among the szlachta that the Commonwealth's government had become corrupt, and presented himself as a disinterested champion of the common good, reaching out to the szlachta as potential partners in government, using the language of virtue? To put it another way, was there an option for Augustus II to offer to reign as a 'republican king', rather than one aiming for *absolutum dominium*?

Despite its 'republican' concern with collective decision-making and with the liberty of the szlachta citizens, it is important to recognize that the ideal of the Commonwealth nevertheless included a significant role for the king in government. The king was, after all, one of the three estates that together shared sovereignty,[10] and as such was accorded considerable dignity as well as substantial power, albeit subject to the limits of the law.

---

[10] Hence Augustus II's representatives at the peace negotiations of 1716 rejected the claim by the Tarnogród confederates that they constituted the 'confederated estates of the Crown and the Grand Duchy of Lithuania' (*Stanow Skonfederowanych Koronnych y WXLitt*), on the grounds that they did not include the king, the Commonwealth's first estate. See Chapter 6.

The king not only chaired the Senate during sessions of the Sejm, but also presided over the activities of ministers, during the periods between Sejms, which given the shortness and infrequency of Sejm sessions accounted for the great majority of any year. In between Sejms, to a great extent the king effectively controlled the, admittedly modest, resources of the Commonwealth's central government.[11] Meanwhile the dignity accorded to the king's office was reflected in very respectful language in which kings were formally addressed, for example by Sejms envoys or other emissaries of the sejmiki, even when they were strongly critical of a particular king's actions or policies.[12]

So even in the 'noble republic', the monarchy retained an important role. It is also significant that not even radical reformers such as Karwicki, whose proposals would have stripped the king of virtually all his powers, went so far as to advocate the abolition of the monarchy.[13] In addition, it was only radicals like Karwicki that proposed the abolition of one of the king's most significant powers, the right to distribute offices and honours. As noted above, the proposal to abolish this power largely failed to resonate among the wider szlachta, despite the fact that numerous sejmiki were urging the king to appoint only worthy (*bene meritis*) men to office, and were (along with their envoys to the Sejm) attacking the licentious conduct of those the king had appointed: both implicit criticisms of the king's previous nominations. This suggests that the great majority of the szlachta remained strongly attached to the idea (articulated by the squire in Łukasz Opaliński's 1641 *Dialogue of a Priest and a Squire*) of the king as the judge of men's virtues who would reward the worthy with honours and offices, thus promoting them to their fellow-citizens as examples to be emulated.[14] Perhaps despite their evident worries about royal patronage as

[11] As royal decisions in between Sejms needed only the signature of any one of the Commonwealth's two Grand Chancellors and two Vice-Chancellors, the king could usually count on getting his way. Frost, *After the Deluge*, and 'The Nobility of Poland-Lithuania', pp. 216–17.

[12] Kings were routinely praised and thanked for their paternal care for the Commonwealth and the public interest. See, for example, resolutions of the sejmiki of Ciechanów, 5 May 1699, TP vol. 1, p. 96; Liw, 2 June 1699, TP vol. 5, p. 280; and Zakroczym, 10 November 1701, TP vol. 36, p. 244. See also Grześkowiak-Krwawicz, 'Anti-Monarchism in Polish Republicanism', pp. 47–8, and Robert Frost, 'Obsequious Disrespect: The Problem of Royal Power in the Polish-Lithuanian Commonwealth under the Vasas, 1587–1668', in Richard Butterwick (ed.), *The Polish-Lithuanian Monarchy in European Context, c.1500–1795* (Basingstoke, 2001), pp. 150–71.

[13] It was not until the 1790s that the abolition of the monarchy was to be proposed, by Felix Potocki, a leader of the Targowice Confederation formed in May 1792 to oppose the reformist constitution of 3 May 1791. Lukowski, *Disorderly Liberty*, pp. 250–1.

[14] Opaliński, *Rozmowa plebana z ziemianinem*, pp. 71–2.

a source of corruption and factionalism, the szlachta nonetheless believed that only a king could fulfil this function.[15]

Given the substantial power that was thus accorded to the monarchy, might Augustus II have chosen to operate within the Commonwealth's existing laws, abiding by the legal restrictions on the throne and collaborating with his szlachta citizens to build an effective government, instead of attempting to overturn the Commonwealth's constitution, break free of the restrictions on his power, and to establish a more authoritarian government centred on his own authority?

A policy of working with the political culture and institutions of the Commonwealth would, of course, have been very different from that which Augustus II actually pursued, and it is likely that in order to secure the support and co-operation of a majority of the szlachta the king would have had to make significant compromises on his own policy objectives. Most obviously, at the beginning of the eighteenth century the great majority of the szlachta strongly desired peace abroad, so collaboration would likely have required Augustus II to drop his activist foreign policy aims, especially as their dynastic component commanded no support among the szlachta. Given szlachta suspicion of foreign influences, and their calls for only szlachta to be appointed to office, the king may also have had to make concessions over the role of loyal supporters from his regime in Saxony such as Flemming. Such compromises may well have been unacceptable (or even unimaginable) to Augustus II, especially given that many other central European princes were at this time working to stamp their authority on their territories, often at the expense of nobilities and their estates.[16]

It should also be borne in mind that Augustus II could not have known for certain in advance that his more authoritarian policy would end in

---

[15] Note also that, as discussed in Chapters 5 and 6, both the envoys to the 1712–13 Sejm and the Tarnogród confederates, who attacked the 'licentious' behaviour of ministers (especially the hetmans), did not press for election to these offices by the szlachta as the solution to this problem, but rather advocated greater accountability to the szlachta of ministers still appointed by the king.

[16] Gierowski, Frost, and Poraziński have each argued that at various points in the early eighteenth century Augustus II was presented with opportunities to work with the Commonwealth's traditional institutions or in alliance with portions of the szlachta, but largely for reasons of personality and ambition chose not to do so. Gierowski, *Między saskim absolutyzmem a złotą wolnością*, p. 156. Frost, '"Everyone understood what it meant"', p. 171. Poraziński, *Epiphania Poloniae*, pp. 191–4. For contemporary princes' efforts to assert their authority against nobilities and estates, see Christopher Clark, *Iron Kingdom: The Rise and Downfall of Prussia* (London, 2006) on the Hohenzollerns in Brandenburg and Ducal (East) Prussia; Francis Ludwig Carsten, *Princes and Parliaments in Germany from the Fifteenth to the Eighteenth Century* (Oxford, 1959) on German princes more generally; and Staszewski, *August II Mocny*, pp. 189–92 on Augustus's efforts to strengthen his position relative to the Saxon estates after 1709.

failure. For example, had his attack on Swedish Livonia been more success-ful (as the mercurial self-proclaimed leader of the Livonian nobility Johann Reinhold Patkul assured him it would be), and had Augustus II been able to acquire Livonia, or a portion of it, as a hereditary territory, he might well have been able to use that success as political leverage to increase his power within the Commonwealth.[17]

In the event, however, the unilateral, authoritarian approach adopted by the king in the early years of his reign did end in failure. By 1717, he had failed to capture any new territories and thus create a permanent link between his own dynasty and the Commonwealth's throne, while virtually all the traditional restrictions on the powers of the monarchy had been restated, and a substantial proportion of the szlachta alienated. For good measure, the Commonwealth itself had been devastated by more than a decade of war and military occupation. So while partnership with the szlachta would likely not have delivered the king's own policy objectives, it has to be noted that the king's alternative strategy also failed to deliver these, as Augustus II made no appreciable progress towards his goal of a stronger monarchy.[18]

Staszewski has argued that 1717 marked a turning point for Augustus II, and that from this point the king did adopt a policy of working with the Commonwealth's traditional institutions, a decision that Staszewski has described as the king's entry into 'political maturity'.[19] The full extent of the king's change of policy is, however, open to doubt, as in the years immediately after 1717 Augustus II both returned to using his Saxon dip-lomatic service to advance his policy with regard to the Commonwealth, and attempted to place a substantial portion of the Commonwealth's new standing army under the command of his loyal supporter Flemming.[20]

---

[17] On Patkul, see Orest Subtelny, *Domination of Eastern Europe: Native Nobilities and Foreign Absolutism, 1500–1715* (Montreal, 1986). Frost has also argued that contemporar-ies expected certain key engagements between the Swedish and Saxon armies (in particular the battle of Kliszów) to end in favour of the Saxons, rather than in the decisive Swedish victory that in fact occurred. Greater success for the Saxon army during the Great Northern War could well have boosted Augustus II's authority within the Commonwealth. Frost, *The Northern Wars*, pp. 271–3.

[18] Gierowski, 'Centralization and Autonomy', pp. 279–82. It could be argued that Augustus II did at least manage to secure the throne for his son, the future Augustus III. Given that the ban on holding royal elections *vivente rege* remained in place, however, and Augustus III was only elected to the throne following an interregnum (and Russian vic-tory in the War of the Polish Succession), it is not clear that the accession of his son can be ascribed to the efforts of Augustus II.

[19] Staszewski, *August II Mocny*, pp. 209–77.

[20] In the field of international affairs, Augustus II negotiated the 1719 Treaty of Vienna, an attempted alliance between Saxony and the Holy Roman Empire against Russia, one of whose purposes was to counter Russian influence in the Commonwealth. Despite the king's efforts, the Sejm did not agree to join the alliance. L. R. Lewitter, 'Poland, Russia and the Treaty of Vienna of 5 January 1719', *Historical Journal*, 13, 1 (1970), pp. 3–30.

In any event, by 1717 it was almost certainly too late for Augustus II to be accepted as a genuine partner in government by the majority of the szlachta, given the mistrust that had been engendered during the preceding 20 years. Indeed, this mistrust allowed foreign powers, especially Russia, to stoke suspicions among the szlachta of their king's 'tyrannical' designs throughout the rest of his reign.[21] By 1717, the opportunity for collaboration with the szlachta had passed: the more feasible moment for the king to have adopted this policy, had he chosen to do so, was at the point of his election to the throne in 1697.

There is a good case that a collaborative policy towards the szlachta was a realistic option at that point. At the turn of the eighteenth century, many sejmiki and szlachta pamphleteers were arguing that the Commonwealth had fallen into corruption and disorder, and called for reform of some sort. This suggests that potential partners for a king appealing to his szlachta citizens to work with him in pursuit of the common good were indeed available. Similarly, institutions such as the sejmiki could probably have provided the means for the new king to reach out to the szlachta citizenry: although Staszewski has argued that kings were largely isolated from the mass of the szlachta and depended on magnates as intermediaries, Poraziński has shown how in the aftermath of the Swedish invasion of the Commonwealth, Augustus II used sejmiki and other ad hoc local assemblies effectively to rally support among the szlachta in defence of his throne.[22] So in all probability there was an opportunity for the king to present himself to the szlachta as a partner in reforming the Commonwealth to restore virtuous government, had he chosen to do so.

Whether such a partnership between the king and the szlachta would have succeeded in implementing reforms to the Commonwealth's government cannot, of course, be known. Substantial obstacles would have to have been overcome, not least the *liberum veto*, which would have given the losers from any changes supported by even a large majority scope to obstruct them in the Sejm. The mistrust of kings that had built up among the szlachta in particular during the previous half century may also have reduced the chances of successful collaboration (though the arrival of a new king proclaiming a sincere desire to work with the szlachta for the common good could perhaps have mitigated this). There can thus be no guarantee that a collaborative policy on the king's part would have

---

[21] Gintautas Sliesoriūnas, 'Changes in Attitudes towards Russia among the Lithuanian-Polish Elite at the Turn of the Seventeenth and Eighteenth Centuries', *Lithuanian Historical Studies*, 9 (2004), pp. 1–18.

[22] Staszewski, *August II Mocny*, p. 75. Poraziński, *Epiphania Poloniae*, pp. 14–50.

yielded better results than the unilateral approach Augustus II in the event adopted.

It is, however, instructive to note that later in the eighteenth century a king (Stanisław August Poniatowski) did succeed in implementing sweeping reform, including the establishment of a hereditary monarchy, the abolition of the *liberum veto*, and the creation of an army of 100,000, by aligning himself with the prevailing mood among the szlachta (in that instance, hostility to Russian interference) and appealing for support with the slogan 'the King with the Nation, the Nation with the King'. The new constitution of 3 May 1791 enacted under Poniatowski was, of course, short-lived, lasting only 18 months before being revoked in 1793 following outside (Russian and Prussian) intervention. Nevertheless, the comparison between the achievements of Poniatowski and Augustus II suggests that, in the absence of overwhelming force (which no Polish-Lithuanian ruler was ever able to bring to bear), working with the szlachta and their political culture and institutions was the only way for a king successfully to bring about reform.[23]

---

[23] Butterwick, 'Political Discourses of the Polish Revolution'. See also Frost, ' "Everyone understood what it meant" ', p. 171.

8

Wider Contexts

The preceding chapters have argued that the idea of virtue was an essential element of early modern szlachta political thought, and an indispensable analytical tool for szlachta politicians and commentators seeking to understand, and respond to, the challenges that their Commonwealth faced, especially during the turbulent early years of the reign of Augustus II. The szlachta concept of virtue also provides a helpful prism for examining szlachta political thought in its wider international context, and for comparing the szlachta tradition with other 'republican' political traditions elsewhere in early modern Europe. As well as showing the various common features shared by szlachta and other European republicanisms, such a comparison also serves to illustrate the distinctive elements of szlachta political thought during this period.

So far, relatively few historians of early modern Poland-Lithuania have adopted an explicitly comparative approach, though Michael Müller has drawn some comparisons between the Commonwealth and the Holy Roman Empire, and Karin Friedrich and Barbara Pendzich have suggested an interpretation of the szlachta state as an example of the wider early modern European phenomenon of the *Ständestaat*.[1]

EXCEPTIONS TO ABSOLUTISM: POLAND-LITHUANIA AND GREAT BRITAIN

Some comparisons have also been drawn between early modern Poland-Lithuania and England/Great Britain. For example, studies by Choińska-Mika, Dean, Hołdys, and Hunt have compared the

[1] Michael Müller, 'Republicanism versus Monarchy? Government by Estates in Poland-Lithuania and the Holy Roman Empire, Sixteenth to Eighteenth Centuries', in Manfred Hildermeier (ed.), *Historical Concepts between Eastern and Western Europe* (New York, 2007), pp. 35–47. Friedrich and Pendzich (eds.), *Citizenship and Identity in a Multinational Commonwealth*. See also Christian Preusse, 'The Scope of Politics in Early Modern Imperial

development of parliamentary systems in the two polities in the sixteenth and seventeenth centuries, and the institutions through which the views and interests of their various regions were represented to the centre. As noted in the Introduction, Grześkowiak-Krwawicz has also drawn heavily on analysis of seventeenth-century English republicanism for her interpretation of the szlachta concept of liberty.[2]

The most notable comparative studies of the constitutions and political ideas of Poland-Lithuania and England/Great Britain in the eighteenth century have been produced by Emanuel Rostworowski and Richard Butterwick. Both have highlighted the institutional similarities between the two 'exceptions to eighteenth-century absolutism'. Both were parliamentary states, in which a single, central bicameral parliament, dominated by owners of landed property, resisted the encroachments of the monarchy to retain a significant role as a partner in government. From 1707, both were also compound states, the products of institutional unions built on earlier dynastic unions, of Scotland and England and of Poland and Lithuania. Perhaps coincidentally, for much of the eighteenth century both polities also had for their kings German princes who retained substantial separate territories within the Holy Roman Empire.[3]

Rostworowski argued that the similar constitutions of the two states were also underpinned by similar political ideas, in particular similar doctrines of resistance to illegitimate rule, expressed in the Commonwealth through the right *de non praestanda obedientia* enshrined in each new king's *pacta conventa*, and expounded in Great Britain in the writings of John Locke. On the basis of the similarities he identified between the two states, Rostworowski even speculated that, but for the *liberum veto* and the Commonwealth's geographical position, Poland-Lithuania might have followed a similar historical path to Great Britain in the eighteenth

Systems: The Holy Roman Empire of the German Nation and Poland-Lithuania in the Seventeenth Century in Comparison' (Oxford University DPhil thesis, 2014).

[2] Jolanta Choinska-Mika and David Dean, 'Representation and Accountability: A Comparison of Early Modern England and Poland', *Parliaments, Estates & Representation*, 21 (2001), pp. 91–101. Choińska-Mika, 'Dwa parlamenty nowożytne—polski i angielski (wieki XVI i XVII)', in Janusz Ekes (ed.), *Dziedzictwo Pierwszej Rzeczypospolitej w doświadczeniu politycznym Polski i Europy* (Nowy Sącz, 2005), pp. 39–53. Sybill Hołdys, 'Sejm polski i parlament angielski w XVI–XVII wieku: porównanie procedury', *Przegląd Historyczny*, 71 (1980), pp. 497–514. William Hunt, 'A View from the Vistula on the English Revolution', in Bonnelyn Kunze and Dwight Brautigam (eds.), *Court, Country and Culture: Essays on Early Modern British History in Honor of Perez Zagorin* (Rochester, NY, 1992), pp. 41–54. Grześkowiak-Krwawicz, 'Quentin Skinner i teoria wolności republikańskiej' and *Regina Libertas*.

[3] In the case of Great Britain, the Hanoverian kings, from the accession of George I in 1714; in Poland-Lithuania the Wettin kings Augustus II (r. 1697–1733) and his son Augustus III (r. 1733–63).

century, and might have developed an effective parliamentary system of government, capable of mobilizing sufficient resources to withstand the encroachments of its powerful neighbours.[4]

While acknowledging the many institutional similarities, Butterwick has sounded a more cautious note. First, he has highlighted several important institutional differences between the two countries, in particular the significantly greater powers of the British monarchy. Unlike their counterparts in the Commonwealth, British monarchs enjoyed hereditary succession (subject to the requirement to be Protestant), the right to dismiss as well as appoint ministers, and substantial ability to determine government policy, in particular foreign policy. For Butterwick, however, the most significant difference between the two states was that while both saw the development of similar 'republican' political ideas, England/Great Britain also had a powerful monarchist tradition that was completely lacking in Poland-Lithuania, where 'Polish political culture had absolutely no equivalent to the Tory doctrine of divine indefeasible hereditary right, non-resistance, and passive obedience.' Thus in early modern England/Great Britain, republicanism was only ever one of several competing political ideologies (and usually one only espoused by a minority of the political nation) rather than being the prevailing orthodoxy, as in the Commonwealth.[5]

Notwithstanding this caveat, striking similarities can nevertheless be seen both between some of the specific policy measures pursued by English/British and szlachta republicans in the late seventeenth and early eighteenth centuries, and between the language and narratives that both groups used to advance and legitimize their political programmes.

Perhaps most notably, both Poland-Lithuania and England/Great Britain during this period had lively discourses of the corruption allegedly prevalent in court circles, and the threat that this posed to their parliamentary constitutions. As discussed in Chapter 3, sejmiki in Poland-Lithuania repeatedly denounced corrupt appointments to high office, accusing the king of rewarding private favourites rather than faithful servants of the common good. In England/Great Britain, opponents of the court similarly charged that the court had succumbed to venality and faction, with supporters of the crown gaining influence and preferment. As a result of this corruption at the centre of power, they particularly feared that

---

[4] Emanuel Rostworowski, 'Republikanizm polski i anglosaski w XVIII wieku', *Miesięcznik Literacki*, 11, 5 (1976), pp. 94–103.
[5] Butterwick, *Poland's Last King and English Culture*, p. 17. See also Butterwick (ed.), *The Polish-Lithuanian Monarchy in European Context* for a comparative study of the Commonwealth's monarchy.

government had fallen under the sway of a 'moneyed interest' that put its own financial agenda ahead of the public good.[6]

In addition to this general fear of the influence of private factions and favourites, in both countries republicans were intensely preoccupied with the threat posed to liberty and parliamentary government by their monarchs' powers of patronage. As noted in Chapter 1, the fear that Polish-Lithuanian kings might use their powers of patronage to suborn or pack a Sejm with their supporters was a key justification for the *liberum veto*. In late Stuart England, 'country republican' politicians were similarly concerned by the crown's ability to influence Parliament through patronage. To guard against this risk, they pressed repeatedly for legislation excluding servants of the crown from the House of Commons (Place Bills: restrictions on placemen sitting in the Commons were eventually included in the 1701 Act of Settlement), and restricting the monarch's power to create new peers (Peerage Bills).[7]

A related concern shared by republicans in both England/Great Britain and Poland-Lithuania was that long parliaments might give the crown the opportunity to win over parliamentarians gradually over time. Hence the requirement in the Commonwealth that ordinary Sejm sessions last for just six weeks, and the strong suspicion among the szlachta of adjournment (*limita*) of the Sejm, a practice banned by the Sejm of 1724. (Note, by contrast, that at the sejmiki, away from the potentially corrupting influence of royal patronage, the *limita* was widely used as a tool to increase the role of local government, as discussed in Chapter 3. This could suggest that had the szlachta been less worried about the threat of corruption from royal patronage, they might have been more willing to accept reforms to increase the effectiveness of the Commonwealth's central government.) Late Stuart England had experienced the so-called 'Cavalier Parliament', which met for 18 years, from 1661 to 1679, during which time King Charles II succeeded in winning the support of a substantial body of members. To avoid a repetition of this precedent, 'country' politicians called

---

[6] Caroline Robbins, *The Eighteenth-Century Commonwealthman: Studies in the Transmission, Development and Circumstance of English Liberal Thought from the Restoration of Charles II until the War with the Thirteen Colonies* (Cambridge, MA, 1959). Blair Worden, *Roundhead Reputations: The English Civil Wars and the Passions of Posterity* (London, 2001). On eighteenth-century accounts of corruption (both political and sexual) at the court of Louis XV of France, see Robert Darnton, *The Forbidden Best-Sellers of Pre-Revolutionary France* (New York, 1995).

[7] Attempts to limit the monarch's ability to create new peers (for which 'country' politicians campaigned particularly energetically following Queen Anne's 'mass' creation of 12 new peers in 1711–12) did not succeed. James Jones, *Country and Court: England, 1658–1714* ('New History of England', vol. 5, London, 1978), p. 31.

for legislation requiring that new parliaments be regularly summoned, a demand that was realized with the passage of the 1694 Triennial Act.

'Country' politicians also successfully pressed for a series of other restrictions on the prerogatives of the crown that in their direction, if not their extent, resembled those that applied in the Commonwealth. Hence the 1701 Act of Settlement, as well as providing for the Protestant succession on the death of Queen Anne, included a ban on foreigners sitting in Parliament or the Privy Council (similar to the requirement in the Commonwealth that only members of the szlachta should serve as Sejm envoys or be appointed to public office), a requirement that all public business be conducted through formal institutions, such as the Privy Council, not informal groups of royal advisers (mirroring szlachta hostility to the alleged usurpation of the Sejm's role in government by 'private' bodies such as the Senate Council), and provision that judges should serve for life rather than be dismissible by the crown (a limited reflection of the life tenure enjoyed by senior magistrates in Poland-Lithuania). The Act of Settlement also imposed some restrictions on the monarch's control over foreign policy, requiring the consent of Parliament before England could go to war on behalf of a monarch's overseas possessions (such as the Electorate of Hanover). This was intended to prevent England fighting solely in the private dynastic interests of the monarch. As noted above, szlachta republicans were similarly strongly opposed to war they believed served only the private interests of the king (most notably Augustus II's invasion of Swedish Livonia), and hence were quick to denounce any perceived violations of the requirement in the *pacta conventa* that the king conduct no foreign diplomacy at all without the consent of the Sejm. The Act of Settlement also banned the monarch from leaving the British Isles without the consent of Parliament, mirroring a similar customary restriction on Polish-Lithuanian kings.[8]

Finally, the Act of Settlement's provision that after the death of Queen Anne the crown should pass to Sophia of Hanover and her heirs 'being Protestant' represented the third in a series of attempts to restrict the hereditary succession to the throne during the late Stuart period. The first such attempt had been in 1679–81, when 'country' politicians campaigned (unsuccessfully) in Parliament for an Exclusion Bill to remove from the line of succession the Catholic James, Duke of York, younger

---

[8] Interestingly, this last restriction was loosened in both Great Britain and Poland-Lithuania almost at the same time, to accommodate their kings' desire to be able to visit their German principalities. In Great Britain, the ban in the Act of Settlement was repealed in 1716. In Poland-Lithuania, the legislation of the 1717 Sejm permitted the king to spend up to six months every two years outside the Commonwealth, whereas previously the king was forbidden to leave the Commonwealth at all without the consent of the Sejm.

brother of King Charles II and (as the king had no legitimate children) next in line to the throne. The attempt to exclude him failed, and James acceded to the throne (as King James II and VII) upon his brother's death in 1685. Three years later, however, 'country' politicians were prominent in the conspiracy that forced James from the throne in the so-called 'Glorious Revolution' of 1688. The Act of Settlement then barred not only James's heirs but all Catholics from the throne, ensuring the Protestant succession.

Although the Act of Settlement did finally establish (as the exclusionists 20 years previously had asserted) that Parliament had the right to determine the succession, it did not, of course, amount to the introduction of a fully elective monarchy as existed in Poland-Lithuania. Nevertheless, Tory opponents, who regarded any interference with strict hereditary succession as anathema, were quick to draw the comparison with Poland-Lithuania, branding the exclusionists as the 'Polish' faction, and lampooning Anthony Ashley-Cooper, 1st Earl of Shaftesbury and the most prominent 'country' politician of the 1670s and 1680s, as 'Anthony, King of Poland'.[9] There is also some evidence that supporters of exclusion did look to Poland-Lithuania as a potential model: in 1674 John Milton published an English translation of the *Letters Patent* proclaiming the election of Jan Sobieski, an act that Nicholas von Maltzahn has argued was probably motivated by a desire to hold up an example of an elective monarchy in support of the exclusionist cause.[10] In many respects, therefore, the programme of the 'country republicans' of late Stuart England was similar at least in direction to that of their szlachta contemporaries, while some may even have consciously sought to emulate the Polish-Lithuanian example.

LIBERTY AS AN ANCIENT INHERITANCE

Beyond the specific political programmes of republicans in England/ Great Britain and Poland-Lithuania, there is also a remarkable similarity

---

[9] Allan Macinnes, 'The Hidden Commonwealth: Poland-Lithuania and Scottish Political Discourse in the Seventeenth Century', in Friedrich and Pendzich (eds.), *Citizenship and Identity in a Multinational Commonwealth*, pp. 233–60 (p. 251). Whig polemicists also deployed the pejorative comparison with Poland to attack their Tory opponents, for example in Daniel Defoe's 1704 satire *The Dyet of Poland*, in which Tory grandees are caricatured as venal and ambitious lords who only 'canted' about liberty while seeking power for themselves but caring nothing for the good of the nation. Anglipoloski [= Daniel Defoe], *The Dyet of Poland, a Satyr* (London, 1704).

[10] Nicholas von Maltzahn, 'The Whig Milton, 1667–1700', in David Armitage, Armand Himy, and Quentin Skinner (eds.), *Milton and Republicanism* (Cambridge, 1995), pp. 229–53.

between the pseudo-historical narratives propagated in the two states to explain and legitimize their 'free' constitutions. As Colin Kidd has shown, in eighteenth-century Britain it was commonplace for liberty and the free constitution to be described as an inheritance from an ancient 'Gothic' past. According to this narrative, based on a reading of Tacitus's *Germania*, once all the 'Goths' had lived in a state of liberty, which their ancient rulers accepted and preserved. Over the centuries, however, other 'Gothic' peoples had seen their liberty gradually eroded by the growing power of monarchs, with the result that by the eighteenth century, only in England or Britain had this ancient liberty been preserved. Kidd has noted how before the Union of 1707, this 'Gothic' narrative was usually used to describe a specifically English inheritance of liberty. During the eighteenth century, however, it was appropriated by writers in Scotland, Ireland, and the colonies of North America, who claimed the 'Gothic' inheritance for Britain more broadly, as part of a more encompassing British identity.[11]

In the case of Poland-Lithuania, Lukowski has similarly shown how szlachta writers typically described their own 'golden freedom' as a precious inheritance from their glorious ancestors. Unlike the English/ British 'Gothic' narrative, for szlachta pseudo-histories of liberty no classical account of the origins of that inheritance was available. Szlachta writers therefore gave different accounts of precisely when and how their liberty had first begun, though the origins of the 'golden liberty' were commonly associated with the introduction of Christianity to Poland in the tenth century.[12]

Like their English/British contemporaries, szlachta writers in the eighteenth century also claimed that liberty had once been enjoyed by other peoples, who had since lost their freedom and fallen beneath the yoke of absolute monarchs.[13] One extensive account of the loss of liberty in other, less fortunate lands, was the anonymous 1701 *History of the Revolution of the Kingdoms of Sweden and Denmark, Told in Polish* (*Historya o Rewolucyi Krolestw Szwedzkiego y Duńskiego Po Polsku Wylozona*).[14] The majority of

---

[11] Colin Kidd, *British Identities before Nationalism: Ethnicity and Nationhood in the Atlantic World, 1600–1800* (Cambridge, 1999). See also Colin Kidd, 'Constitution and Character in the Eighteenth-Century British World', in Paschalis Kitromilides (ed.), *From Republican Polity to National Community: Reconsiderations of Enlightenment Political Thought* (Oxford, 2003), pp. 40–61.

[12] Lukowski, 'The Szlachta and their Ancestors', and *Disorderly Liberty*, pp. 13–32.

[13] For a survey of eighteenth-century szlachta portrayals of contemporary European monarchies, see Anna Grześkowiak-Krwawicz, 'Polish Views on European Monarchies', in Butterwick (ed.), *The Polish-Lithuanian Monarchy in European Context*, pp. 116–31.

[14] Gierowski has suggested that the author of this work may have been Franciszek Poniński. Gierowski, *Rzeczpospolita w dobie upadku*, p. 198 n.

this work, whose preface explicitly stated it was intended as a cautionary tale for the szlachta, was devoted to Sweden, recounting its history from ancient times until the accession of Gustav Vasa, and his seizure of 'absolute' power in the sixteenth century. The 'ancient' Swedish constitution is first described, and presented as a paradise of liberty with a constitution remarkably similar to that of early eighteenth-century Poland-Lithuania: an elective monarchy whose prerogative powers were strictly limited by a powerful parliament. The kings possessed extensive powers of patronage, but their love of liberty prevented them from using these in a corrupt or self-interested way, and they appointed only worthy Swedes to offices. Meanwhile, a Senate led by the Archbishop of Uppsala was charged with watching over the king, and warning him should he ever overstep the limits set on his office. In the event that he did, it was generally accepted that his subjects had the right to join together to oppose and, if necessary, dethrone him.[15]

This ancient free constitution allegedly survived more or less unchanged until the sixteenth century and the arrival of two mortal threats: the Lutheran 'heresy' and King Gustav Vasa. Gustav is presented in this account as a pure villain, intent only on securing absolute and hereditary power for himself. Upon his election to the throne, he immediately set about undermining the institutions that checked his power and guaranteed Swedish liberty. His chief target was the Catholic Church, which Gustav attacked politically (rolling back the jurisdiction of ecclesiastical courts), economically (seizing the income from Church estates to pay for an enlarged army), and above all doctrinally, by encouraging the spread of Lutheranism, including by promoting a Swedish translation of the Bible.

According to this account, Gustav's attacks on the Church and its wealth won him great popularity among the common people, as well as the growing number of Swedish Lutherans. Gustav also used his powers of patronage to promote a faction of personal supporters, led by his low-born Chancellor Anderson, a closet Lutheran. Aided by this faction and the powerful army he had built up with expropriated Church funds, Gustav was able to intimidate the Swedish Parliament into supinely agreeing to all of his demands. In 1527, Parliament ratified Gustav's seizure of Church property, agreed to the production of a Swedish Bible, and declared that henceforth only members of the Vasa dynasty could be

---

[15] Jan Jakub Potulicki [pseud.], *Historya o Rewolucyi Krolestw Szwedskiego y Duńskiego Po Polsku Wylozona* (1701), pp. 3–5. To emphasize the parallel between 'ancient' Sweden and the Commonwealth of his own day, the author uses Polish terms to describe the main institutions of the Swedish government, such as *Seym* for the Swedish parliament.

elected to the throne. At this point the king formally declared his conversion to Lutheranism and took unlimited power. The journey to absolutism was then completed in 1544 when Parliament, by now completely packed with supporters of the king, unanimously declared the monarchy hereditary.[16]

Having charted the downfall of ancient Swedish liberty, the author then gives a much shorter account of the Danish 'revolution', the establishment of hereditary absolute monarchy in Denmark by King Frederik III in 1660. As in the Swedish case, the author emphasizes the roles played by a self-serving royal faction, a nobility complacent in its defence of liberty, and a standing army (though the religious aspect of the Swedish narrative is not present in the Danish case). Interestingly, this szlachta account of the coming of absolutism in Denmark appeared just a few years after Viscount Molesworth's *Account of Denmark*, recounting the same events for an English/British audience, was published in 1694. Like its Polish counterpart, Molesworth's cautionary tale of the Danish 'revolution' also emphasized the role of the moral decline of the Danish nobility and the king's possession of a standing army in the loss of Danish liberty.[17]

These descriptions of the loss of Swedish and Danish liberty served to emphasize how the szlachta had uniquely managed to preserve the precious inheritance of liberty that had once been shared by many peoples. Szlachta accounts of the present state of those unfortunate foreigners similarly note how the loss of liberty had, over the ages, wrought changes to the character and customs of those living under *absolutum dominium*, who had degenerated from their former state into one of servility.[18] The claim that the szlachta were the sole inheritors of a once-shared ancient liberty is also virtually identical to that made by English/British contemporaries

---

[16] Potulicki [pseud.], *Historya o Rewolucyi Krolestw Szwedzkiego y Duńskiego*, pp. 189–269. The portrayal of Gustav Vasa as a one-dimensional villain was, of course, as much a caricature as the description of the idealized ancient Swedish constitution. Any positive achievements of Gustav's, such as his liberation of Sweden from foreign (Danish) rule, or his delivery of the kingdom from the murderous rule of King Kristian II, were entirely glossed over. For a modern scholarly account of the accession and reign of Gustav Vasa, see Michael Roberts, *The Early Vasas: A History of Sweden, 1523–1611* (Cambridge, 1968).

[17] Robert, 1st Viscount Molesworth, *An Account of Denmark as It Was in the Year 1692* (London, 1694). There is no evidence to suggest that the author of the 1701 Polish history of the Danish 'revolution' had read Molesworth's account. On English/British perceptions of the establishment of absolutism in Denmark, see Blair Worden, 'Republicanism and the Restoration, 1660–1683', in David Wootton (ed.), *Republicanism, Liberty and Commercial Society, 1649–1776* (Stanford, 1994), pp. 139–93.

[18] Grześkowiak-Krwawicz, 'Polish Views on European Monarchies'. Note also the parallel drawn by Grześkowiak-Krwawicz with mid-seventeenth-century English republicans who described those subject to arbitrary power as 'dis-heartened', 'dis-couraged', and 'dis-spirited'. Grześkowiak-Krwawicz, 'Quentin Skinner i teoria wolności republikańskiej' and 'Deux libertés'. Skinner, 'A Third Concept of Liberty'.

that the English or British were the only people to have retained their own primeval 'Gothic' liberty.

Another remarkable similarity between the szlachta and English/British accounts of the preservation of their own people's ancient liberty concerns the role of religion in the two narratives. The author of the *Historya o Rewolucyi* repeatedly emphasizes the link between the absolutism of Gustav Vasa and his Lutheran faith. Gustav Vasa's supporters are virtually all described as Lutherans, and the propagation of a Lutheran Bible was a key part of Gustav's campaign to undermine Sweden's ancient constitution and amass greater power for himself. By contrast, the Catholic Church is presented as a bulwark of the traditional constitution and one of the principal checks on the power of the throne. This connection between Catholicism and liberty was in line with the claim repeated by szlachta writers throughout the eighteenth century that the szlachta had retained their 'golden liberty' thanks to Divine Providence, as a reward for their adherence to the Catholic faith.[19] Given this connection, deviating from the Catholic faith would have terrible political as well as spiritual consequences. Indeed, one pamphlet published in 1713 or 1714, as szlachta anger was mounting at the 'occupation' of Poland-Lithuania by troops from Lutheran Saxony, referred directly to the Swedish and Danish experience in warning its readers of the link between 'a change of faith and [the coming of] a despotic regime'.[20]

Late seventeenth- and early eighteenth-century English/British writers also commonly ascribed their own retention of 'Gothic' liberty to faith and Providence. In England/Great Britain, however, it was Catholicism that was associated with royal despotism, in particular following the Jacobite alliance with the arch-absolutist Louis XIV of France.[21] The English/British and szlachta providential claims were thus almost perfect mirror images of each other. Writers in both states propagated strikingly similar accounts of liberty as an ancient inheritance that had been lost by the bulk of humanity, and only retained by a single chosen people.

---

[19] Lukowski, 'The Szlachta and their Ancestors', and, for the role of Catholic piety in szlachta identity, *Disorderly Liberty*, chapter 3. See also Wagner-Rundell, 'Holy War and Republican Pacifism'.

[20] 'odmiana wiary et despoticum imperium'. *Przestroga generalna stanów Rzeczypospolitej z docieczonej na zgubę wolności u dworu rad*, reproduced in Gierowski (ed.), *Rzeczpospolita w dobie upadku*, pp. 197–210 (p. 198). The irony that the king being complained about, Augustus II, was himself only a recent convert to Catholicism (and was attempting to increase his power over his Lutheran Saxon subjects as well as in the Commonwealth) does not appear to have struck the author of this pamphlet, or indeed any other contemporary szlachta observers.

[21] Robbins, *The Eighteenth-Century Commonwealthman*.

VIRTUE RETAINED OR VIRTUE ABANDONED?

Whether similarities between the narratives and political programmes of English/British and szlachta republicans in the late seventeenth and early eighteenth centuries reflect the two traditions' adherence to a common set of underlying ideas and values is, however, debatable. As discussed in earlier chapters, during this period szlachta politicians and commentators continued to analyse their own political system in terms of the virtues of its rulers and citizens, and to assume that the preservation of the szlachta state depended upon the maintenance of public virtue, and the willingness of all to subordinate their private interests to the common good. Szlachta republicanism thus remained firmly rooted in the concepts of classical political thought.

In his seminal work *The Machiavellian Moment*, J. G. A. Pocock argued that during the seventeenth and eighteenth centuries English/British (and later North American) republicans similarly remained true to the ideas and values of classical republicanism, including the classical concept of virtue. In particular, Pocock argued that the key tenets of classical republicanism were transmitted to the English/British tradition via the work of James Harrington (1611–77), prominent republican thinker of the Interregnum period and author of the 1656 treatise *The Commonwealth of Oceana*, and then a group of republicans at the end of seventeenth century, including Henry Neville and John Toland, whom Pocock termed 'neo-Harringtonians'.

Pocock argued that the proposals of Harrington's *Oceana* were firmly rooted in the classical republican tradition, noting the influence on Harrington of the ideas of Niccolò Machiavelli, and citing Harrington's adoption of the classical language of virtue and corruption, and his support for measures such as rotating magistracies and a citizens' militia. Pocock argued that the 'neo-Harringtonians' took up both Harrington's classical vocabulary and ideas, and became the intellectual driving force behind the attacks by 'country' politicians such as Shaftesbury on the power of the court, and especially on the corrupting influence of royal patronage. Thus the 'neo-Harringtonians' 'restated the old antithesis of "Court" and "Country" in a new form', from the standpoint of the classical ideal of self-sacrificing virtue, and their demand for regular, frequent parliaments and for the exclusion of placemen 'was designed to secure the same principle as Harrington had aimed at with his mechanisms of rotation, namely the perpetual renewal of independence, freedom and virtue'. Similarly, their opposition to royal proposals to maintain a peacetime standing army was the ideological heir to Harrington's (and before him Machiavelli's) support for a citizens' militia. Pocock therefore argued that classical ideas, including that of virtue, remained central to English republican thought during this period, which he described as constituting a 'chapter in the continuing history of civic humanism', that would culminate at the end of the eighteenth century in the American Revolution. According to this analysis, the English/British republican tradition continued during this period to share with its szlachta counterpart a common foundation in the values and ideas of classical republicanism.[22]

Pocock's argument has, however, been challenged, most notably by David Wootton and Paul Rahe, who have argued that over the course of the late seventeenth and eighteenth centuries English/British republican thinkers gradually abandoned the precepts of classical political thought in favour of a more 'modern' republicanism based on the preservation of life and material well-being, rather than on virtue. Wootton has first questioned Pocock's general thesis that a single, continuous tradition of 'civic humanism' can be identified linking the ideas of the Italian Renaissance to seventeenth-century England and on to the American Revolution. He has highlighted a number of discontinuities between the political thought of Machiavelli and the Florentine tradition and the Anglo-American republicanism of the seventeenth and eighteenth centuries, in particular emphasizing the importance in the latter tradition of the concept of representation, a crucial mechanism through which republicanism could be adapted from the context of the city-state to that of a larger territorial state, and which was wholly absent from Florentine political discourse. Wootton has also noted that especially during the eighteenth century English/British and later American republican writers had to engage with the new phenomenon of rapidly increasing wealth generated by economic and particularly commercial growth. Partly in response to this challenge, Wootton claimed, they tended increasingly to emphasize the importance of negative, 'civil liberty', rather than the active, 'political liberty' so prized by Machiavelli and the classical and Florentine republican traditions.[23]

In addition to this general critique of Pocock's thesis, Wootton has also challenged the claim that virtue was central to the ideas of James Harrington, and to the design of his ideal constitution set out in *The Commonwealth of Oceana*. This argument has been made at much greater length by Rahe, who has claimed that instead of being founded on the classical idea of virtue, Harrington's political thought was in fact based on a complete rejection of classical assumptions about human nature, and

---

[22] Pocock, *The Machiavellian Moment*, especially Part III.
[23] David Wootton, 'Introduction: The Republican Tradition: From Commonwealth to Common Sense', in David Wootton (ed.), *Republicanism, Liberty and Commercial Society, 1649–1776* (Stanford, 1994), pp. 1–41 (pp. 14–17).

that his proposed political system was based instead on the harnessing of selfish interests.

Rahe has noted that Harrington followed Thomas Hobbes (1588– 1679) in rejecting the classical premise that men were naturally sociable and that they were endowed with the capacity to discern rationally what was right and good. Rather, Harrington proceeded on the assumptions that men were naturally wicked and would tend always to pursue their own interests. It would be unrealistic to expect essentially selfish individuals to act in a virtuous way: the task of the lawgiver was therefore to establish laws and institutions that would induce individuals to act well not out of any virtuous concern for the common good, but because it was in their selfish interests to do so. Harrington termed the construction of such laws and institutions 'political architecture', and offered the charming example of an agreement by two girls needing to share a cake that one will divide it and the other will decide who gets which piece. According to this arrangement, it is in both girls' selfish interest to act as fairly as possible, as if they cared about the other. Similarly but on a grander scale, Harrington envisaged that a political system could be constructed that did not require individuals to be virtuous and to desire the common good, but instead incentivized even bad men to act according to the public interest.[24]

So according to Rahe, despite Harrington's 'wrapping himself in a toga' and pervasive use of classical vocabulary (a device that Rahe suggested he adopted deliberately to mislead his readers), the central premises of classical political thought were in fact absent from Harrington's work. Rather than being grounded in classical ideas, as the szlachta political tradition continued to be, the driving force behind Harrington's ideal constitution was rather what Rahe has termed the principle of 'humanity', that is the claim that the chief goal of all political systems should be the preservation of human life and material well-being. This principle, Rahe has argued, was first articulated by the sixteenth-century French essayist Michel de Montaigne (1533–92). It was subsequently adopted in England at the turn of the seventeenth century by Francis Bacon (1561–1626), who argued that a central task of government was to encourage the development of the arts and sciences through which improvements in the material lot of humanity could be produced. The principle of 'humanity' was then central to the political philosophy of Thomas Hobbes, who argued that government was established in order to preserve human life by ending the 'war of all against all' that characterized the state of nature.

---

[24] Paul Rahe, *Republics Ancient and Modern: Classical Republicanism and the American Revolution* (Chapel Hill, 1992), pp. 410–22.

Rahe has argued that Harrington accepted Hobbes's basic premises, but whereas Hobbes had claimed that only an absolute monarchy—Leviathan—was capable of producing the order on which security and hence human life depended, Harrington set out in *The Commonwealth of Oceana* to argue that a republican constitution was also capable of delivering this goal. After Harrington, the principle of 'humanity' was also accepted by John Locke (who similarly made the preservation of human life his chief moral and political imperative), and, despite their classical rhetoric, by those Pocock had termed 'neo-Harringtonians'. Court apologists, responding to 'country' polemics, also based their arguments on similar premises, leading Rahe to claim that the principle of 'humanity' became the dominant orthodoxy among the political nation of Great Britain during this period.[25] In line with Rahe's argument, Shelly Burtt has also argued that the concept of virtue in early eighteenth-century English political thought was transformed, with both court apologists and their opponents arguing that it was possible for an individual to act virtuously but to do so for 'private' reasons such as a concern for the happiness and security of the individual, rather than out of 'public spirit'.[26] The adoption of the principle of 'humanity' could also be seen as having encouraged the development later in the eighteenth century of the idea of 'politeness' as a set of rules according to which fundamentally self-interested individuals could still live together harmoniously in society.[27] The invention of 'politeness' was also accompanied both by a gradual shift in the use of classical examples in British political discourse, with the austere virtuous Cato being gradually displaced as a political hero by the more pragmatic figure of Cicero, and by increasing rejection of self-sacrificing classical virtue as barbaric, rather than civilized.[28]

Finally, over the course of the eighteenth century, the focus on material well-being and the idea that self-interest could be harnessed for the well-being of all would be key to the emerging discipline of political

[25] Rahe, *Republics Ancient and Modern*, pp. 409–37.

[26] Shelly Burtt, *Virtue Transformed: Political Argument in England, 1688–1740* (Cambridge, 1992).

[27] Rahe, *Republics Ancient and Modern*, p. 321. See also Nicholas Phillipson, 'Politeness and Politics in the Reigns of Anne and the Early Hanoverians', in J. G. A. Pocock (ed.), *The Varieties of British Political Thought, 1500–1800* (Cambridge, 1993), pp. 211–45; Laurence Klein, *Shaftesbury and the Culture of Politeness: Moral Discourses and Cultural Politics in Early Eighteenth-Century England* (Cambridge, 1994); Philip Carter, *Men and the Emergence of Polite Society: Britain, 1660–1800* (Harlow, 2001); and Iain Hampsher-Monk, 'From Virtue to Politeness', in van Gelderen and Skinner (eds.), *Republicanism*, vol. 2, pp. 85–106.

[28] Reed Browning, *Political and Constitutional Ideas of the Court Whigs* (Baton Rouge, 1982). See also Rahe, *Republics Ancient and Modern*, pp. 269f., and 'Antiquity Surpassed: The Repudiation of Classical Republicanism', in Wootton (ed.), *Republicanism, Liberty and Commercial Society*, pp. 233–69.

economy. The claim that individual selfishness could yield common prosperity, while austerity would conversely only produce general poverty was central to Bernard Mandeville's 1714 pamphlet *The Fable of the Bees*, and would be most famously articulated in Adam Smith's dictum that 'it is not from the benevolence of the butcher, the brewer, or the baker that we expect our dinner, but from their regard to their own self-interest'.[29]

In contrast with these developments in English/British political (and political economic) thought, there is very little evidence of any similar evolution in szlachta republicanism. Rather, as discussed in earlier chapters, szlachta political writers and commentators continued to argue that the preservation of virtue was essential to good government, whose ultimate goal was moral rather than material. Szlachta politicians also continued to demand that private interests always be subordinated to the common good, as well as to proclaim their willingness to sacrifice even their very lives to that cause.[30] Thus despite the apparent similarities between English/British and szlachta republicanism in this period, over the course of the late seventeenth and eighteenth centuries a wide gulf gradually opened up between the intellectual foundations of the two traditions.

THE GODLY COMMONWEALTH?

Ironically, perhaps, the part of Great Britain where the influence on republican thought of classical ideas of virtue persisted the longest may have been Adam Smith's native Scotland. Allan Macinnes has argued that in the late seventeenth and early eighteenth centuries, much closer parallels can be seen between the szlachta republican tradition and its contemporary Scottish counterpart than with republicanism south of the border in England. In particular, Macinnes has argued that in Scotland, as in Poland-Lithuania, the concept of the 'commonwealth' was articulated more in opposition to the monarchy than in England, where it 'was applied to celebrate the harmonious operation of a mixed monarchy . . . where sovereignty was exercised by the king or queen in parliament'.[31]

---

[29] Bernard Mandeville, *The Fable of the Bees: or, Private Vices, Public Benefits*, (London, 1714). Adam Smith, *An Inquiry into the Nature and Causes of the Wealth of Nations* (London, 1776).

[30] Lukowski, 'The Szlachta and their Ancestors'.

[31] Macinnes, 'The Hidden Commonwealth'. The opposition between monarchy and 'commonwealth' should not be over-emphasized in the case of Poland-Lithuania, as the king was himself one of the three estates that together constituted the Rzeczpospolita (a point that Augustus II's representatives negotiating with the Tarnogród Confederates attempted to use to challenge the legitimacy of the Confederates claim to represent the Commonwealth, as discussed in Chapter 6 above). By the beginning of the eighteenth century, however, the perceived threat to the Commonwealth and to szlachta liberty from the monarchy undermined

Macinnes has ascribed the difference in this regard between the English and Scottish conceptions of the 'commonwealth' to the two kingdoms' different experiences of the Reformation. Whereas in England, the Reformation was largely driven by the crown, in Scotland Protestantism was introduced in defiance of the monarchy, which resulted in Scottish political thinkers articulating to a much greater extent than their English counterparts 'the commonwealth's right to resist an ungodly monarch'. Macinnes has compared Scottish thinkers' claim to a right of resistance to the szlachta's right *de non praestanda obedientia* to withdraw their allegiance from a king who violated their laws and liberties.[32]

In Scotland, the conception of the 'commonwealth' as separate from the monarchy, and superior at least to an ungodly monarch was central to the mid-seventeenth-century Covenanting Movement, which overthrew the rule of King Charles I in both Kirk and state, and established a new government which demanded loyalty to the commonwealth and the National Covenant, rather than the king.[33] Macinnes and John Young have argued that this conception of the 'commonwealth' as distinct from and superior to the monarchy persisted well beyond the Restoration of King Charles II in 1660 and into the early eighteenth century. In particular, Young has emphasized the 'covenanting heritage' of the group of radical politicians known as the 'Club' who in the aftermath of the 1688 Glorious Revolution sought a series of constitutional reforms aimed at restricting the powers of the monarchy, such as the passage of a Triennial Act to protect the Scottish Parliament against royal influence, an increase in parliamentary representation for the shires, and the abolition of the Lords of Articles, a committee appointed by the crown to control the agenda of each parliamentary session. The 'Club's covenanting heritage was further displayed in their assertion that King James VII had not abandoned his throne (as his English subjects maintained) but had "forfeited" the crown as a result of his misrule, and that the 1689 Parliament, though not summoned by the king, was nevertheless a "free" and "lawful meeting of the Estates" '.[34]

---

the idea of the Commonwealth as a partnership of the three estates, and encouraged a conception of the Commonwealth in opposition to the monarchy (or needing to be preserved against the incursions of the monarchy), for example by the Tarnogród Confederates.

[32] Macinnes, 'The Hidden Commonwealth'. See also Roger Mason, *Kingship and the Commonweal: Political Thought in Renaissance and Reformation Scotland* (East Linton, 1998); Allan Macinnes and Jane Ohlmeyer (eds.), *The Stuart Kingdoms in the Seventeenth Century: Awkward Neighbours* (Dublin, 2002); and Allan Macinnes, *The British Revolution, 1629–1660* (Basingstoke, 2005).

[33] For example, in 1640 the Covenanting government redefined the crime of treason as betrayal of the Covenant, not of the king. Macinnes, *The British Revolution*, p. 129.

[34] John Young, 'The Scottish Parliament and the Covenanting Heritage of Constitutional Reform', in Macinnes and Ohlmeyer (eds.), *The Stuart Kingdoms*, pp. 226–50.

Young and John Robertson have similarly noted the Covenanting heritage of the group of Scottish radicals in the early eighteenth century led by the republican writer Andrew Fletcher of Saltoun, who in 1703 and 1704 attempted to pass legislation imposing further limitations on the powers of the monarchy. Under this legislation, the monarch's power to prorogue Parliament would be abolished and all crown placemen were to be excluded, while in future Parliament, not the crown, would have the power to appoint public officials. Should the monarch fail to abide by these restrictions, he or she would be deemed to have forfeited the crown.[35]

At the same time, the Scottish Parliament agreed an Act Anent Peace and War that banned future monarchs from declaring war, making peace, or entering into any diplomatic or commercial treaties without the consent of Parliament, and an Act of Security that reserved for the Scottish Parliament the right to elect a Protestant successor to Queen Anne from the Stuart dynasty unless 'there be such condicions of government settled and enacted, as may secure the honour and soveraignty of this Crown and Kingdom, the freedom frequency and power of Parliaments . . . with power [being given] to the said meeting of [Parliament] to add such further condicions of government as they shall think necessary'.[36]

Like those sought by English 'country' politicians, these proposed restrictions on the powers of the crown were similar in direction, if not extent, to those that applied to the kings of Poland-Lithuania. Arguably, these attempts to restrict the powers of the monarchy should be seen primarily in the context of the anticipated childless death of Queen Anne, and the debate on Union with England. A key objective of this package of reforms was to limit the powers of a future 'foreign' monarch and thus ensure that Scotland was governed according to its own interests and not those of England or any foreign dynasty. At the same time, however, Scottish constitutional radicalism in the late seventeenth and early eighteenth centuries remained firmly rooted in the ideas of the Covenanting Movement, whose primary desire was to establish and preserve a godly (Calvinist) commonwealth. Macinnes has noted that, in line with these Covenanting roots, one of the chief aims of the early eighteenth-century radicals was to 'promote the probity and accountability' of government.

[35] John Robertson, 'Introduction' to Andrew Fletcher, *Political Works* (ed. John Robertson, Cambridge, 1997), p. xxv. Young, 'The Scottish Parliament and the Covenanting Heritage', p. 244.
[36] Quoted in William Dickinson, Gordon Donaldson, and Isabel Milne (eds.), *A Source Book of Scottish History* (3 vols., Edinburgh, 1954), vol. 3, pp. 472–7.

Robertson has similarly argued that Andrew Fletcher was profoundly concerned with promoting virtue among the citizens as the best means of resisting royal tyranny. Perhaps most notably, Fletcher argued for the establishment of a citizens' militia whose Spartan training regimen was to be 'a right method for disposing the minds of men, as well as forming their bodies, for military and virtuous actions'.[37]

So unlike the English republican tradition, which had come to accept the fallibility of human nature and to look to 'political architecture' as the basis for good government, Scottish republicanism in the early eighteenth century retained a strong preoccupation with maintaining the character and virtue of the citizens, to ensure that government remained in the hands of worthy men. Although its moral base was Calvinist rather than classical, Scottish republicanism in the early eighteenth century was, like its szlachta counterpart, to a large extent a moral enterprise.

This similarity between Scottish and szlachta republicanism did not, however, persist long into the eighteenth century. In practical politics, the Covenanting tradition in Scotland was largely brought to an end by the Union of 1707, which established London as the primary centre of political activity for the whole of Great Britain, and led to an increasing number of Scots adopting a new British, rather than specifically Scottish, identity. In this context, the English concept of the 'commonwealth' largely prevailed.[38]

Meanwhile the ascetic ideal of civic virtue endorsed by Fletcher was increasingly challenged by the growing prosperity of Great Britain's commercial economy, and the ever-greater opportunities for luxury that ensued. As Robertson has shown, these were developments that Fletcher, a devotee of refined urban living even while preaching the austere virtues of the militia training camp, was well aware of, and yet struggled to reconcile with his 'ancient', virtue-based republican political ideas. Eventually, the self-sacrificing virtue of classical republicanism was to be decisively rejected in favour of the material opportunities offered by the modern commercial economy by the leading figures of the Scottish Enlightenment, in particular David Hume and Adam Smith. Like its English counterpart, the Scottish political tradition eventually rejected the republicanism of the ancients, and its moralistic preoccupation with preserving civic virtue in order to ensure good government.

---

[37] Fletcher, *Discourse of Government with relation to Militia's* (1698) in Fletcher, *Political Works*, p. 24. See also Robertson, 'Introduction' in Fletcher, *Political Works*, p. xxi.
[38] Kidd, *British Identities before Nationalism*. Young, 'The Scottish Parliament and the Covenanting Heritage', pp. 249–50. See also Macinnes, 'The Hidden Commonwealth'.

UNIQUELY VIRTUOUS?

It is very difficult to detect any comparable shift in szlachta republican thought during this period. In contrast, at the beginning of the eighteenth century, Stanisław Herakliusz Lubomirski was still hoping that good government could be restored through reform of the character and behaviour of those in power, just as Łukasz Opaliński had some 60 years before. Similarly, the calls from the sejmiki throughout this period for only worthy men to be appointed to high office presumed that such worthy men could be found to act as the basis for a virtuous government. They did not call for the creation of structures that would induce even bad men to act in the common interest.

Even those in the early eighteenth century who did propose constitutional reform did not adopt 'political architecture' as their method. Rather, the aim of radicals such as Stanisław Dunin Karwicki was to construct institutions that would teach men to *be* virtuous, not simply to incentivize them to act *as if they were so*. The radicals' proposals presumed that the szlachta citizenry could be educated to become virtuous: unlike their British contemporaries, they did not accept that all men were inherently selfish.

One specific contrast neatly illustrates the gulf in assumptions between szlachta republicans and their English/British contemporaries. The *Eclipsis Poloniae* proposed the establishment of a postal service to provide every szlachcic with accurate information on public business and the state of the Commonwealth and the wider world. Armed with this information, the szlachta would be able to discuss any matters of policy and collectively agree on what course of action would serve the common good. In *The Commonwealth of Oceana*, however, Harrington proposed that the Senate be silent, able to vote but not debate on any decisions. Harrington claimed that debate would only lead to faction and civil strife, as a result of men's ambition and fractiousness. The *Eclipsis Poloniae* by contrast presumed that informed discussion could lead to consensus, given men's ability to use their reason to seek out what was right and good.

As the eighteenth century progressed, there is little evidence that this presumption changed. Grześkowiak-Krwawicz has shown how throughout the eighteenth century szlachta writers and politicians remained intensely concerned with the moral character of their fellow citizens. Hence their particular interest in the appropriate education for future generations of citizens. This concern with civic virtue was also shared by reformers later in the eighteenth century. For example even Stanisław Konarski (1700–73) the Piarist priest and political and educational reformer, whom Lukowski has described as an arch-realist in his analysis of the Commonwealth and its citizens, was in designing the curriculum for his new 'Noble Academy' (*Collegium Nobilium*) deeply concerned with moulding the characters of his students and instilling in them a love of their fatherland and the common good.[39]

The szlachta republican tradition was thus marked out from other contemporary European republicanisms by its retention of classical ideas about virtue as both the foundation and the objective of good government. While elsewhere in Europe republican writers gradually accepted as unchangeable the basic fallibility of human nature, and responded by turning to 'political architecture' and attempting to construct laws and institutions that would make it in individuals' selfish interests to act for the common good, szlachta republicans retained a focus on preserving the moral character of the citizenry, presuming that individuals could be virtuous, and attempting to find ways to make them be so, and to maintain good government by ensuring that only good men occupied positions of power. Szlachta republicanism's continuing concern with preserving civic virtue was thus its distinctive feature.

[39] Lukowski, *Disorderly Liberty*, pp. 77–97. Grześkowiak-Krwawicz, *Regina Libertas*, pp. 269–77. Rose, *Stanislas Konarski*.

Conclusion

THE POLITY OF VIRTUE?

Throughout the early modern period, a central feature of the szlachta political tradition was its continuing preoccupation with the concept of virtue, understood as the sacrifice by individuals and groups of their private interests to the common good. From at least Modrzewski in the mid-sixteenth century, szlachta political thinkers approached their Commonwealth as a fundamentally moral enterprise, a polity established not for a material purpose, such as the preservation of life or property, but for a moral one, that of living virtuously according to the public interest. As classical authors such as Aristotle and Cicero had argued, only thus could men realize their natures as political, rather than solitary, beings.

This moral perspective was not confined to the realm of abstract political theory. Rather, as the turbulent early years of the reign of Augustus II illustrate, for szlachta politicians and commentators it was an indispensable analytical tool for understanding the Commonwealth and its actual condition, and for interpreting the disorder and disarray into which by the turn of the eighteenth century a wide range of contemporary observers agreed the szlachta state had fallen. With virtue at the centre of their analysis, szlachta writers and political activists identified the dysfunction of the Commonwealth as rooted in the moral failings of its citizens, and especially those occupying positions of power, who had abandoned the common good in favour of their private interests in accumulating greater personal wealth or power. From this it followed that the solution to the Commonwealth's problems was a moral one: a revival of virtue among the citizenry as a whole, but especially those in government.

This focus on the moral qualities of citizens and rulers was not merely an evasion of the challenges facing the szlachta state, or a rhetorical cover for opposition to any change in its form of government. Admittedly, some szlachta politicians and commentators at the turn of the eighteenth century, such as Stanisław Herakliusz Lubomirski, did indeed restrict themselves to calling for reform only of the intentions and behaviours of those in power. Others, however, during this 'reforming moment' offered a variety of different proposals for constitutional reform to restore virtuous government, ranging from grassroots efforts to build a government of worthy men at the local level, to attempts to institutionalize greater accountability for ministers, to the blueprint for comprehensive reform produced by Stanisław Dunin Karwicki.

These attempts at reform at the beginning of the eighteenth century largely failed. This failure was not only due to innate conservatism on the part of the szlachta, or foreign intervention, but at least in part the result of tension and conflict between different programmes for reform, including the monarchical model pursued by the king. Ironically, therefore, it could be argued that the Commonwealth's failure to reform in this period was the result not of too little reforming energy, but too much. It is impossible to know whether reform might have succeeded in the absence of this division between rival agendas for change. The widespread agreement on the need for reform, however, suggests that some potential for success existed, had the szlachta been able to unite behind a single programme for reform.

The continuing concern with virtue was also one of the distinctive features of the early modern szlachta political tradition. Elsewhere in Europe, during the seventeenth and in particular the eighteenth century, republican political thinkers increasingly rejected the propositions that virtuous living was the ultimate purpose of political society, and that the survival of a commonwealth depended on the maintenance of virtue among rulers and citizens. Rather, they began to see the preservation of life and the promotion of material prosperity as the objective of government, and to accept private self-interest as a natural characteristic of humanity, and one that could be harnessed for the well-being of all. The task of the lawgiver was therefore not to suppress self-interest, but to channel it as a positive social, political, and economic force. This was to be achieved through 'political architecture', that is, the construction of laws and institutions that would incentivize selfish individuals to act for the good of all, not out of regard for the common good but because such behaviour was also in the individuals' private interests. By the end of the eighteenth century, this approach was perhaps most clearly expressed in the political sphere in James Madison's advocacy of a constitution in which 'Ambition must be made to counteract ambition' and the competition between multiple private (or factional) interests would check each one and thus produce government in the public interest. In political economy, Adam Smith similarly argued that individuals' pursuit of their private interests could, in the right institutional and market context, lead to general prosperity.[1]

---

[1] James Madison, *The Federalist* 51 (ed. William Brock, London, 2000, pp. 265–9). Adam Smith, *An Inquiry into the Nature and Causes of the Wealth of Nations* (London, 1776).

Resonances of 'ancient' ideas about virtue can also be seen in modern political and social science. In recent decades, alongside the analysis of institutions and incentives that is the modern heir to Harrington's art of 'political architecture', political and social science, in particular the study of 'civil society', has increasingly emphasized the importance of citizens' values and behaviours for the maintenance of democracy. Citizens, it has been argued, must actively participate in the political process, and keep governments under constant scrutiny to prevent their capture by special (or particular) interests. They must also respect the boundaries imposed by the democratic political process, such as accepting the legitimacy of election results and of decisions made or legislation passed according to established constitutional rules, while still respecting the rights of minorities and dissenters. In the words of one commentator:

> democracies need citizens. Citizens are not only people who engage in public life, though they are also that. Above all, citizens accept that their loyalty to the processes they share must override loyalty to their own political side. Citizens understand the idea of a 'loyal opposition'. They accept the legitimacy of government run by and even for their opponents, confident that they may have their own turn in time. Citizens, it follows, do not use the political process to destroy the ability of their opponents to operate in peace.

At the same time, those in government must also accept the limits set on their own power, not least the requirement that they leave office at the end of their terms.[8]

It is thus argued that democratic political systems cannot be maintained without a common acceptance of certain norms of behaviour by citizens and rulers. In a similar vein, modern economic thought has recognized that functioning markets also depend on common standards of behaviour among participants, such as fair dealing and abiding by agreed terms of trade, and mutual trust that these standards will be generally adhered to.

---

example the argument that its commitment to participation and consensus makes effective decision-making impossible, or that beyond a general dissatisfaction with contemporary social and political order, it lacks specific aims or a clear vision of the new society it wishes to create, also have parallels with criticisms of the Polish-Lithuanian Commonwealth.

[8] Gabriel Almond and Sidney Verba, *The Civic Culture: Political Attitudes and Democracy in Five Nations* (Princeton, 1963). Robert Putnam, 'Bowling Alone: America's Declining Social Capital', *Journal of Democracy*, 6, 1 (1995), pp. 65–78. Jane Jacobs, *Systems of Survival: A Dialogue on the Moral Foundations of Politics and Commerce* (New York, 1992). Quotation from Martin Wolf, 'There is No Easy Path to Democracy', *Financial Times*, 4 March 2014.

Low levels of trust can prevent trades that would otherwise be mutually profitable, and thus inhibit economic growth and prosperity.[9]

So even modern political and economic systems whose design is informed by the assumption that individuals will naturally tend to follow their selfish interests depend on all (or at least an overwhelming majority of) agents acknowledging a common interest in preserving the system itself and acting according to its rules—even when it might be in individual agents' private interests to cheat. Or as a szlachta commentator might have put it, all commonwealths depend on some degree of virtue among their citizens.

This would imply that the early modern Polish-Lithuanian Commonwealth was not unique in demanding that its citizens and rulers subordinate their private interests to a common good and adhere to a common set of values and behaviours. Rather, it was distinctive in the degree to which it demanded, and depended upon, virtue from its citizens. In particular, the Commonwealth's constitution required an unusual degree of consensus among citizens for its government to function effectively. The Commonwealth was also unusual in the extent to which it lacked effective mechanisms to sanction individuals who failed to display sufficient virtue. At the same time, it is striking that the Commonwealth's political discourse drew little distinction between what might today be termed 'constitutional' and 'political' issues, and between disputes over the right process for making policy decisions and disputes over the policy decisions themselves. Perhaps as a result, the Commonwealth never developed a concept of the 'loyal opposition' who disagreed over what policy to pursue, while still upholding the basic tenets of the szlachta state's constitution. On the contrary, the common good that virtuous citizens were required to pursue was usually presented in the singular, and it was assumed, for example by the *Eclipsis Poloniae*, that if only the szlachta could set aside private interests and deliberate rationally they would all agree over what course to adopt: from which it followed that dissenters must be self-interested, corrupt, and potentially a threat to the Commonwealth itself. This attitude was particularly applied to the policies of the Commonwealth's kings, which by the early eighteenth century were virtually all interpreted by szlachta commentators from a constitutional perspective, as part of an 'absolutist' plot to undermine the Commonwealth's traditional laws and liberties (sometimes with good reason).

---

[9] Francis Fukuyama, *Trust: The Social Virtues and the Creation of Prosperity* (London, 1996). Paul Zak and Stephen Knack, 'Trust and Growth', *The Economic Journal*, 111 (2001), pp. 295–321.

The Commonwealth's political system was thus unusually dependent upon mutual trust between rulers and citizens to function effectively. The extended political crisis of the late seventeenth and early eighteenth centuries can therefore be seen as the result of a breakdown of that trust, which was arguably only restored (if at all) at the very end of the Commonwealth's existence. The szlachta state's experience of protracted political paralysis thus illustrates the risks and vulnerabilities facing political systems with weak institutions that are over-reliant upon mutual trust. The Commonwealth was not, however, unique in this vulnerability: arguably, recent experience of bitter partisanship and political deadlock in the United States, including the repeated failures of the different parts of its government to agree budgets, pass major legislation, or make senior public appointments, shows how even a political system based on carefully designed 'political architecture' is, in the absence of a certain degree of mutual trust and co-operation, at risk of lapsing into dysfunction. In its dependence on the common acceptance of a set of shared values, that is on virtue and mutual trust, the Commonwealth was therefore an outlier, but not a case *sui generis*.

Chronological Table of Key Events

1674–96	Reign of King Jan III Sobieski.
17 June 1696	Death of Jan III Sobieski.
26 June 1697	Rival elections of Prince François de Conti of France and Elector Friedrich August of Saxony as king.
15 September 1697	Coronation of Friedrich August of Saxony as King Augustus II in Kraków.
9 November 1697	de Conti leaves Commonwealth and returns to France.
14 August 1698	Lithuanian 'Republicans' form Confederation against Sapieha clan.
26 January 1699	Peace of Karlowitz ends war with Ottoman Empire. Commonwealth recovers city of Kamieniec Podolski.
16–30 June 1699	Pacification Sejm. Supporters of de Conti formally accept election of Augustus II.
February 1700	Saxon army invades Swedish Livonia.
17 November 1700	Battle of Olkieniki. Lithuanian 'Republicans' defeat Sapieha forces.
May 1701	Publication of so-called 'Wilno Resolution'.
December 1701	Swedish armies invade Commonwealth.
May 1702	Swedish troops occupy Warsaw.
19 July 1702	Battle of Kliszów. Crushing Swedish victory over Polish and Saxon forces.
19 June–12 July 1703	Extraordinary Sejm meets in Lublin.
16 February 1704	Establishment of Swedish-supported General Confederation of Warsaw in opposition to 'tyranny' of Augustus II. Warsaw Confederates declare Augustus II dethroned.
27 May 1704	Establishment of General Confederation of Sandomierz in support of Augustus II against Sweden.
12 July 1704	Swedish-promoted election of Stanisław Leszczyński as king.
August–September 1706	Swedish armies invade Saxony.
24 September 1706	Treaty of Altranstädt. Augustus II forced to abdicate as King of Poland.
8 July 1707	Sandomierz Confederation declares interregnum.

July 1708	Swedish armies invade Russia.
8 July 1709	Battle of Poltava. Swedish armies defeated by Russian forces. Charles XII of Sweden flees to Bender in Ottoman territory.
August 1709	Augustus II returns to the Commonwealth.
2 February – 16 April 1710	General Council of Warsaw. Augustus II reaffirmed as lawful King of Poland.
5–19 April 1712	Extraordinary Sejm meets in Warsaw. Sejm session adjourned to reconvene on 31 December 1712.
31 December 1712 – 18 February 1713	Second session of 1712–13 Extraordinary Sejm. Sejm finally broken by supporters of Lithuanian Grand Hetman Ludwik Pociej.
Autumn 1713	Augustus II departs the Commonwealth for Saxony to confer with his closest advisers.
Winter 1713–14	Large numbers of Saxon troops move into Commonwealth.
Summer 1714	Abortive szlachta uprisings against Saxon occupation quickly crushed by Saxon army.
Summer 1715	Renewed szlachta uprisings against Saxon army.
2 October 1715	Crown Army forms Confederation against Saxon occupation. Crown Grand Hetman Adam Sieniawski arrested by Army Confederates.
26 November 1715	Establishment of General Confederation of Tarnogród against Saxon occupation.
January 1716	Treaty of Rawa signed between Saxon army and województwa of Małopolska, but rejected by Tarnogród Confederates.
23 March 1716	Establishment of Lithuanian Confederation against Saxon army. Lithuanian Confederates accept authority of Tarnogród Confederation.
June–November 1716	Negotiations held between Tarnogród Confederates and representatives of Augustus II.
25 July 1716	Lithuanian army rejects authority of Grand Hetman Pociej and forms Confederation against Saxon occupation. Pociej narrowly escapes arrest.
3 November 1716	Treaty of Warsaw agreed between Augustus II and Tarnogród Confederates.
1 February 1717	Treaty of Warsaw ratified by one-day 'Silent Sejm'.
5 January 1719	Augustus II, as Elector of Saxony, signs Treaty of Vienna with Hanover and Habsburg Monarchy, but fails to persuade the Commonwealth to join the treaty.
Summer 1719	Russian troops withdraw from Commonwealth.
30 August 1721	Treaty of Nystad formally ends Great Northern War.
1 February 1733	Death of Augustus II.

Note on Names and Glossary of Polish Terms

NOTE ON PERSONAL AND PLACE NAMES

For the sake of consistency, throughout this study personal names have been rendered in the primary language of the individual concerned, with the exception of the regnal names of monarchs, which have generally been Anglicized.

Historical names of places within the borders of the Commonwealth have been given in their modern Polish forms (e.g. Lwów, Gdańsk, and Wilno not Lviv, Danzig, and Vilnius), except here familiar English forms are available (e.g. Warsaw).

In references to modern places (for example when referring to places of publication), present modern names have, with the exception of Warsaw, usually been preferred.

GLOSSARY OF POLISH TERMS

Below is a short glossary of the key Polish terms for the key offices and institutions of the early modern Commonwealth. Throughout this study institutional terms are rendered in their modern Polish spelling (e.g. Sejm not Seym or Diet and Województwo not Woiewództwo or Palatinate) except when quoted from primary sources.

Castellan (*Kasztelan*)	Originally governors of royal cities, by the eighteenth century Castellans had few administrative responsibilities. Castellans sat *ex officio* in the Senate.
Chamber of Envoys (*Izba Poselska*)	The lower chamber of the Sejm. When (rarely) fully attended, the Chamber was made up of 182 Envoys (*Posłowie*) elected by the Sejmiki of the Crown and the Grand Duchy, along with an indeterminate number of envoys from Royal Prussia.
Chancellor (*Kanclerz*)	Ministers responsible for overseeing the activities of the king and counter-signing all royal edicts. In theory the Chancellors (Poland and Lithuania each had a Grand Chancellor and a Vice Chancellor) were also responsible for conducting foreign policy.
Confederation (*Konfederacja*)	A league or union of the *szlachta*, either of a particular region or of the whole Commonwealth (known as a General Confederation). Confederations were temporary, emergency institutions established in response to a particular crisis or threat, either external or internal.

Fiscal Tribunal (*Trybunał Skarbowy*)	Central institution responsible for overseeing the fiscal administration of the Commonwealth, assigning tax quota to particular regions, and judging disputes over tax payments.
Henrician Articles (*Artykuły henrykowskie*)	Set of conditions to which every newly elected king was obliged to agree before his coronation. Named after the first elected king, Henri de Valois (r. 1573), the Henrician Articles were the same for every king and guaranteed the basic constitutional rights of the szlachta. They were supplemented by particular conditions set for individual kings in their *Pacta Conventa*.
Hetman	Commanders-in-chief of the Commonwealth's armies. Poland and Lithuania each had a Grand Hetman and a subordinate Field Hetman. Grand Hetmans were usually succeeded in their office by their Field Hetman.
Komput	The established strength and make-up of the Commonwealth's armies.
Liberum veto	Derived from the principle that all laws must be agreed unanimously, the right of any individual Sejm Envoy to veto any proposed bill. Since all bills were formally passed in a single package at the very end of a Sejm, a single veto invalidated all of the legislation agreed by a particular Sejm. The *liberum veto* also applied at Sejmiki, where any individual nobleman could block proceedings.
Pacta Conventa	Particular conditions set for each newly elected king and sworn along with the Henrician Articles before his coronation.
Pospolite ruszenie	A general levy of the szlachta, either of a particular region or of the entire Commonwealth. Of little actual military value, the *Pospolite ruszenie* symbolized the szlachta's responsibility to defend the Commonwealth and their willingness to do so even at the cost of their own lives.
Rokosz	Szlachta rebellion against royal authority. Such rebellions usually claimed to be defending szlachta liberty against tyrannical royal ambitions and declared themselves to be Confederations.
Sejm	The Commonwealth's parliament, considered to be made up of three estates: the King, the Senate (chaired by the king), and the Chamber of Envoys.
Sejmik	Local assembly, at which all members of the szlachta could attend.

Senate (*Senat*)	The upper chamber of the Sejm. Chaired by the king, the Senate was made up of the Commonwealth's chief ministers along with the Roman Catholic Bishops, Wojewodas and Castellans.
Senate Council (*Senatus Consilium*)	Council of senators called together to advise the king. The Senate Council, whose membership was largely decided by the king, possessed no legal power to decide government business and could only take interim decisions that had to be ratified by the next Sejm.
Starosta	Originally a royal official in the provinces, by the seventeenth century starostas retained only a few local judicial functions. More importantly, they also controlled portions of royal land, whose revenues they were supposed to pay to the king.
Tribunal (*Trybunał*)	The highest szlachta courts in the Commonwealth (one existed for each of Poland and Lithuania), made up of judges or deputies (*deputaci*) elected by the Sejmiki.
Wojewoda	Originally royal regional governors, by the eighteenth century Wojewodas retained only ceremonial and a few local judicial powers. Wojewodas did, however, sit in the Senate.
Województwo	Principal administrative division of the Commonwealth. In most cases one Sejmik met for each Województwo, but in some regions smaller units such as districts (*ziemie*) or even parishes (*powiaty*) also had their own Sejmiki.

Bibliography

MANUSCRIPT SOURCES

Note: Many of the manuscript sources used here are substantial collections of various documents, which have subsequently been assembled and bound together into large numbered volumes, each of which contains a large number of different documents. These large volumes generally either have no title or else only a vague title (e.g. 'Various Historical Documents from the period 1700–2'). As a result, they will be listed in this bibliography by their manuscript numbers only, with the titles of individual documents (where they exist) being given in footnotes when each document is first referred to.

From the Library of the Princes Czartoryski Foundation (Biblioteka Fundacji im. XX Czartoryskich [Bibl. Czart.]), Kraków:
196, 202, 203, 204, 205, 206, 440, 473, 489, 541, 545, 546, 548, 580, 1164, 1167, 1679, 1682, 2447, 2880, 2881, 2882, 2883, 2884, 3599.

From the Library of the Ossoliński National Foundation/Ossolineum (Biblioteka Zakładu Narodowego im. Ossolińskich/Ossolineum [Bibl. Ossol.]), Wrocław:
233, 271, 701, 2088, 2620, 3345, 3561.

From the Gdańsk State Archive (Archiwum Państwowe w Gdańsku [APG]):
300.29.208.
300, R/Ff, 1.

From the Central State Archive (Archiwum Główne Akt Dawnych [AGAD]), Warsaw:
Archiwum Radziwiłłów [Arch. Radz.] section VI MSS II:36; II:45, II:52, 2305.

From the Kraków State Archive (Archiwum Państwowe w Krakowie [APKr]):
Collection 'Akta grodzkie krakowskie [Castr. Crac.]' MS 761.

From the Library of the Polish Academy of Sciences in Kórnik (Biblioteka Polski Akademii Nauk (PAN) w Kórniku [Bibl. PAN Kórnik]):
409, 434, 1216, 1345, 1767.

From the National Library (Biblioteka Narodowa [BN]), Warsaw:
6650, 6652, 6654, 6668.

Biblioteka Ordinacji Zamoyskiej [BOZ] MS 937.
From the Library of the University of Warsaw (Biblioteka Uniwersytetu Warszawskiego [BUW]):
352.

From the Library of the Polish Academy of Sciences in Kraków (Biblioteka Polski Akademii Nauk (PAN) w Krakowie [Bibl. PAN Krak.]):
The 'Teki Pawińskiego' [TP]—collections of sejmik records assembled in the nineteenth century by Adolf Pawiński:

TP vol. 1 (= Bibl. PAN Krak. MS 8318)

TP vol. 3 (= MS 8320)

TP vol. 4 (= MS 8321)

TP vol. 5 (= MS 8322)

TP vol. 8 (= MS 8325)

TP vol. 9 (= MS 8326)

TP vol. 11 (= MS 8328)

TP vol. 12 (= MS 8329)

TP vol. 15 (= MS 8332)

TP vol. 16 (= MS 8333)

TP vol. 17 (= MS 8334)

TP vol. 18 (= MS 8335)

TP vol. 19 (= MS 8336)

TP vol. 20 (= MS 8337)

TP vol. 21 (= MS 8338)

TP vol. 22 (= MS 8339)

TP vol. 23 (= MS 8340)

TP vol. 26 (= MS 8343)

TP vol. 27 (= MS 8344)

TP vol. 29 (= MS 8346)

TP vol. 30 (= MS 8347)

TP vol. 31 (= MS 8348)

TP vol. 32 (= MS 8349)

TP vol. 33 (= MS 8350)

TP vol. 34 (= MS 8351)

TP vol. 35 (= MS 8352)

TP vol. 36 (= MS 8353)

TP vol. 37 (= MS 8354)

TP vol. 38 (= MS 8355)

TP vol. 39 (= MS 8356)

PRINTED SOURCES

Anglipoloski [= Defoe, Daniel], *The Dyet of Poland, A Satyr* (London, 1705).

Aristotle, *The Politics* and *The Constitution of Athens* (ed. Stephen Everson, Cambridge, 1996).

Bobrzyński, Michał, *Dzieje Polski w zarysie* (Kraków, 1879).

Candidus Veronensis [pseud.], *Eclipsis Poloniae Orbi Publico Demonstrata* (1709).

Censura Pewnego Republikanta na dwa uszczypliwe Manifesty Strony Przeciwney, raz w Brzesciu Litewskim die 11 Julij, drugi raz w Tykocinie die 11 Octobris 1705 zaniesione (1705).

Cicero, *The Republic* and *The Laws* (trans. Niall Rudd, Oxford, 1998).

Confutatio Manifesti a D. Leduchowski vulgati. Die 27 Janurarij Anno 1716 (1716).

Considerationes Circa Electionem futuri Regnantis (1697).

Copia Listu od Szlachcica do znaiomego swego pisanego (1710).

Dębiński, Jan, *Rozne mowy publiczne, seymikowe, y seymowe* (Częstochowa, 1727).

Dickinson, William, Donaldson, Gordon, and Milne, Isabel (eds.), *A Source Book of Scottish History* (3 vols., Edinburgh, 1954).

Dzieduszycki, Jerzy, *Traktat o elekcyi królów polskich* (1707) (ed. Teodor Wierzbowski, Warsaw, 1906).

Fletcher, Andrew, *Political Works* (ed. John Robertson, Cambridge, 1997).

Fredro, Andrzej Maksymilian, *Gestorum Populi Poloni sub Henrico Valesio, Polonorum, postea vero Galliae Rege* (2nd edition, Gdańsk, 1660).

Fredro, Andrzej Maksymilian, *Scriptorum Seu Togae & Belli Notationum Fragmenta Accesserunt Peristromata Regum Symbolis expressa* (Gdańsk, 1660).

Gierowski, Józef (ed.), *Rzeczpospolita w dobie upadku 1700–1740: Wybór źródeł* (Wrocław, 1955).

Gordon, Thomas and Trenchard, John, *Cato's Letter: or Essays on Liberty, Civil and Religious, And other Important Subjects* (London, 1720–3) (ed. Ronald Hamowy, Indianapolis, IN, 1995).

Hamilton, Alexander, Jay, John, and Madison, James, *The Federalist or, The New Constitution* (ed. William Brock, London, 2000).

Hejnosz, Wojciech (ed.), *Akta Grodzkie i Ziemskie z Archiwum Państwowego we Lwowie* (vol. 25, Lwów, 1935).

Karwicki, Stanisław Dunin, *De Ordinanda Republica seu de corrigendis defectibus in statu Reipublicae Polonae* (c.1705), in *Stanisław Dunin Karwicki: dzieła polityczne z początku XVIII wieku* (ed. and trans. (into Polish) Adam Przyboś and Kazimierz Przyboś, Wrocław, 1992).

Kluczycki, Franciszek (ed.), *Lauda Sejmików Ziemi Dobrzyńskiej* (Kraków, 1887).

Kołudzki, Augustyn, *Thron oyczysty albo Pałac wiecznosci w krotkim zebraniu Monarchow, Xiążąt y Krolow Polskich* (Poznań, 1727).

Konfederacya Generalna Nierozdzielnie Całey Prowincyey Wielkiego Księstwa Litewskiego z Woyskiem, zgodnie od Woiewodztw, Ziem, y Powiatow Uczyniona w Wilnie Anno Domini 1716. Mśca Marca dnia 23 (Wilno, 1716).

Krzywda nad wszystkie krzywdy niesprawiedliwosc nad wszystkie niesprawiedliwosci zgorszeni nad wszystkie zgorszenia hiberna w Polszcze (1712).

Kutrzeba, Stanisław and Przyboś, Adam (eds.), *Akta sejmikowe województwa kra-kowskiego* (5 vols., Kraków and Wrocław, 1932–84).

Lettre d'un gentil homme Polonois a un de ses amis, sur l'état present de la Pologne (Cologne, 1704).

Lettre d'un Gentilhomme Polonois à un Gentilhomme de ses amis de la même Nation, sur le sejour des Troupes Saxones en Pologne (c.1713).

List Szlachcica Polskiego do Confidenta (1711).

List Szlachcica Polskiego, do swego Konfidenta w Litwie mieszkaiącego, z pod Warszawy (Warsaw, 1716).

Lubomirski, Stanisław Herakliusz, *De Vanitate Consiliorum Liber Unus* (Warsaw, 1700).

Milton, John, *A Declaration, or Letters Patents of the Election of this Present King of Poland John the Third* (July 1674), in *Complete Prose Works* (8 vols., New Haven, CT, 1982), vol. 7, pp. 441–53.

Modrzewski, Andrzej Frycz, *De Emendanda Republica* (1551–9), in *Andreae Fricii Modrevii Opera Omnia* (ed. Kazimierz Kumaniecki, 3 vols., Warsaw, 1953).

Molesworth, Robert 1st Viscount, *An Account of Denmark as It Was in the Year 1692* (London, 1694).

Nobilis Poloni Epistola ad Amicum Varsaviae commorantem, Qua literi Czari Moscoviae Ad Foederatos Reipublicae Ordines respondetur (1705).

Opaliński, Łukasz, *Rozmowa Plebana z Ziemianinem* (1641), in *Łukasz Opaliński: Wybór pism* (ed. Stanisław Grzeszczuk, Wrocław, 1959).

Petrycy, Sebastian, *Przydatki do Polityki Aristotelesowej* (1605), in *Pisma Wybrane* (ed. Wiktor Wąsik, 2 vols., Kraków, 1956), vol. 2.

Potulicki, Jan Jakub [pseud.? = Poniński, Franciszek], *Historya o Rewolucyi Krolestw Szwedzkiego y Duńskiego Po Polsku Wylozona* (1701).

Prochaska, Antoni (ed.), *Akta Grodzkie i Ziemskie z Archiwum Państwowego we Lwowie* (vol. 20, Lwów, 1909–14).

Przebendowski, Piotr, *Mémoires sur les dernières Revolutions de la Pologne où on justifie le Retour du Auguste, par un gentilhomme polonnois* (Amsterdam, 1710).

Racyński, Edward (ed.), *Dziennik konfederacyi tarnogrodzkiej przeciw wojskom saskim zawiązany w Polsce, 1715–1717 r. Wydany z rękopismu współczesnego w Bibliotece Publicznej w Poznaniu znajdującego się* (Poznań, 1841).

Reflexya Iednego Senatora Koronnego Na zgromadzenie y Postanowienie Niektorych W. X. L. Woiewodztw y Powiatow Pod Grodnem miane, y Odprawione (1699).

Reflexya pewnego ziemianina na seymiki (1705).

Respons Szlachcica Pewnego Na Manifest Pseudo-Principis J. W. I. M. P. Woiewody Poznanskiego (1704).

Sapieha, Jan, *Mowa Jasnie Wielmożnego Imci Pana JANA SAPIEHI, Kasztelana Trockiego, Starosty Brzeskckiego delegowanego, do J. K. Mci od Trybunału Skarbowego, Prowincyi W. X. L. Miana na publiczney Audyencyi w Dreznie Die 2 Novemb: 1717* (1717).

Smith, Adam, *An Inquiry into the Nature and Causes of the Wealth of Nations* (London, 1776).

Smolarek, Przemysław (ed.), *Diariusz Sejmu Walnego 1701–1702* (Warsaw, 1962).

Szujski, Józef, *Dzieje Polski według ostatnich badań* (Lwów, 1866).

Szujski, Józef, *Historii polskiej treściwie opowiedzanej ksiąg dwanaście* (Kraków, 1880).

Volumina Legum: Przedruk zbioru praw (11 vols., St Petersburg and Kraków, 1859–89, reprinted Warsaw, 1980).

Węgierski, Andrzej, *Classicum Wolnosci Polskiey. w Ruinie Oyczyzny, na odgłos lamentuiącego Ubostwa Otrąbione Niedostrzymaniem poprzysięzonych Paktow Oliwskich, przez KAROLA XII Krola Szwedzkiego, złamaney Wiary. stwierdzone* (1703).

Załuski, Andrzej, *Mowy seymowe Jaśnie Oświeconego Xiażęcia Biskupa Warminskiego Andrzeia Chryzostoma Na Załuskach y Błędowie Załuskiego Kanclerza Wielkiego Koronnego* (Kalisz, 1734).

Zawisza, Krzysztof, *Pamiętniki Krzysztofa Zawiszy, Wojewody Mińskiego (1661–1721)* (ed. Julian Bartoszewicz, Warsaw, 1862).

SECONDARY LITERATURE

Almond, Gabriel and Verba, Sidney, *The Civic Culture: Political Attitudes and Democracy in Five Nations* (Princeton, 1963).

Bailyn, Bernard, *The Ideological Origins of the American Revolution* (enlarged edition, Cambridge, MA, 1992).

Banning, Lance, *The Jeffersonian Persuasion: Evolution of a Party Ideology* (Ithaca, NY, 1978).

Bardach, Juliusz, 'Czy istniało obywatelstwo w szlacheckiej Rzeczypospolitej?', *Czasopismo Prawno-Historyczne*, 17, 2 (1965), pp. 261–6.

Bardach, Juliusz (ed.), *Historia państwa i prawa Polski*; vol. 2, Zdzisław Kaczmarczyk and Bogusław Leśnodorski (eds.), *Od połowy XV wieku do r. 1795* (Warsaw, 1966).

Barycz, Henryk (ed.), *Sebastian Petrycy: uczony doby Odrozenia* (Wrocław, 1957).

Behrens, B., 'The Whig Theory of the Constitution in the Reign of Charles II', *Historical Journal*, 7, 1 (1941), pp. 42–71.

Bieniarzówna, Janina, 'Projekty reform magnackich w Połowie XVIII wieku (Nowe dążenie ekonomiczne)', *Przegląd Historyczny*, 42 (1951), pp. 304–30.

Bieńkowski, Tadeusz (ed.), *Andrzej Frycz Modrzewski i problemy kultury Polskiego Odrozenia* (Wrocław, 1974).

Biskupski, Mieczysław and Pula, James (eds.), *Polish Democratic Thought from the Renaissance to the Great Emigration: Essays and Documents* (New York, 1990).

Black, Jeremy, *Robert Walpole and the Nature of Politics in Early Eighteenth Century England* (London, 1990).

Bogucka, Maria, *Dzieje Polski do 1795 r.* (Warsaw, 1964).

Bogucka, Maria, *The Lost World of the "Sarmatians": Custom as the Regulator of Polish Social Life in Early Modern Times* (Warsaw, 1996).

Bogucka, Maria, *Dawna Polska: Narodziny, rozkwit, upadek* (Warsaw, 1998).

172 *Bibliography*

Borkowska-Bagieńska, E., 'Nowożytna myśl polityczna w Polsce 1740–1780', in Jacek Staszewski (ed.), *Studia z dziejów Polskiej myśli politycznej IV: od reformy państwa szlacheckiego do myśli o nowoczesnym państwie* (Toruń, 1992), pp. 31–45.

Boulton, James (ed.), *Daniel Defoe* (London, 1965).

Boulton, James, *Arbitrary Power: An Eighteenth-Century Obsession* (Nottingham, 1967).

Browning, Reed, *Political and Constitutional Ideas of the Court Whigs* (Baton Rouge, LA, 1982).

Burtt, Shelly, *Virtue Transformed: Political Argument in England, 1688–1740* (Cambridge, 1992).

Butterwick, Richard, *Poland's Last King and English Culture: Stanisław August Poniatowski, 1721–1798* (Oxford, 1998).

Butterwick, Richard (ed.), *The Polish-Lithuanian Monarchy in European Context, c.1500–1795* (Basingstoke, 2001).

Butterwick, Richard, 'Political Discourses of the Polish Revolution, 1788–92', *English Historical Review*, 120, 487 (2005), pp. 695–731.

Carsten, Francis Ludwig, *Princes and Parliaments in Germany from the Fifteenth to the Eighteenth Century* (Oxford, 1959).

Carter, Ian, *A Measure of Freedom* (Oxford, 1999).

Carter, Philip, *Men and the Emergence of Polite Society: Britain, 1660–1800* (Harlow, 2001).

Choińska-Mika, Jolanta, *Sejmiki mazowieckie w dobie Wasów* (Warsaw, 1998).

Choińska-Mika, Jolanta, *Między społeczeństwem szlacheckim a władzą: problemy komunikacji społeczności lokalne władza w epoce Jana Kazimierza* (Warsaw, 2002).

Choińska-Mika, Jolanta, 'Dwa parlamenty nowożytne—polski i angielski (wieki XVI i XVII)', in Janusz Ekes (ed.), *Dziedzictwo Pierwszej Rzeczypospolitej w doświadczeniu politycznym Polski i Europy* (Nowy Sącz, 2005), pp. 39–53.

Choinska-Mika, Jolanta and Dean, David, 'Representation and Accountability: A Comparison of Early Modern England and Poland', *Parliaments, Estates & Representation*, 21 (2001), pp. 91–101.

Clark, Christopher, *Iron Kingdom: The Rise and Downfall of Prussia* (London, 2006).

Clark, Jonathan, *English Society, 1660–1832: Religion, Ideology and Politics during the Ancien Régime* (2nd edition, Cambridge, 2000).

Collini, Stefan, *Matthew Arnold: A Critical Portrait* (Oxford, 1994).

Conrads, Norbert, *Ritterakademien der frühen Neuzeit: Bildung als Standesprivileg im 16. und 17. Jahrhundert* (Göttingen, 1982).

Cynarski, Stanisław, 'The Shape of Sarmatian Ideology in Poland', *Acta Poloniae Historica*, 19 (1968), pp. 5–17.

Cynarski, Stanisław, 'Sarmatyzm: ideologia i styl życia', in Janusz Tazbir (ed.), *Polska XVII wieku: Państwo, społeczeństwo, kultura* (Warsaw, 1969), pp. 220–43.

Czapliński, Władysław, *O Polsce siedemnastowiecznej: Problemy i sprawy* (Warsaw, 1966).

Czapliński, Władysław, 'Polish Seym in the Light of Recent Research', *Acta Poloniae Historica*, 22 (1970), pp. 180–92.

Darnton, Robert, *The Forbidden Best-Sellers of Pre-Revolutionary France* (New York, 1995).

Davies, Norman, *God's Playground: A History of Poland* (2 vols., Oxford, 1981).

Dickinson, H., *Liberty and Property: Political Ideology in Eighteenth Century Britain* (London, 1977).

Doyle, William, *The Old European Order, 1660–1800* (Oxford, 1978).

Dworzaczek, Włodzimierz, 'La mobilité sociale de la noblesse polonaise aux XVIe et XVIIe siècles', *Acta Poloniae Historica*, 36 (1977), pp. 147–61.

Dybaś, Bogusław, *Sejm Pacyfikacyjny w 1699 r.* (Toruń, 1991).

Evans, Robert J. W., *Austria, Hungary and the Habsburgs: Essays on Central Europe, c.1683–1867* (Oxford, 2006).

Fedorowicz, Jan (ed.), *A Republic of Nobles: Studies in Polish History to 1864* (Cambridge, 1982).

Feldman, Józef, *Polska w dobie wielkiej wojny północnej 1704–1709* (Kraków, 1925).

Feldman, Józef, *Polska a sprawa wschodnia 1709–1714* (Kraków, 1926).

Feldman, Józef, 'Geneza konfederacji tarnogrodzkiej', *Kwartalnik Historyczny*, 42 (1928), pp. 493–531.

Fiszman, Samuel (ed.), *Constitution and Reform in Eighteenth-Century Poland: The Constitution of 3 May 1791* (Bloomington, IN, 1997).

Friedrich, Karin, *The Other Prussia: Royal Prussia, Poland and Liberty, 1569–1772* (Cambridge, 2000).

Friedrich, Karin and Pendzich, Barbara (eds.), *Citizenship and Identity in a Multinational Commonwealth: Poland-Lithuania in Context, 1550–1772* (Leiden, 2009).

Frost, Robert, '"Liberty without License?" The Failure of Polish Democratic Thought in the Seventeenth Century', in Mieczysław Biskupski and James Pula (eds.), *Polish Democratic Thought from the Renaissance to the Great Emigration: Essays and Documents* (New York, 1990), pp. 29–54,

Frost, Robert, *After the Deluge: Poland-Lithuania and the Second Northern War, 1655–1660* (Cambridge, 1993).

Frost, Robert, 'The Nobility of Poland-Lithuania, 1569–1795', in Hamish Scott (ed.), *The European Nobilities in the Seventeenth and Eighteenth Centuries* (2 vols., London, 1995), vol. 2 (*Northern, Central and Eastern Europe*), pp. 183–222.

Frost, Robert, *The Northern Wars: War, State and Society in Northeastern Europe, 1558–1721* (Harlow, 2000).

Frost, Robert, 'Obsequious Disrespect: The Problem of Royal Power in the Polish-Lithuanian Commonwealth under the Vasas, 1587–1668', in Richard Butterwick (ed.), *The Polish-Lithuanian Monarchy in European Context, c.1500–1795* (Basingstoke, 2001), pp. 150–71.

Frost, Robert, '"Everyone understood what it meant": The Impact of the Battle of Poltava on the Polish-Lithuanian Commonwealth', in Serhii Plokhy (ed.), *Poltava 1709: The Battle and the Myth* (Cambridge, MA, 2012), pp. 159–76.

Fukuyama, Francis, *Trust: The Social Virtues and the Creation of Prosperity* (London, 1996).

Gelderen, Martin van and Skinner, Quentin (eds.), *Republicanism: A Shared European Heritage* (2 vols., Cambridge, 2002).

Gibbs, G. C., Oresko, Robert, and Scott, Hamish (eds.), *Royal and Republican Sovereignty in Early Modern Europe: Essays in Memory of Ragnhild Hatton* (Cambridge, 1997).

Gierowski, Józef, *Sejmik generalny Księstwa Mazowieckiego na tle ustroju sejmikowego Mazowsza* (Wrocław, 1948).

Gierowski, Józef, *Między saskim absolutyzmem a złotą wolnością: z dziejów wewnętrznych Rzeczypospolitej w latach 1712–1715* (Wrocław, 1953).

Gierowski, Józef, 'Pruskie i saskie projekty zamachu stanu w Polsce w 1715 r.', *Przegląd Historyczny*, 50 (1959), pp. 753–67.

Gierowski, Józef, 'From Radoszkowice to Opatów: The History of the Decomposition of the Stanisław Leszczyński Camp', in *Poland at the XIth International Congress of Historical Sciences in Stockholm* (Warsaw, 1960), pp. 217–37.

Gierowski, Józef, '"Opisanie" urzędów centralnych przez konfederatów tarnogrodzkich', in Józef Gierowski, Adam Kersten, Jarema Maciszewski, and Zbigniew Wójcik (eds.), *O naprawę Rzeczypospolitej XVII–XVIII: Prace ofiarowane Władysławowi Czaplińskiemu w 60 rocznicę urodzin* (Warsaw, 1965), pp. 193–211.

Gierowski, Józef, 'La France et les Tendances Absolutistes du Roi de Pologne, Auguste II', *Acta Poloniae Historica*, 17 (1968), pp. 49–70.

Gierowski, Józef, 'Wokół mediacji w Traktacie Waszawskim 1716 roku', *Zeszyty naukowe Uniwersytetu Jagiellońskiego, Prace Historyczne*, 26 (1969), pp. 57–68.

Gierowski, Józef, *W cieniu ligi północnej* (Wrocław, 1971).

Gierowski, Józef, 'Rzeczpospolita szlachecka wobec absolutystycznej Europy', in Antoni Mączak (ed.), *Pamiętnik X Powszechnego Zjazdu Historyków Polskich w Lublinie 9–13 września 1969r. Referaty i dyskusja III Referaty Plenarne sekcje I–IV* (Warsaw, 1971), pp. 99–126.

Gierowski, Józef (ed.), *Dzieje kultury politycznej w Polsce* (Toruń, 1974).

Gierowski, Józef, 'Centralization and Autonomy in the Polish-Saxon Union', *Harvard Ukrainian Studies*, 3/4, pt. 1 (1979–80), pp. 271–84.

Gierowski, Józef, 'Stanisław Herakliusz Lubomirski jako polityk', in Wanda Roszkowska (ed.), *Stanisław Herakliusz Lubomirski: Pisarz—polityk—mecenas* (Wrocław, 1982), pp. 9–24.

Gierowski, Józef, *The Polish-Lithuanian Commonwealth in the XVIIIth Century: From Anarchy to Well-Organised State* (Kraków, 1996).

Gierowski, Józef, 'Prokejt układu Piotra I z Adamem Sieniawskim z 1707 roku', *Śląski Kwartalnik Historyczny Sobótka*, 51, 1–3 (1996), pp. 210–20.

Gierowski, Józef, 'August II Wettyn', in I. Kaniewska (ed.), *Królowie Elekcyjni: Leksykon biograficzny* (Kraków, 1997), pp. 163–85.

Gierowski, Józef, *Rzeczpospolita w dobie złotej wolności (1648–1763)*, in Stanisław Grodziski, Jerzy Wyrozumski, and Marian Zgórniak (eds.), *Wielka Historia Polski* (2nd edition, 5 vols., Kraków, 2003), vol. 3, part 1.

Gierowski, Józef, Kersten, Adam, Maciszewski, Jarema, and Wójcik, Zbigniew (eds.), *O naprawę Rzeczypospolitej XVII–XVIII: Prace ofiarowane Władysławowi Czaplińskiemu w 60 rocznicę urodzin* (Warsaw, 1965).

Gieysztor, Aleksander, Kieniewicz, Stefan, Rostworowski, Emanuel, Tazbir, Janusz, and Wereszycki, Hernyk (eds.), *History of Poland* (Warsaw, 1968).

Góralski, Zbigniew, *Urzędy i godności w dawnej Polsce* (Warsaw, 1983).

Grabski, Andrzej, 'Historyzm sarmacki a historyzm oświecenia', *Przegląd Humanistyczny*, 16 (1972), no. 5 (92), pp. 1–15.

Grodziski, Stanisław, *Obywatelstwo w szlacheckiej Rzeczypospolitej* (Kraków, 1963).

Grodziski, Stanisław (ed.), *Księga pamiątkowa ku czci Konstantego Grzybowskiego* (Kraków, 1971).

Grodziski, Stanisław, 'Les Devoirs et les Droits Politiques de la Noblesse Polonaise', *Acta Poloniae Historica*, 36 (1977), pp. 163–76.

Grześkowiak-Krwawicz, Anna, *O formie rządu czy o rząd dusz: Publicystyka polityczna Sejmu Czteroletniego* (Warsaw, 2000).

Grześkowiak-Krwawicz, Anna, 'Quentin Skinner i teoria wolności republikańskiej', *Archiwum historii filozofii i myśli społecznej*, 45 (2000), pp. 165–74.

Grześkowiak-Krwawicz, Anna, 'Polish Views on European Monarchies', in Richard Butterwick (ed.), *The Polish-Lithuanian Monarchy in European Context, c.1500–1795* (Basingstoke, 2001), pp. 116–31.

Grześkowiak-Krwawicz, Anna, 'Anti-Monarchism in Polish Republicanism in the Seventeenth and Eighteenth Centuries', in Martin van Gelderen and Quentin Skinner (eds.), *Republicanism: A Shared European Heritage* (2 vols., Cambridge, 2002), vol. 1, pp. 43–59.

Grześkowiak-Krwawicz, Anna, 'Deux libertés, l'ancienne et la nouvelle, dans la pensée politique polonaise du XVIIIe siècle', in Grześkowiak-Krwawicz and Izabella Zatorska (eds.), *Liberté: Héritage du Passé ou Idée des Lumières?* (Kraków, 2003), pp. 44–59.

Grześkowiak-Krwawicz, Anna, *Regina Libertas: Wolność w polskiej myśli politycznej XVIII wieku* (Gdańsk, 2006).

Grześkowiak-Krwawicz, Anna and Zatorska, Izabella (eds.), *Liberté: Héritage du Passé ou Idée des Lumières?* (Kraków, 2003).

Gunn, John, *Beyond Liberty and Property: The Process of Self-Recognition in Eighteenth-Century Political Thought* (Montreal, 1983).

Halecki, Oskar, *A History of Poland* (2nd edition, with additional material by Antony Polonsky, London, 1978).

Hampsher-Monk, Iain, 'From Virtue to Politeness', in Martin van Gelderen and Quentin Skinner (eds.), *Republicanism: A Shared European Heritage* (2 vols., Cambridge, 2002), vol. 2, pp. 85–106.

Hirst, Derek, *England in Conflict, 1603–1660: Kingdom, Community, Commonwealth* (London, 1999).

Holborn, Hajo, *A History of Modern Germany, 1648–1840* (London, 1965).

Hołdys, Sybill, 'Sejm polski i parlament angielski w XVI–XVII wieku: porównanie procedury', *Przegląd Historyczny*, 71 (1980), pp. 497–514.

Hunt, William, 'A View from the Vistula on the English Revolution', in Bonnelyn Kunze and Dwight Brautigam (eds.), *Court, Country and Culture: Essays on Early Modern British History in Honor of Perez Zagorin* (Rochester, NY, 1992), pp. 41–54.

Jacobs, Jane, *Systems of Survival: A Dialogue on the Moral Foundations of Politics and Commerce* (New York, 1992).

Jeudwine, John, *Religion, Commerce, Liberty: A Record of a Time of Storm and Change, 1683–1793* (London, 1925).

Jones, James, *Country and Court: England, 1658–1714* ('New History of England', vol. 5, London, 1978).

Kamiński, Andrzej S., *Konfederacja Sandomierska wobec Rosji w okresie poaltransztadzkim* (Wrocław, 1969).

Kamiński, Andrzej S., 'Polish-Lithuanian Commonwealth and Its Citizens (Was the Commonwealth a Stepmother for Cossacks and Ruthenians?)', in Peter Potichnyj (ed.), *Poland and Ukraine Past and Present* (Edmonton, 1980), pp. 32–57.

Kamiński, Andrzej S., 'The *Szlachta* of the Polish-Lithuanian Commonwealth and Their Government', in Ivo Banac and Paul Bushkovitch (eds.), *The Nobility in Russia and Eastern Europe* (New Haven, CT, 1983), pp. 17–45.

Kamiński, Andrzej S., *Republic vs Autocracy: Poland-Lithuania and Russia, 1686–1697* (Cambridge, MA, 1993).

Kamiński, Andrzej S., *Historia Rzeczypospolitej wielu Narodów 1505–1795: Obywatele, ich państwa, społeczeństwo, kultura* (Lublin, 2000).

Kenyon, John, *Revolution Principles: The Politics of Party, 1689–1720* (Cambridge, 1977).

Kersten, Adam, 'Les Magnats—Elite de la société nobiliaire', *Acta Poloniae Historica*, 36 (1977), pp. 119–33.

Kidd, Colin, *British Identities before Nationalism: Ethnicity and Nationhood in the Atlantic World, 1600–1800* (Cambridge, 1999).

Kidd, Colin, 'Constitution and Character in the Eighteenth-Century British World', in Paschalis Kitromilides (ed.), *From Republican Polity to National Community: Reconsiderations of Enlightenment Political Thought* (Oxford, 2003), pp. 40–61.

Király, Béla, 'War and Society in Western and East Central Europe in the Pre-Revolutionary Eighteenth Century', in Béla Király, Gunther Rothenberg, and Peter Sugar (eds.), *East Central European Society and War in the Pre-revolutionary Eighteenth Century* (New York, 1982), pp. 1–25.

Király, Béla, Rothenberg, Gunther, and Sugar, Peter (eds.), *East Central European Society and War in the Pre-Revolutionary Eighteenth Century* (New York, 1982).

Kitowicz, Jędrzej, *Opis obyczajów za panowania Augusta III* (Warsaw, 1985).

Klein, Laurence, *Shaftesbury and the Culture of Politeness: Moral Discourses and Cultural Politics in Early Eighteenth-Century England* (Cambridge, 1994).

Konopczyński, Władysław, *Liberum veto: studium porównawczo-historyczne* (Kraków, 1918, 2nd edition Kraków, 2002).

Konopczyński, Władysław (ed.), *Czasy saskie w Polsce* (Kraków, 1923).

Konopczyński, Władysław, *Polska a Szwecja: od pokoju Oliwskiego do upadku Rzeczypospolitej, 1660–1795* (Warsaw, 1924).

Konopczyński, Władysław, 'Stanisław Dunin Karwicki (1640–1724)', *Przegląd Historyczny*, 37 (1948), pp. 261–75.

Konopczyński, Władysław, *Polscy pisarze polityczni XVIII wieku (do Sejmu Czteroletniego)* (Warsaw, 1966).

Konopczyński, Władysław, *Dzieje Polski Nowożytnej* (2nd edition, Warsaw, 1986).

Kosińska, Urszula, 'Kwestyje Polityczne, Obojętne [Franciszka Radzewskiego]: Traktat polityczny z roku 1699', *Kwartalnik Historyczny*, 102 (1995), pp. 91–112.

Kriegseisen, Wojciech, 'Walka polityczna w województwach małopolskich w roku 1708', *Kwartalnik Historyczny*, 92 (1985), pp. 3–31.

Kriegseisen, Wojciech, *Samorząd szlachecki w Małopolsce w latach 1669–1717* (Warsaw, 1989).

Kriegseisen, Wojciech, *Sejmiki Rzeczypospolitej szlacheckiej w XVII i XVIII wieku* (Warsaw, 1991).

Kriegseisen, Wojciech, *Sejm Rzeczypospolitej Szlacheckiej (do 1763 roku): Geneza i kryzys władzy ustawodawczej* (Warsaw, 1995).

Kriegseisen, Wojciech, *Ewangelicy polscy i litewscy w epoce saskiej (1696–1763): Sytuacja prawna, organizacja i stosunki międzywyznaniowe* (Warsaw, 1996).

Kriegseisen, Wojciech, 'Zmierzch staropoliskiej polityki, czyli o niektórych cechach szczególnych polskiej kultury politycznej przełomu XVII i XVIII wieku', in Urszula Augustyniak and Adam Karpiński (eds.), *Zmierzch Kultury Staropolskiej: Ciągłość i kryzysy* (Warsaw, 1997), pp. 15–39.

Kutrzeba, Stanisław, *Historia ustroju Polski* (8th edition, Warsaw, 1949).

Langford, Paul, *A Polite and Commercial People: England, 1727–1783* (Oxford, 1989).

Langford, Paul, *The Eighteenth Century, 1688–1815* ('Short Oxford History of the British Isles', Oxford, 2002).

Leith, James (ed.), *Facets of Education in the Eighteenth Century* (Oxford, 1977).

Lepszy, Kazimierz, *Andrzej Frycz Modrzewski* (Warsaw, 1954).

Leśniewski, Sławomir, *Poczet Hetmanów Polskich i Litewskich XVIII wiek* (Warsaw, 1992).

Lewitter, L. R., 'Poland, the Ukraine and Russia in the Seventeenth Century', *Slavonic and East European Review*, 27 (1948), pp. 157–71.

Lewitter, L. R., 'Peter the Great and the Polish Election of 1697', *Historical Journal*, 12, 1 (1956), pp. 126–43.

Lewitter, L. R., 'Russia, Poland and the Baltic 1697–1721', *Historical Journal*, 11 (1968), pp. 3–34.

Lewitter, L. R., 'Poland, Russia and the Treaty of Vienna of 5 January 1719', *Historical Journal*, 13, 1 (1970), pp. 3–30.

Link-Lenczowski, Andrzej, *Rzeczpospolita na rozdrożu: 1696–1736* (Kraków, 1994).

Link-Lenczowski, Andrzej, 'Wokół zabiegów o 'jedność' Rzeczypospolitej. Z dziejów współpracy Adama Sieniawskiego i Stanisława Denhoffa w latach 1706–1709', *Śląski Kwartalnik Historyczny Sobótka*, 51, 1–3 (1996), pp. 204–9.

Link-Lenczowski, Andrzej and Markiewicz, Mariusz (eds.), *Rzeczpospolita wielu Narodów i jej tradycje* (Kraków, 1999).

Lityński, Adam, 'Małopolskie sądy skarbowe do roku 1717', *Czasopismo Prawno-Historyczne*, 24, 2 (1972), pp. 107–24.

Lityński, Adam, 'Problem szlacheckiego prawa zgrodadzeń ziemskich w Polsce w XVII i XVIII wieku', *Czasopismo Prawno-Historyczne*, 26, 1 (1974), pp. 175–83.

Lityński, Adam, *Szlachecki samorząd gospodarczy w Małopolsce (1606–1717)* (Katowice, 1974).

Lityński, Adam, 'Sejmiki dawnej Rzeczypospolitej (na marginesie pracy J. Włodarczyka, *Sejmiki łęczyckie*, Wydawnictwo Uniwersytetu Łódzkiego, Łódź 1973, s. 336)', *Przegląd Historyczny*, 66, 3 (1975), pp. 295–304.

Lityński, Adam, 'Samorząd szlachecki w Polsce XVII–XVIII wieku', *Kwartalnik Historyczny*, 99, 4 (1992), pp. 17–34.

Lukowski, Jerzy, *Liberty's Folly: The Polish-Lithuanian Commonwealth in the Eighteenth Century* (London, 1991).

Lukowski, Jerzy, *The Partitions of Poland: 1772, 1793, 1795* (London, 1999).

Lukowski, Jerzy, *The European Nobility in the Eighteenth Century* (Basingstoke, 2003).

Lukowski, Jerzy, 'Political Ideas among the Polish Nobility in the Eighteenth Century (to 1788)', *Slavonic and East European Review*, 82, 1 (2004), pp. 1–26.

Lukowski, Jerzy, 'The Szlachta and their Ancestors in the Eighteenth Century', *Kwartalnik Historyczny*, 111, 3 (2004), pp. 161–82.

Lukowski, Jerzy, *Disorderly Liberty: The Political Culture of the Polish-Lithuanian Commonwealth in the Eighteenth Century* (London, 2010).

Macinnes, Allan, *The British Revolution, 1629–1660* (Basingstoke, 2005).

Macinnes, Allan, 'The Hidden Commonwealth: Poland-Lithuania and Scottish Political Discourse in the Seventeenth Century', in Karin Friedrich and Barbara Pendzich (eds.), *Citizenship and Identity in a Multinational Commonwealth: Poland-Lithuania in Context, 1550–1772* (Leiden, 2009), pp. 233–60.

Macinnes, Allan and Ohlmeyer, Jane (eds.), *The Stuart Kingdoms in the Seventeenth Century: Awkward Neighbours* (Dublin, 2002).

Mączak, Antoni (ed.), *Encyklopedia historii gospodarczej Polski do 1945 roku* (2 vols., Warsaw, 1981).

Mączak, Antoni, *Rządzący i rządzeni: Władza i społeczeństwo w Europie wczesnonowożytnej* (Warsaw, 1986).

Mączak, Antoni, *Klientela: Nieformalne systemy władzy w Polsce i Europie XVI–XVIII w.* (Warsaw, 1994).

Maltzahn, Nicholas von, 'The Whig Milton, 1667–1700', in David Armitage, Armand Himy, and Quentin Skinner (eds.), *Milton and Republicanism* (Cambridge, 1995), pp. 229–53.

Mańkowski, Tadeusz, *Genealogia sarmatyzmu* (Warsaw, 1946).

Markiewicz, Mariusz, *Rady senatorskie Augusta II (1697–1733)* (Wrocław, 1988).

Mason, Roger, *Kingship and the Commonweal: Political Thought in Renaissance and Reformation Scotland* (East Linton, 1998).

Melton, James van Horn, *Absolutism and the Eighteenth-Century Roots of Compulsory Schooling in Prussia and Austria* (Cambridge, 1988).

Michalski, Jerzy, 'Plan Czartoryskich naprawy Rzeczypospolitej', *Kwartalnik Historyczny*, 63 (1956), pp. 29–44.

Michalski, Jerzy, 'Les Diétines Polonaises au XVIIIe Siècle', *Acta Poloniae Historica*, 12 (1965), pp. 87–107.

Michalski, Jerzy, 'Z problematyki republikańskiego nurtu w polskiej reformatorskiej myśli politycznej w XVIII wieku', *Kwartalnik Historyczny*, 90 (1983), pp. 327–38.

Michalski, Jerzy, *Historia Sejmu Polskiego* (Warsaw, 1984).

Motley, Mark, *Becoming a French Aristocrat: The Education of the Court Nobility, 1580–1715* (Princeton, 1990).

Müller, Michael, 'Wielkie miasta Prus Królewskich wobec parlamentaryzmu polskiego po Unii Lubelskiej', *Czasopismo Prawno-Historyczne*, 45 (1993), pp. 257–67.

Müller, Michael, 'Republicanism versus Monarchy? Government by Estates in Poland-Lithuania and the Holy Roman Empire, Sixteenth to Eighteenth Centuries', in Manfred Hildermeier (ed.), *Historical Concepts between Eastern and Western Europe* (New York, 2007), pp. 35–47.

Nagielski, Mirosław (ed.), *Hetmani Rzeczypospolitej Obojga Narodów* (Warsaw, 1995).

Nycz, Michał, *Geneza reform skarbowych Sejmu Niemego: Studium z dziejów skarbowo-wojskowych z lat 1697–1717* (Poznań, 1938).

Ochmański, Władysław, 'Zwalczanie zbójnictwa góralskiego przez szlachtę w XVII i XVIII wieku', *Czasopismo Prawno-Historyczne*, 3 (1951), pp. 193–242.

Olszewski, Henryk, *Dokryny prawno-ustrojowe czasów saskich 1697–1740* (Warsaw, 1961).

Olszewski, Henryk, 'Praktyka limitowania sejmików', *Czasopismo Prawno-Historyczne*, 13 (1961), pp. 33–55.

Olszewski, Henryk, *Sejm Rzeczypospolitej epoki oligarchii 1652–1763: Prawo Praktyka Teoria Programy* (Poznań 1966).

Olszewski, Henryk, 'Ideologia Rzeczypospolitej—przedmurza chrześciaństwa', *Czasopismo Prawno-Historyczne*, 35, 2 (1983), pp. 1–19.

Olszewski, Henryk, 'Sejm konny. Rzecz o funkcjonowaniu ideologii demokracji szlacheckiej w dawnej Polsce', *Czasopismo Prawno-Historyczne*, 37, 2 (1985), pp. 225–42.

Olszewski, Henryk, 'The Essence and Legal Foundations of the Magnate Oligarchy in Poland', *Acta Poloniae Historica*, 56 (1987), pp. 29–49.

Opaliński, Edward, *Kultura polityczna szlachty polskiej w latach 1587–1652: System parlamentarny a społeczeństwo obywatelskie* (Warsaw, 1995).

Opaliński, Edward, 'Civic Humanism and Republican Citizenship in the Polish Renaissance', in Martin van Gelderen and Quentin Skinner (eds.), *Republicanism: A Shared European Heritage* (2 vols., Cambridge, 2002), vol. 1 (*Republicanism and Constitutionalism in Early Modern Europe*), pp. 147–66.

Pawiński, Adolf, *Dzieje ziemi kujawskiej oraz akta historyczne do nich służące* (4 vols., Warsaw, 1888).

Pawiński, Adolf, *Rządy sejmikowe w Polsce 1572–1795 na tle stosunków województw kujawskich* (1st edition 1888, 2nd edition ed. Henryk Olszewski, Warsaw, 1978).

Perłakowski, Adam, *Jan Jerzy Przebendowski jako podskarbi wielki koronny (1703–1729): Studium funkcjonowania ministerium* (Kraków, 2004).

Phillipson, Nicholas, 'Politeness and Politics in the Reigns of Anne and the Early Hanoverians', in J. G. A. Pocock (ed.), *The Varieties of British Political Thought, 1500–1800* (Cambridge, 1993), pp. 211–45.

Pocock, J. G. A., *The Ancient Constitution and the Feudal Law* (Cambridge, 1957).

Pocock, J. G. A., *The Machiavellian Moment: Florentine Political Thought and the Atlantic Republican Tradition* (Princeton, 1975).

Pocock, J. G. A., *Virtue, Commerce and History: Essays on Political Thought and History, Chiefly in the Eighteenth Century* (Cambridge, 1985).

Pocock, J. G. A. (ed.), *The Varieties of British Political Thought, 1500–1800* (Cambridge, 1993).

Poraziński, Jarosław, 'Funkcje polityczne i ustrojowe rad senatu w latach 1697–1717', *Kwartalnik Historyczny*, 91, 1 (1984), pp. 25–44.

Poraziński, Jarosław, 'Stanisław Leszczyński na tle orientacji politycznych szlachty w latach 1704–1705', *Rocznik Gdański*, 46 (1986), pp. 7–14.

Poraziński, Jarosław, *Sejm Lubelski w 1703 roku i jego miejsce w konfliktach wewnętrznych na początku XVIII wieku* (Warsaw, 1988).

Poraziński, Jarosław, *Epiphania Poloniae: orientacje i postawy polityczne szlachty polskiej w dobie wielkiej wojny północnej, 1702–1710* (Toruń, 1999).

Pośpiech, Andrzej and Tygielski, Wojciech, 'The Social Role of Magnates' Courts in Poland (From the End of the 16th up to the 18th Century)', *Acta Poloniae Historica*, 43 (1981), pp. 75–100.

Pryszlak, Maria, '"Forma Mixta" as a Political Ideal of a Polish Magnate: Łukasz Opaliński's "Rozmowa plebana z ziemianinem"', *Polish Review*, 3 (1981), pp. 26–42.

Przyboś, Kazimierz, *Sejmik województwa krakowskiego w czasach saskich (1697–1763)* (Kraków, 1981).

Putnam, Robert, 'Bowling Alone: America's Declining Social Capital', *Journal of Democracy*, 6, 1 (1995), pp. 65–78.

Rachuba, Andrzej, *Wielkie Księstwo Litewskie w systemie parlamentarnym Rzeczypospolitej w latach 1569–1763* (Warsaw, 2002).

Rahe, Paul, *Republics Ancient and Modern: Classical Republicanism and the American Revolution* (Chapel Hill, NC, 1992).

Rahe, Paul, 'Antiquity Surpassed: The Repudiation of Classical Republicanism', in David Wootton (ed.), *Republicanism, Liberty and Commercial Society, 1649–1776* (Stanford, 1994), pp. 233–69.

Robbins, Caroline, *The Eighteenth-Century Commonwealthman: Studies in the Transmission, Development and Circumstance of English Liberal Thought from the Restoration of Charles II until the War with the Thirteen Colonies* (Cambridge, MA, 1959).

Roberts, Clayton, *The Growth of Responsible Government in Stuart England* (Cambridge, 1966).

Roberts, Michael, *On Aristocratic Constitutionalism in Swedish History, 1520–1720* (London, 1966).

Roberts, Michael, *The Early Vasas: A History of Sweden, 1523–1611* (Cambridge, 1968).

Roberts, Michael, *Swedish and English Parliamentarism in the Eighteenth Century* (Belfast, 1973).

Ronikier, Jerzy, *Hetman Adam Sieniawski i jego regimentarze: Studium z historii mentalności szlachty polskiej 1706–1725* (Kraków, 1992).

Rose, William, *Stanislas Konarski: Reformer of Education in XVIIIth Century Poland* (London, 1929).

Rosner, Anton, 'Wolność polska rozmową Polaka z Francuzem roztrząśniona', in Antoni Mączak (ed.), *Francja—Polska XVIII–XIX w. Studia z dziejów kultury i polityki poświęcone Profesorowi Andrzejowi Zahorskiemu w sześćdziesiątą rocznicę urodzin* (Warsaw, 1983), pp. 120–9.

Rostworowski, Emanuel, *Legendy i Fakty XVIII w.* (Warsaw, 1963).

Rostworowski, Emanuel, 'Republikanizm polski i anglosaski w XVIII wieku', *Miesięcznik Literacki*, 11, 5 (1976), pp. 94–103.

Rostworowski, Emanuel, *Historia powszechna wiek XVIII* (Warsaw, 1977).

Rostworowski, Emanuel, 'Czasy Saskie i Oświecenie', in Janusz Tazbir (ed.), *Zarys Historii Polski* (Warsaw, 1980), pp. 295–370.

Rostworowski, Emanuel, 'Ilu było w Rzeczypospolitej obywateli szlachty?', *Kwartalnik Historyczny*, 94, 3 (1988), pp. 3–40.

Roszkowska, Wanda (ed.), *Stanisław Herakliusz Lubomirski: Pisarz—polityk—mecenas* (Wrocław, 1982).

Rynduch, Zbigniew, *Andrzej Maksymilian Fredro: Portret Literacki* (Gdańsk, 1980).

Scott, Hamish, *The Emergence of the Eastern Powers, 1756–1775* (Cambridge, 2001).

Skinner, Quentin, 'Meaning and Understanding in the History of Ideas', *History and Theory*, 8 (1969), pp. 3–53.

Skinner, Quentin, *The Foundations of Modern Political Thought* (2 vols., Cambridge, 1978).

Skinner, Quentin, *Liberty before Liberalism* (Cambridge, 1998).

Skinner, Quentin, 'A Third Concept of Liberty', Berlin Lecture to the British Academy 2001, *Proceedings of the British Academy*, 117 (2002), pp. 237–68.

Sliesoriūnas, Gintautas, 'Problem separatyzmu Wielkiego Księstwa Litewskiego w końcu XVII wieku', in Andrzej Link-Lenczowski and Mariusz Markiewicz (eds.), *Rzeczpospolita wielu Narodów i jej tradycje* (Kraków, 1999), pp. 85–94.

Sliesoriūnas, Gintautas, 'Changes in Attitudes towards Russia among the Lithuanian-Polish Elite at the Turn of the Seventeenth and Eighteenth Centuries', *Lithuanian Historical Studies*, 9 (2004), pp. 1–17.

Sochaniewicz, Stefan, 'Z dziejów sejmiku wiszeńskiego (1673–1732)', *Kwartalnik Historyczny*, 29, 1/4 (1915), pp. 17–54.

Sowa, Andrzej, *Świat ministrów Augusta II: Wartości i poglądy funkcjonujące w kręgu ministrów Rzeczypospolitej w latach 1702–1728* (Kraków, 1995).

Stańczak, Edward, *Kamera saska za Augusta III* (Warsaw, 1973).

Stanek, Wojciech, *Konfederacje generalne koronne w XVIII wieku* (Toruń, 1991).

Starnawski, Jerzy, *Andrzej Frycz Modrzewski: Żywot, dzieło, sława* (Łódź, 1981).

Stasiewicz-Jasiukowa, Irena (ed.), *Wkład Pijarów do nauki i kultury w Polsce XVII–XIX wieku* (Warsaw, 1993).

Staszewski, Jacek, 'Pomysły reformatorskie czasów Augusta II', *Kwartalnik Historyczny*, 82 (1975), pp. 736–65.

Staszewski, Jacek, 'La Culture Polonaise durant la crise du XVIIIe siècle', *Acta Poloniae Historica*, 55 (1987), pp. 107–32.

Staszewski, Jacek, *August III Sas* (Wrocław, 1989).

Staszewski, Jacek (ed.), *Studia z dziejów Polskiej myśli politycznej—tom IV* (Toruń, 1992).

Staszewski, Jacek (ed.), *Elity mieszczańskie i szlacheckie prus królewskich i kujaw w XIV–XVIII wieku* (Toruń, 1995).

Staszewski, Jacek, *Jak Polskę przemienić w kraj kwitnący: Szkice i studia z czasów saskich* (Olsztyn, 1997).

Staszewski, Jacek, *August II Mocny* (Wrocław, 1998).

Stefanowska, Zofia (ed.), *Swojskość i cudzoziemszczyzna w dziejach kultury polskiej* (Warsaw, 1973).

Stone, Lawrence (ed.), *An Imperial State at War: Britain from 1689 to 1815* (London, 1994).

Subtelny, Orest, *Domination of Eastern Europe: Native Nobilities and Foreign Absolutism, 1500–1715* (Montreal, 1986).

Sucheni-Grabowska, Anna and Żaryn, Małgorzata (eds.), *Między monarchą a demokracją: Studia z dziejów Polski XV–XVIII wieku* (Warsaw, 1994).

Szcząska, Zbigniew, 'Sąd sejmowy w Polsce, od końca XVI do końca XVIII wieku', *Czasopismo Prawno-Historyczne*, 20, 1 (1968), pp. 93–124.

Szijártó, István, 'The Diet: The Estates and the Parliament of Hungary, 1708–1792', in Gerhard Ammerer, William D. Godsey, Martin Scheutz, Peter Urbanitsch, and Alfred Stefan Weiß (eds.), *Bündnispartner und Konkurrenten der Landesfürsten? Die Stände in der Habsburgermonarchie* (Vienna, 2007), pp. 151–71.

Szpilczyński, Stanisław, *Doktor Sebastian Petrycy z Pilzna (1554–1626)* (Warsaw, 1961).

Tazbir, Janusz (ed.), *Polska XVII wieku: Państwo, społeczeństwo, kultura* (Warsaw, 1969).

Tazbir, Janusz, *Rzeczpospolita i świat: studia z dziejów kultury XVII wieku* (Wrocław, 1971).

Tazbir, Janusz, *A State without Stakes: Polish Religious Toleration in the Sixteenth and Seventeenth Centuries* (Warsaw, 1973).

Tazbir, Janusz, *Kultura szlachecka w Polsce: rozkwit, upadek, relikty* (Poznań, 1998).

Uruszczak, Wacław, 'Kultura polityczna i prawna w sejmie polskim czasów odrodzenia', *Czasopismo Prawno-Historyczne*, 32, 2 (1980), pp. 47–62.

Vasiliauskas, Artūras, 'The Practice of Citizenship among the Lithuanian Nobility c.1580–1630', in Karin Friedrich and Barbara Pendzich (eds.), *Citizenship and Identity in a Multinational Commonwealth: Poland-Lithuania in Context, 1550–1772* (Leiden, 2009), pp. 71–102.

Voisé, Waldemar, *Andrzej Frycz Modrzewski 1503–1572* (Wrocław, 1975).

Wagner-Rundell, Benedict, 'Liberty, Virtue and the Chosen People: British and Polish Republicanism in the Early Eighteenth Century', in Richard Unger (ed.), *Britain and Poland-Lithuania: Contact and Comparison from the Middle Ages to 1795* (Leiden, 2008), pp. 197–214.

Wagner-Rundell, Benedict, 'A Missed Opportunity? Conflicting Programmes for Reform at the Sejm of 1712–13', *Central Europe*, 6, 1 (2008), pp. 3–16.

Wagner-Rundell, Benedict, 'Holy War and Republican Pacifism in the Early-Eighteenth-Century Commonwealth of Poland-Lithuania', in David Onnekink and Gijs Rommelse (eds.), *Ideology and Foreign Policy in Early Modern Europe (1650–1750)* (Farnham, 2011), pp. 163–79.

Walicki, Andrzej, *The Three Traditions in Polish Patriotism and their Contemporary Relevance* (Bloomington, IN, 1988).

Walicki, Andrzej, *The Enlightenment and the Birth of Modern Nationhood: Polish Political Thought from Noble Republicanism to Tadeusz Kościuszko* (Notre Dame, IN, 1989).

Wąsik, Wiktor, *Sebastjan Petrycy z Pilzna i epoka* (Warsaw, 1923).

Wimmer, Jan, *Wojsko polskie w drugie połowie XVII wieku* (Warsaw, 1965).

Wojtasik, Janusz, 'Walka Augusta II z obozem kontystowsko-prymasowskim w pierwszym roku panowania (1697–98)', *Przegląd Historyczny*, 60 (1969), pp. 24–44.

Wolff, Larry, *Inventing Eastern Europe: The Map of Civilization on the Mind of the Enlightenment* (Stanford, 1994).

Worden, Blair, 'Republicanism and the Restoration, 1660–1683', in David Wootton (ed.), *Republicanism, Liberty and Commercial Society, 1649–1776* (Stanford, 1994), pp. 139–93.

Wootton, David (ed.), *Republicanism, Liberty and Commercial Society, 1649–1776* (Stanford, CA, 1994).

Worden, Blair, *Roundhead Reputations: The English Civil Wars and the Passions of Posterity* (London, 2001).

Wrede, Marek and Wrede, Maria (eds.), *Sejmy i sejmiki pierwszej Rzeczypospolitej: Dokumenty w zbiorach Biblioteki Narodowej* (Warsaw, 1999).

Wyczański, Andrzej, 'La Structure de la Noblesse Polonaise aux XVIe–XVIIIe siècles (Remarques méthodiques)', *Acta Poloniae Historica*, 36 (1977), pp. 109–17.

Wyczański, Andrzej, *Polska rzeczą pospolitą szlachecką* (Warsaw, 1991).

Young, John, 'The Scottish Parliament and the Covenanting Heritage of Constitutional Reform', in Allan Macinnes and Jane Ohlmeyer (eds.), *The Stuart Kingdoms in the Seventeenth Century: Awkward Neighbours* (Dublin, 2002), pp. 226–50.

Zajączkowski, Andrzej, *Szlachta polska: Kultura i struktura* (Warsaw, 1993).

Zak, Paul and Knack, Stephen, 'Trust and Growth', *The Economic Journal*, 111 (2001), pp. 295–321.

Zakrzewski, Andrzej, *Sejmiki Wielkiego Księstwa Litewskiego XVI–XVIII w. Ustrój i funkcjonowanie: sejmik trocki* (Warsaw, 2000).

Zamoyski, Adam, *The Last King of Poland* (London, 1992).

Zielińska, Teresa, *Magnateria polska epoki saskiej: Funkcje urzędów i królewszczyzn w procesie przeobrażeń warstwy społocznej* (Wrocław, 1977).

Zielińska, Zofia, 'Mechanizm sejmikowy i klientela radziwiłłowska za Sasów', *Przegląd Historyczny*, 62 (1971), pp. 397–419.

Zielińska, Zofia, *Studia z dziejów stosunków polsko-rosyjskich w XVIII wieku* (Warsaw, 2001).

UNPUBLISHED THESES

Gromelski, Tomasz, 'The Social and Political Values of Gentry Elites in Poland, England and Wales in the Later Sixteenth Century' (Oxford University DPhil thesis, 2007).

Preusse, Christian, 'The Scope of Politics in Early Modern Imperial Systems: The Holy Roman Empire of the German Nation and Poland-Lithuania in the Seventeenth Century in Comparison' (Oxford University DPhil thesis, 2014).

Index

Lightning Source UK Ltd.
Milton Keynes UK
UKOW04n1259281217
315001UK00001B/16/P